LIBRARY BOUND

LIBRARY BOUND

A Saratoga Anthology

Edited by
Linda Bullard

SARATOGA SPRINGS PUBLIC LIBRARY
Saratoga Springs, New York

ISBN 0-9650300-0-8

Library of Congress Catalog Card Number: 95-72815

Printed in the United States of America

Cover design by Valerie Collins

CONTENTS

PREFACE

Bound in this volume are works which were read at the Saratoga Springs Public Library as part of a series called "Writers on Reading." Supported by the Literature Program of the New York State Council on the Arts, the library invited guest writers to present their original works and lead discussions of favorite books. Compiling this anthology of the authors' writings, which happily represent many different genres of literature, was a logical next step.

The writers are diverse; in the good company of poets and fiction writers there are writers for children, essayists, journalists and a playwright. Though from many different backgrounds all these writers share a devotion to the power and magic of words. The gift of their work for this anthology is only one of the many ways each has been supportive of this library. It has been a supreme pleasure to work with and for them.

Linda Bullard
Editor

ACKNOWLEDGEMENTS

In all cases, unless otherwise noted, permission to reprint previously published works in this anthology has been granted by the individual authors.

Jennifer Armstrong: *Little Salt Lick and the Sun King* copyright © 1994 by Jennifer M. Armstrong. Reprinted by permission of Crown Publishers, Inc.

Maria McBride Bucciferro: "Upstairs/Downstairs at Sagamore" is reprinted courtesy of *Adirondack Life*, September/October 1990, Volume XXI, Number 6.

Michael Burkard: "The Bridge" and "Entire Dilemma" first appeared in *The American Poetry Review*, "Red Leaf" in *The North American Review*, "Clothes Which Are Moonlit" in *Zone 3*, and "A Raincoat" in *Ironwood*.

Ken Denberg: "Winter Hawks" first appeared in *The Southern Poetry Review*, "Common Birds" in *The Denver Quarterly*, "Nocturne" in *The Berkshire Review*, "Clouds and Crows" in *The Little Magazine*, and "Blueberry Pie" in *The Agni Review*.

Douglas Glover: "La Corriveau" was previously published in *Descant* and *Best Canadian Stories*.

Amy Godine: "Foreign Aid" originally appeared in *TriQuarterly*, a publication of Northwestern University.

Barry Goldensohn: "Rediscovering Wonder: Santa Cruz Mts, California, 1989" and "Song to A Porcupine In Mating Season" previously appeared in *Salmagundi*. "Thelonius Monk Dancing" appeared in *The Harvard Review*.

Lorrie Goldensohn: "Clear Water" and "L'Esprit de L'Escalier" first appeared in *Salmagundi*. "Bald Eagle With A Six-Foot Wingspan" first appeared in *Racoon*. "Anesthesia" first appeared in *Poetry* copyright © 1988 by The Modern Poetry Association, and is reprinted by permission of the Editor of *Poetry*. "Saratoga Ballet" first appeared in *Ploughshares*, Vol. 17/No. 243.

William Hathaway: "Mirth," "Guillotine," and "The Texaco Opera" all appeared in Mr. Hathaway's book *Churlsgrace*, published by the University of Florida Press, 1992. "Selfsame Songs" first appeared in *Confluence*, and "The Last Cowboy" first appeared in *The Chariton Review*.

Bruce Hiscock: "Winter Scenes" is from *Tundra: The Arctic Land* copyright © 1986 by Bruce Hiscock reprinted by permission of Atheneum.

Dennis Loy Johnson: "Second Language" is reprinted by permission of *The Black Warrior Review*.

Naton Leslie: "Affirmation" first appeared in *Puerto Del Sol*, "Charles Dickens Travels To Cleveland" in *Yarrow*, "The Darker Excursions" in the *California Quarterly*, "Mercy" in the *Cimmaron Review*, and "Late Freeze" in *Ironwood*.

F. R. Lewis: "Bread" first appeared in *Ascent*.

George Liaskos: "On The Second Time Looking Into Caesar's Gallic War" previously appeared in the collection *If Only It Were A Beast* copyright © 1983 by George Liaskos.

Ron MacLean: "Where Morning Finds You" first appeared in *Reed* (San Jose).

Shirley Nelson: "The Search Begins" is from her novel *Fair Clear and Terrible: The Story of Shiloh, Maine*, British American Publishing, 1989.

Paul Pines: "The Crab" was previously published in *First Intensity*.

Jay Rogoff: "Aesthetics" was first published in *The Kenyon Review—New Series*, Summer 1992, Vol. XIV, No. 3, copyright © 1992 by Kenyon College. "How We Came To Stand On That Shore" first appeared in *The Quarterly* 20 (Winter 1991).

Hollis Seamon: "Meanwhile, What The Old Women Were Up To: A Revisitation Of "Indian Camp" by Ernest Hemingway" first appeared in *The American Voice*.

Nancy Seid: *Parents* Magazine (March 1994) first published "How I Learned To Live Without A Paycheck."

Joanne Seltzer: "Illumination" and "Amber" were first published in *Waterways*, "Half Moon Beach: Piseco Lake" in *Adirondack Lake Poems*, Loft Press, 1985, "As The Hudson Is Swept Through The Locks" in *From The Hudson To The World: The Voices Of A River*, Clearwater Sloop Restoration, Inc. 1978, and "Mohawk Music" in *The MacGuffin*.

Jordan Smith: "Job" and "Lilac" first appeared in the *New England Review*. "Tristan" first appeared in *Poetry* and was copyrighted © 1994 by The Modern Poetry Association, and is here reprinted by permission of the Editor of *Poetry*. "The Dream of Horses" first appeared in the *Paris Review*.

Marilyn Stablein: *The North American Review* first published "Picnic In Bodh Gaya."

Steve Stern: "Lazar Malkin Enters Heaven" is copyright ©1986 by Steve Stern and reprinted by permission of Viking Penguin, Inc.

Susan Thames: "Gone" is from *As Much As I Know* copyright © 1992 by Susan Thames, reprinted by permission of Random House, Inc.

Beth Weatherby: "Sun-Dialing" first appeared in *The Little Magazine*.

Matthew Witten: "Washington Squares Moves" is copyright © 1994 by Matthew Witten and is reprinted by permission of the author and Dramatists Play Service, Inc.

LITTLE SALT LICK
AND THE SUN KING

JENNIFER ARMSTRONG

THE PALACE AT VERSAILLES was busier than an anthill. Wherever you looked, servants and courtiers scurried to and fro, here and there, upstairs and downstairs, back and forth. There were maids putting candles in the crystal chandeliers and lads polishing brass doorknobs, washerwomen scrubbing lace hankies and grooms braiding horses' manes. There were topiarists pruning ivy swans, perfumers strewing potpourri, and groundsmen raking white gravel.

And down in the kitchen, standing by the fire, was Little Salt Lick, the Second Assistant Rotisserie Turner in the Department of Roasted Meats.

Little Salt Lick should properly have been known by his given name, Paul, but nobody was proper in those days, at that palace. His job was turning the rotisserie. He sweated at it all day long, and when he left his post by the fire, the dogs would follow after him, rudely licking the salt from his arms. This was highly irritating to him.

"Shoo!" Little Salt Lick scolded. "Begone you filthy *chiens!*"

But Little Salt Lick was such a tiny chap that the dogs had no fear of him. They pestered him all the time, and the other kitchen servants were no help. "There goes Little Salt Lick!" they would laugh as poor Paul raced to escape the dogs. He liked dogs, as far as dogs went, but dogs and his job together did not make a good match.

For days and days, all the palace had been humming with work as everyone prepared for the arrival of King Louis, who was returning after a journey. This meant more meats than ever must be roasted for the great banquets and assemblies. And so, Little Salt Lick had scarcely a moment's peace.

The Cook of Roasted Meats clasped his hands in ecstasy. "For our most delightful Sun King, I will prepare such delicious venison, pork, and beef!" he exclaimed, kissing his fingers. "*Magnifique!*"

But to Little Salt Lick, it was no occasion for joy. He sweated at his post—and kept an eye out for the dogs.

Finally, at four o'clock on Thursday, the poor boy had had enough.

"Enough!" he cried out. "*C'est intolérable!*"

And with that Little Salt Lick ran to the stables, climbed up a ladder to the haylofts, and thumbed his nose at the dogs yelping their futile yelps down below. Way up there, he was Paul, and he liked it that way. He gazed out a window and imagined himself a tall person with elegant cats. Idly, he picked bits of straw from his hair.

Suddenly, there was a blaring and blasting of trumpets. Clouds of dust came rolling toward Versailles from a distance.

"The King!" the grooms below gasped, bumping into one another. In their haste and excitement they dropped tack and currycombs on the heads of the dogs. "It is the King!"

From his perch, Little Salt Lick saw the great Sun King, Louis, descend from a golden coach, stepping daintily in high-heeled slippers, a large footman with a tiny dog on a satin pillow following behind.

Little Salt Lick pouted. Because of the King he had a palace to work in. Yet now, because of the King, he had an excess of sweaty work to do. All in all, Little Salt Lick was a practical fellow, but very tired of being hounded.

He knew the Cook of Roasted Meats would be searching for him, brandishing a basting spoon and uttering angry oaths. And so Little Salt Lick trod forlornly back to the kitchen, shooing off dogs as he went.

That night, there was a tremendous feast. The Department of Pastry presented fancy pies with live birds inside. The Department of Fish and Seafood served jellied eels and pink lobsters dressed in cardinals' robes, and the tables were adorned with immense ice sculptures that changed from winged horses to mermaids as they melted.

The King sat on his sparkling throne, waving distantly to his favorites and sampling one bite of every dish placed before him. From time to time, he fed a morsel of meat to the tiny dog that sat beside him on a tasseled pillow, and smiled an absent smile as the musicians fussed with their butterfly costumes.

Little Salt Lick watched from one of the many peepholes, until he was shoved aside by a bigger boy from the Department of Piquant Sauces. Then he scuffed away down the corridor, with his hands in his pockets, keeping a sharp lookout for dogs.

On the following day, there was a great hullabaloo throughout Versailles. The King's precious pet, Chou-Chou, was missing! Who had seen the Sun King's dog? It was *un désastre!*

The fact was, the little dog was oppressed by all the great huge people who constantly surrounded it. It had fled in terror of all the big feet. But this was not known to Versailles, which was in an uproar over Chou-Chou's inexplicable disappearance.

High and low, near and far, from top to bottom, the servants and courtiers searched for the petite Chou-Chou.

They searched among topiaries and marble nymphs, under buffets and petitpoint footstools, inside the urns and the harpsichords. But not a glimpse of Chou-Chou's curly little tail did they see.

The Sun King was despondent and sat languishing on his throne. Rumor spread that he was ready to take drastic measures. Versailles held its breath and peeked behind the drapes.

Of this great tragedy, however, Little Salt Lick was quite ignorant. News and reports of state business did not penetrate to the level of the Second Assistant Rotisserie Turner in the Department of Roasted Meats.

There he stood, beside the huge fireplace in the kitchen beneath the palace, turning and turning the rotisserie.

In the hottest part of the day, Little Salt Lick slipped away from his post. All the dogs were sleeping in the heat, and this was his chance to elude them. He scampered up the stone steps to the courtyard and ran to the stables to hide.

Yap! Le Yap!

Little Salt Lick froze in his tracks. Slowly he turned and beheld the King's tiny dog mincing toward him, nose aquiver at the scent of salt.

"Shoo!" Little Salt Lick yelled. "Shoo! Shoo!"

Thinking it had heard its name, the tiny dog instantly sat down and cocked its head, awaiting a command. It was delighted to find a small human French person. Its tail went *tip-tip-tip* on the ground.

"Aha, what is this?" Little Salt Lick exclaimed. "What a nice dog this is!"

So delighted was he to encounter a dog that did not slurp all over him, that he scooped the beast up in his arms.

"*Ah! Voilà!*" came a shout of triumph. "The Second Assistant Rotisserie Turner has rescued the King's dog!"

To his amazement, Little Salt Lick found himself at the center of a throng of elated servants and courtiers, who bore him and Chou-Chou along like grains of pepper on a flood of *sauce Hollandaise*. And then, to his further amazement, Little Salt Lick was served up before the Sun King himself.

"*Merci! Formidable!*" King Louis sighed, clapping his hands with relief. "And you, young fellow, may name your reward."

The Cook of Roasted Meats sidled up beside Little Salt Lick and whispered in his ear. "Riches are yours for the asking, and authority and power. Choose wisely and remember your friends!"

"Ah," said Little Salt Lick, scratching his head. He was not sure what he wanted. Chou-Chou's tail went *tip-tip-tip*. "Umm. . ."

"I have it!" the King broke in with a snap of his fingers. "You shall from this day cease to be the Second Assistant Rotisserie Turner, but shall instead be the First Assistant Bearer of the King's Dog. How does that suit you—uh, what is your name?"

Little Salt Lick blinked in surprise. But then he smiled. "Your Majesty, my name is Paul. And that job suits me fine.

HE USED TO SAY

Mae Guyer Banner

HE USED TO SAY, "In my village, the richest man owned a horse; here, I have a car." By the world's measure, my father was not rich, but by his own reckoning, he had wealth enough. So, when our enormous family gathered in Detroit to mourn his death in August, 1984—sisters, brothers, cousins from Chicago and California, from Arizona and New Jersey—we told over and over the stories of his journey in 1922 from the shtetl of Gombin in central Poland to the city of Detroit and, in the telling, confirmed the sufficiency of his life.

It was a life of contradictions. As a young man in Gombin, he and his friends successfully petitioned the Czarist Russian officials who ruled the town before World War I for the establishment of a library and a theatrical group. But in this country, he could barely read English. Before he left the old country at the age of 21, he broke with his father's Orthodoxy and embraced the thinking of Darwin and Engels. But in his first twenty years in Detroit, with his tailor's needle, he earned the money to bring his father and mother, three brothers and two sisters, one by one, to a new home in America.

More contradictions. His politics were socialist, but he was fiercely determined to own his own business. He did custom tailoring in his own shop on 14th Street, staying at that address for more than forty years, until the city government finally bought the property, now ravaged by street gangs and robberies, in the 1970's. Then, he set up his sewing machines and ironing boards at home and continued to work until a few weeks before his death.

When we went through his house in the week of mourning, we felt like archeologists, uncovering layer after layer of
immigrant history. On every table, in every bureau drawer,
under the hand-made tissue patterns and bolts of cloth, were
letters, photographs, certificates, notices of meetings. We
found his gasoline ration book from World War II and the certificate that declared him a volunteer air raid warden for his
block, and I remembered him in white helmet and carrying a
flashlight, going out to check compliance with the blackouts.

We found his certificate from night school, saying he had
passed the course for citizenship, and I remembered that
though he read English haltingly, he bought me the complete
works of Shakespeare, a thick volume bound in royal blue
and gold, when I was eight years old, and listened proudly to
my chant, "Double, double, toil and trouble, fire burn and
cauldron bubble," from the witches who open "Macbeth." A
reader in Yiddish of Isaac Bashevis Singer and Sholem Asch,
he would come home with books for me by Mark Twain,
Louisa May Alcott, Zane Grey.

We found bundles of canceled checks, tuition payments
and room and board installments that mark the education of
four children, who between us have two Ph.D.'s, a law
degree and an M.D., all from his needle and thread. Beneath
the checks, we found a small bound notebook, his accounting
of money collected from the Gombiners in America and sent
during the Depression to their impoverished neighbors in the
home village.

We found theater programs listing the parts he had
played and photographs of him in snappy American clothes,
a sharp crease in his trousers, a rakish tilt to his hat. We found
our parents' marriage contract, a large parchment, hand lettered in formal Hebrew, inside a border of angels and clasped
hands. Beneath everything else, we found a letter to his uncle
(the first of the family to reach America) dated 1919, saying
in Yiddish, "Life is impossible here. I am as a bird without a
resting place. I must come to America."

He came from Poland, but he never thought of himself as
Polish. Indeed, there scarcely was a Poland during his life-

time. The Gombiner Jews spoke Yiddish, Polish, Russian, German. They had to. Their province of Warsaw was controlled first by one, then another of these warring nations. At best, the rulers tolerated the Jews in their midst; at worst, they killed them.

In America, in 1969, the Gombiners made a book—the most important book my father gave me. It is called, "Gombin: the Life and Destruction of a Jewish Town in Poland." It is a heavy book, 400 pages in Yiddish and English, filled with maps hand drawn from memory, photographs and rememberings that talk of daily life and, finally, daily terror, from the 18th Century to World War II, when the Nazis demolished the town and murdered all who still lived there. Those who had come to America made this book for their children and grandchildren, so that we would always know where we came from. In it, they speak of the River Vistula, seven miles to the north, and of the pine forest which bordered the town. They describe the main street, with its tailor shops and bakeries, and on the hill, a wooden synagogue.

The town is gone; the book remains. My father is dead; his legacy survives, firmly lodged in his acts and his papers. They tell us what he knew for sure: that he had two homes— Gombin and America—and that he had stitched them together, as he stitched coats and trousers, finely, so the seams never showed.

UPSTAIRS/DOWNSTAIRS AT SAGAMORE
The millionaire's son and the caretaker's daughter shared a Great Camp childhood

MARIA MCBRIDE BUCCIFERRO

WORD THAT Alfred Gwynne Vanderbilt Sr. had gone down with the *Lusitania* when it was torpedoed by a German U-boat in May of 1915 shocked the staff at Sagamore Lodge, the Vanderbilts' fifteen-hundred-acre Great Camp near Raquette Lake.

"Everyone stopped short in their tracks and mourned," recalls eighty-two-year-old Margaret Collins Cunningham. She was seven years old at the time of the tragedy, the daughter of the camp's caretakers. "It was a very sad day. Mr. Vanderbilt was well liked by everybody. He was tall, well built, handsome. He was a very good friend as well as the boss of my mother and father."

Alfred Gwynne Vanderbilt Jr., who will be seventy-eight in September, has no memories of his father. But he does remember Margaret, "the young black-haired girl," and her father, Richard, who carried him around Sagamore in a pack basket when injury and illness made him too weak to walk.

Though the Vanderbilts' and Collinses' paths diverged in 1924, when Margaret's parents opened a place of their own in Blue Mountain Lake, the two families shared their lives, and Alfred and Margaret shared a childhood, at Sagamore. Their stories are intertwined like the twisted twigs of the rustic furniture that furnished the Great Camp they all called home.

Alfred Vanderbilt Sr. bought Sagamore from its architect, William West Durant, in 1901. That same year, he married his first wife, Elsie French; in fact, they honeymooned at the camp. The marriage ended in 1908 (amidst charges of Alfred Sr.'s infidelity), but in 1911, Alfred Sr. married again, this time taking Margaret Emerson McKim, the heiress to the Bromo-Seltzer fortune, as his bride. The wedding took place in Surrey, England. Alfred Jr. was born in London the following year, and his brother George was born there in 1914.

The family lived in England for the first two years of Alfred Jr.'s life. There, his father pursued his favorite hobby: show horses. The family then moved to Lenox, Massachusetts, and later finally settled on Long Island. But no matter what location the Vanderbilts called home, Sagamore would always remain their special retreat.

Margaret Cunningham's father, Richard, grew up on a farm along the Hudson River in North Creek and was on the crew that built Sagamore, in 1897. Her mother, also named Margaret, was a teacher from Chestertown. Richard and Margaret were married in 1901 (the same year as the ill-fated Vanderbilt/French nuptials), and were hired by Alfred Sr. as the caretakers for Sagamore, in 1902. In January 1908, while her employers were embroiled in divorce proceedings, Margaret Collins took a three-week "vacation" from her duties at Sagamore to give birth to her daughter. It was one of the few breaks she had while working at the Great Camp.

Sagamore was a place far removed from the world in its early days. Young Alfred rode in the "Wayfarer," his father's private railroad car, from Lenox to Raquette Lake, where two matching teams of horses would pull the Vanderbilts' custom carriages the remaining four miles to the settlement. The Vanderbilts' Great Camp was like a self-sufficient village in the wilderness, with a staff of artisans to produce furniture, hardware and food. It even, for a time, had its own school, housed in a cottage that was formerly used for the help. Margaret Cunningham remembers that one of her cousins, from Corinth, was the teacher.

Corn and potatoes were grown across the lake from the camp, where there was a cow pasture, and sheds for milking in the summer and for making maple syrup in the spring. "We loved maple-sugar time," says Margaret. "When the syrup wasn't all boiled down, we'd make jackwax. We'd put [the syrup] on the snow to harden into a brittle, thin candy." She recalled that Mrs. Vanderbilt wanted the maple syrup to be as lightly colored as the maple table in her dining room.

Life at Sagamore operated on two levels: upstairs/downstairs and up the hill/down the hill. The Vanderbilts and their guests inhabited the main lodge and cottages on the peninsula on the lake; the workers' enclave was up the hill, where there were barns for horses, cows and carriages, and shops for the blacksmith, painters and carpenters. A letter written in 1913 gives an idea of the staff required to run Sagamore. It reads, "Help who will arrive at 'Sagamore Lodge' Monday eve.: Butler, 2 Footmen, 1 Chambermaid, 2 Laundresses, Chef, 2nd Cook, Kitchenmaid. The other footman, 2nd chambermaid and another kitchenmaid will arrive Wednesday."

Richard Collins was in charge of the outside maintenance of the camp, which grew to include twenty-nine buildings. Margaret Collins took care of the inside. While Mrs. Vanderbilt played croquet on the lawn that she insisted be mowed each morning by eight o'clock, Mrs. Collins was busy overseeing the cooking, cleaning, washing and ironing for the Vanderbilts, their fifteen or so personal servants, an average of thirty, but sometimes as many as fifty, guests and nearly twenty resident staff members. Margaret Collins raised her own five children in her spare time; she and her family lived in four rooms over the kitchen until a separate building for the help was built up the hill sometime around 1913.

Life at Sagamore couldn't have been more bucolic than it was in 1915, when the sinking of the *Lusitania* suddenly shattered the calm.

Alfred Jr. was just two and a half years old when his father drowned off the Irish coast. Thirty-eight-year-old Alfred Sr., who could not swim, was last seen giving his life jacket to an old woman and helping children into the lifeboats, which carried only 761 of the *Lusitania's* nearly two thousand passengers to safety. (When Alfred Sr.'s death was confirmed, Margaret Vanderbilt halted the construction of a large sports center at Sagamore; a new men's camp was later built on part of that foundation.)

Two years later, in 1917, tragedy once again struck the camp. A horrific carriage accident killed Sagamore coachman Johnny Hoy, and nearly killed Alfred, his brother George and their nurses. Alfred still remembers the incident vividly.

"I was about five years old, and my younger brother and I had gone up to Sagamore while I was recovering from mastoiditis. We were out for our afternoon carriage drive around the lake. The coachman, myself and the nurse were in front and my brother George and his nurse were in back. A birch tree fell and killed the coachman. It knocked my head open, and broke both my knees and the ankles of my nurse."

Margaret Cunningham remembers the stillness of that August afternoon. Alfred's mother was playing croquet when the team of horses, carriageless, rushed back to the barn. One of the nurses shouted across the lake for help.

Johnny Hoy's widow stayed on at Sagamore as cook for the men's camp (and Margaret's schoolmate, Elizabeth Hoy, didn't have to move away). Margaret remembers her father carrying Alfred around in a pack basket well into spring as he recovered from the accident.

But despite the misfortunes, Margaret and Alfred have grand memories of life at Sagamore.

Margaret still has a gold heart and chain from one of Alfred's birthday parties. She remembers that he ordered the chef not to cut the spaghetti so that he could watch his young guests struggle with it.

Alfred recalls that the only automobiles present at the camp were the toy cars owned by the Vanderbilt children. "No cars were allowed in any of the camps until the late forties and early fifties," says Alfred. "We took the train and were met by horse and carriage."

During the winter, the sleighs that met the train at Raquette Lake would be filled with fur robes, bearskin coats and heated bricks, Margaret says. When a party was being held at Sagamore, the road to the camp would be lit with torches.

Winter was a favorite time of both Margaret and Alfred. They remember riding the toboggan slide onto the lake and bobsledding on the snow-covered roads between the camps. Margaret especially liked skijoring—being pulled on skis behind a horse-drawn sleigh.

In the summer the Collins children would take the Vanderbilt boys on hikes. "They were nice kids," says Alfred. "They'd take us on picnics and cookouts—they were much better woodsmen than we were. We didn't know anything."

The pictures in Margaret's photo album capture her and her brothers fishing, hunting, horseback riding, and feeding their pet fawn. The photos show the hard work, too: shoveling snow off the camp roofs, cutting ice from Raquette Lake. But unlike her parents, Margaret wasn't buried by chores; setting the bowling pins at Sagamore's open-air bowling alley was one of her favorites. ("After dinner everyone would bowl," Alfred recalls.) Arranging colored pins in pincushions for the guests' rooms was another duty Margaret remembers.

"I probably did the same amount of work all twelve- to fifteen-year-olds do—not much. I didn't have any job I *had* to do, only the tasks I was assigned by my parents," says Margaret.

While her oldest brother, John, had to go live with relatives in Corinth to attend high school, Margaret and her brothers drove a buggy to the new school in Raquette Lake. There were three students in her graduating class: her brother Dick, who was class president, her brother Pat and herself. "We all had an office," she recalls.

Alfred went to private schools, but spent about five weeks a year at Sagamore, from mid-July to Labor Day, and also came up to the camp for Christmas when his father was alive.

In 1922 the Collinses bought a Great Camp of their own—the former Duryea camp on Blue Mountain Lake. They left Sagamore in 1924 to operate The Hedges as a guest hotel.

"When we moved to Blue Mountain Lake, my father told Mrs. Vanderbilt that he wanted to buy something that was his own so *he* could turn the key and take my mother and himself off for a change," Margaret says.

Alfred recalls that the Vanderbilts' lives also took a new direction in 1924, when his mother pooled some money with a few friends to buy steeplechase horses.

"My mother picked a winner and that hooked her," Alfred remembers. Her father built her a racing stable outside of Baltimore, which she named Sagamore.

Alfred, after attending Yale University for a year and a half, also caught the horse-racing bug, and he decided to leave the school. "My mother thought I was making a terrible mistake," he says.

When Alfred was nineteen years old, he bought his first racehorse, which won $725 in eight races. Three years later his horses ran in 569 races and won $303,705. In 1935 and 1953 Alfred was the leading money-winning thoroughbred owner in the country. His horse Native Dancer was named Horse of the Year in 1954. It was in that same year that his mother gave Sagamore to Syracuse University.

The Great Blowdown of 1950 had caused heavy damage to Sagamore. "We lost a lot of trees," Alfred recalls. "Mother called us together and said, 'Are any of you going to keep this up?' No one was."

Alfred Vanderbilt Jr. was twelve years old and Margaret Cunningham was sixteen when their paths parted in 1924. More than six decades later, in 1986, Margaret and her brothers stopped by Alfred's box at Saratoga racecourse to say hello.

"He remembered me at once and invited me to his box," Margaret recalls. "He always asked for every one of us individually. The Vanderbilts were real people," she says.

Alfred relived more of his own history that same summer when he, his son Michael and their good friend Anne LaBastille visited Sagamore. Alfred and Michael marked their initials and heights on the door frame where, Alfred says, "Mother used to back me up to the wall with a flat book."

Today, Alfred has reduced his racing stable from eighty horses to six, and he's having trouble reading the racing program. His eyesight has deteriorated in the past year or so from macula degeneration. "There's nothing to be done, it's the aging process," he says. The binoculars in his box are for his guests.

Margaret still comes up to Sagamore from North Creek several times a year to give friends and family a personal tour.

Both Alfred and Margaret planned to return to the camp this year, to experience a small taste of their pasts and in the process prove that sometimes the lines between upstairs and downstairs are inextricably interwoven. Despite the plain differences between a millionaire's son and a caretaker's daughter, Sagamore was a home to both.

THE BRIDGE

Michael Burkard

Despite our protestations
the bridge is approved.
The mayor examines
the breasts of the participants,

and the sadder breasts
are sung to.
The men and the boys,
the women and the children—

these pairs are not used to
singing together. Sung to,
yes. Manipulated
from song, yes.

But to be gently paired,
to have their breasts, the breasts
they themselves have disliked,
serenaded—

this they are not used to.

A RAINCOAT

My mother kisses me goodnight for the thousandth time.
I am always wondering now, is this the last kiss?
Is this the end—for I have begun to see the face of the end
and it is not such a dark end, nor wholly white with light.
It is as if one will don a raincoat for a journey into eternity.
That is the most I can say about this face.
My mother's face—ahh! Now that I forgave myself I can see
      her face

and it is more beautiful now
than ever before in its seventy years.
And to think I worry about my face, and you
yours! How foolish.
My darling I told you my memory was forming in a central
      place
around a raincoat. And my young friend, whom I feuded with
as only friends will, walking to school with me in abject silence

(we were feuding but walking together!)

and my brother attempting to break this silence for us.
It broke, I know it broke, I don't know when and where
but yes it broke. . .

and did I tell you I might see death before any of us. . . and I
      say this
not to frighten us but to tell you it is alright, to tell myself
it is alright. . . it is believable

and death is so broke it needs us. . .
I believe the momentum of a life never, never stops. . .

the breath never ceases. . . the moon and the sycamore never
    cease to
miss us as we miss them. . .

A raincoat—I cannot even begin to articulate this coat. . .
the lives it saw, the leaves it saw orphaned at the school,
the words like orphans which fell against the silent night
from a child's mouth. The breath of the closet like a stone filled
with light as the closet knew the moon or sun rose. . .

the paint which married one of its sleeves. . .
the coy view the raincoat possessed of my mother and my
    sister. . .
if this raincoat could have met you darling. . .

people's faces. . . in the square, in the school, in the window
    our souls
climbed at night when we slept in each other's arms. . . the
    faces at sea
accompanying the faces on the roads to the sea. . . the face of
    your
sons and your daughter, my mother and my father, the lost
    ones who
love us without our ever knowing. . . how constant they are

in this life and death which is one beauty. . .
Shh! A child is hanging his raincoat. . . my mother
kisses us goodnight. . .

ENTIRE DILEMMA

I wish you had knocked on my door today,
because I've realized I've had the entire dilemma
upside down. It will not seem important to you,
but you see, it has not been my parents who have
made me lonely, deeply deeply cold, over many

years and bridges, it was never them at all.
All this time I thought so, but I've had the entire dilemma
upside down. It will not seem important to you,
which is why you did not knock, but it has been the town
I was born in, town my parents remained in, town I returned

to like a dead bird still flying in search of a dead bell,
a soundless one the town likes to ring coldly out into the sky
at five o'clock or six o'clock or whenever one of the
    important
persons wants someone less important to know they are
    counting
money so they ring the bell—it is the town which has made

me sick all these, a town! And it made my parents sick,
and it made my brothers sick, and it made my sisters sick,
perhaps my sisters sickest of all—for they were always the
    ones
who were told you have nothing to be sick about, stick
    around
and see. They saw! Their poor eyes hardened like coins on a
    shelf,

and my relatives walked into our house to count these coins,
and slowly but surely they took my sisters apart, my little
 sisters!
And my brothers and I have returned and returned—because
 my
father was there, because my mother was there, and she is still
and is now very sick indeed and old, and yet we never knew

we had the entire dilemma upside down. It will not seem
 important
to you, but you see it has been the town all these years.
It was not the roads we loved, it was not the houses,
—we actually hated the houses but we could not tell,
we hated the roads there but we walked upon them like ghosts

of deep habit, searching for passports, illegal passports, which
would place us in another country where someone is
 important
for you, knocks at your door, and whispers get out, get out,
long before you have heard the rivers in the words, the words
which come close, only to stray, only to judge you like the
 person

you are not, like the person on the top of a bell, being told
now, now, come down, come down from your bell you little
 dead bird.
It is five or six o'clock. The blackbird is sewing a song for you
to wear. A heavy song. All the heavier, for it is a song you will
always wear, and wear it upside down.

It has been the town I was born in.
It has made me sick. It has killed people, over and over.
Everyone tells everyone you are nothing in my town, and it
 is meant.
I wish you had knocked on my door today,
because I've realized I've had the entire dilemma upside down.

CLOTHES WHICH ARE MOONLIT

Ada's decision to have the barn painted has not created
an affinity with the sky. The family is troubled.
When they visit they now see this lack of an affinity,
but they are not sure of what they are seeing
so it is very uncomfortable.

Ada's brother-in-law Curtis is picking blueberries
from the blueberry bushes. He is also picking them
from the porches of his youth: and Ada is calling to her
    husband
Irving, and Irving is calling to no one,
—the clothes which are moonlit

are like the jokes about his uncle
who has become so plump that when he wears a dark blue
    shirt
he resembles a blueberry, and when the uncle is told this
he is offended; his clothes are moonlit
but he is offended.

There is not much affinity between blueberries and money.
Oh, Ada makes some money from the blueberries, people
    come to pick,
but she misplaces the blueberry money as often as she
    banks it.
And the banks are miles away anyway, as far as the
    mountain
is from the sea, as far as the bra is from the socks

on the clothesline, as far as the uncle's dark blue shirt
is from the cat at the edge of the field,
as far as
the plump fossils of the moon are from the bed we sleep in.
But we dream. We dream.

RED LEAF

You have come to the end and there is a red leaf—it is staring
across the chasm where your friend is dreaming—before the
    two of you,
your friend and you, your alias and your bridge, fell into
    poison.

A sunset is a neck.
A rain is falling outside no one.
Upon god's mother there was a spider
but Helen killed it.

And she is not your memory nor her own.
And the dream is as ill as someone else.
And no one in the world now seems as alone as your friend.
And the world is hard on your friend when your friend is
    feeling alone.

You have come to the end and there is a red leaf—it is the one
your friend blew from a palm in laughter, laughter about
    the mission of god, and the leaf
fell but you took it. But you took it and placed it away.
And tonight you have found it—by accident—in your book.

A book you stole.
A book you will never return.
A book belonging to those you called your tormentors
on a small day in a small spring when it was hot then cold.
    And no one knew what was coming next.

The red leaf is beautiful.
Intact. Intact red.
Your belief in it is as important as your belief in your friend.
For that reason alone you hold it to your heart, and to your
    head.

Poison seems more invisible than death. No.
No.
You have come to the end and there is this red leaf—it is the
    one
you press to your heart as if it could be the world.

ONCE YOU HAVE LET SADNESS GO THE WAY OF LOST GEESE

Albino Carrillo

There's a wilderness
no rationality can touch—
good fear will stick to you
in the woods, the tracks
beneath you.

In another decade
flowing with red wine
and the voices of a girls' choir
behind me, I held my head down,
I climbed a tree.

I knew its dark limbs
like I knew maps of my city:
what I don't know were shadows
crying beyond me
like broken animals.

When I confront
the wild body thrashing
inside, the sweetest songs
of medieval Europe, I must give up loneliness.
Lost geese float everywhere.
I cannot name each one.
Traveling south in late winter

I saw them. One night
in March I heard their calls,
traced their shadows
in gray moonlight.

A FLAME TOUCHING MY LIPS

I wrestled with the gray
Canadian ghost who spoke through
pines tracing ridges, precipice. Far below
men carved into the earth.
The city they loved
lay several miles east, a reflection
of its makers, who in building
the railroad cut into several
miles of high alpine fields.

Here blind
young men climbed
the granite face of the world. Broken
tools and flags jutted like rotten hair.
One morning after walking seven
miles into the Rockies
I found an outcrop
covered in ladybugs.
I watched rain
fill the world. From what I know
it fell evenly. The woods'
reflections fell evenly.

EL OTRO LADO

Already my language is translated
into elegiacally moving pulses,
a static my father couldn't imagine.

While living in New England
I listened to the radio, trying to dial-in
outposts of my desert
where Mexican voices ride
the high voltage wires of Chihuahua:

there's a song about a lost sparrow
that drops into a sweet, hidden spring.
This other world
resonates like the clear bottom
note of a bass guitar. The same world

contains evening: the airwaves are ultraviolet streets,
promoting connections, ringing bells
like errant boys in the afternoon.

In small cities the words hang
like ripe fruit, vanishing
translators of the possible: at night
the disk jockey spins guarachas,
canciones premiadas de Celia Cruz—
I'm warm, falling asleep
with my palms
pressed between my knees.

STRUCTURES AND HABITATS

1. Stretching in the Lightning Storm

This morning it rained as I wrote
a world into your life of hillside,
deep thickets of syllabic columbine.
The storm moved in; I wrote to ease
my entrance into the weather, and later
slid along the streets
with big drops soaking my jacket,
the Mexican student who smiled
at me through her umbrella.

O sullen friend who does not leave me abandoned,
I am thinking of you as the perfect
stranger who wants only my
odd assortments of poems to read at moments
when, undressing, we realize
windows and shutters are moving with the grace of air.

Tonight
slow to admit to love or boredom,
I am thinking of calling
the mysterious animal who waits
beyond my headlights when I drive
through the southwest, the sky
darkened by the absence of moon.

2. Church of Empty Fields

Where I write this
the land is epistle yellow.
I dreamt readily about it
under rain clouds, sleeping near Cerrillos.

That night
there was a sense I would disappear:
the western rhetoric of pine ceilings,
the small blue-bellied lizards
living in the honeysuckle,
they'd leave with the rain.

Before I loved you that night
I dragged a dry stump
away from a clearing,
the chain cutting into my hands.
Somewhere along these lines, again waiting,
is the swiftness of your gesture
dragging the emerald heart to rest.

3. Centuries of Music

The planting was late,
taking place in June. The music
wrapped the room
like a Navajo blanket.
You'd chosen the peppers carefully—
deep red pods to cook during Winter.

Only days before
I burned dried Russian thistle,
crab-grass and pale lilac
branches in the dark yard
where I'd set-up my telescope at night.

The distance created in the flames
was the cold elm covered in hoarfrost.
It beat me one January. June was late
and music took the place of air.

THE KISS

LÂLE DAVIDSON

SIMON DUPRAS was the kind of man who was nicer to the woman behind the counter than to his own wife because she reminded him of his wife but wasn't. His impulses to anger were interrupted by sudden and acute fixations on irrelevant details: a loose thread on his vest pocket, a cap set askew on the ketchup bottle. His wife was a peripheral figure with whom he only had the most utilitarian exchanges. Memory of a time when things were briefly different belonged to another world. A time such as that was impossible now, and indeed, he doubted if it ever was.

Much larger on the horizon was his love of detail, which was profound. This made Christmas presents easy for everyone. He collected miniatures of everything: paintings, carvings, figurines, train sets, doll house furniture. The placement of objects was a matter of world harmony and peace of mind. Ritual was a matter of beauty and repetition, a matter of truth. He took great pride in working out his daily routines to the last movement. Not one minute or motion was ever wasted. He never took extra steps to get into the car, rather the process was one fluid motion from pivoting hips to turning key. In the office his efficiency was extreme and greatly admired.

His life was so precise that the placement of the toothpaste tube on the wrong side of the sink was the sign of an inner disturbance or mental imbalance. Small wonder, then, that he had no room in his life for his wife. He hated nothing more than having to pause and wonder whether the displacement of his wallet or coffee cup was a message from himself or the effects of his wife. He didn't blame her, no. The particular pattern of movement unique to each individual was the result of a million possibilities falling into a particular system shaped by chance, will, immediate circumstance, body chemistry and an infinite variety of incalculable factors. That was the beauty of it. And that was the shame. For his wife naturally had a different pattern, and matching them was as likely as reversing time.

Separate bathrooms and bedrooms had taken care of most of these problems, and separate work realms had taken care of the rest. This meant that the chaotic results of their interrelations were a matter of choice, not chance. And gradually they chose to meet less.

He distrusted alcohol and did not partake of it despite the frequent and overbearing insistence of his associates during business lunches. The one time he'd given in resulted in such a serious departure from the routine placement of his clothing that the next morning he'd stumbled over his shoes, banged his knee on the dresser, found his watch on the window sill and lost a full eight minutes from his morning ablutions. Most disturbing was that it took him a good part of the morning, even after he'd found his footing again, to see and feel his life as he had always seen and felt it. It took him hours to shake the feeling that he inhabited the same place, life and world.

As the years passed and his routine became ever more polished, he got so that he could perform at full capacity without being truly aware. Through repetition and the methodic tailoring of time and movement, he gained speed and through speed he achieved a kind of stasis. For though he whirled with plantagenate celerity, he himself was completely at rest. The world spun, and he spun with it, but from his inner eye he watched it all with a Buddha calm, trusting that he had reached a form of enlightenment.

Until one day. There must have been a blip in his consciousness. He was never to know. It was a sort of bubble, a pocket of air in the smooth stream of his existence. No one else could have noticed it. No one but him. It happened first at the office. He was processing a few papers when all at once something snapped and he realized he had no idea what he was doing. He was paralyzed for a second and then it all came back to him. It hadn't lasted long, and it was just a small dip in his flight of efficiency, but for Simon Dupras, it was the first crack in a crumbling empire. Of course he regained his calm almost immediately and was able to lay this worry aside.

Until one morning. When he woke up, everything had changed. He was still sleeping in his customary position, on his back with one arm on his stomach, the other under his pillow, one leg straight, the other bent. BUT, he had the distinct impression that everything had shifted a little to the left, and consequently he was lying just a little bit to the right of his customary spot, thus leaving his elbow edging out of the covers and over the mattress. When he got out of bed, he nearly fell off it, as the edge came too soon. Once out of bed, it seemed, to his increasing alarm,that it had not been a uniform shift, for not only had his bed shifted to the left leaving him to the right, but it seemed that the room had shifted a little bit to the left of the bed. For no sooner had he nearly fallen out of bed, but he almost toppled into his dresser. And when he went into the bathroom he scraped his right shoulder on the door frame. And as he shaved he seemed to have to constantly crane his head to the left to catch the mirror, and when he set down his razor it fell off the edge of the sink, and at breakfast when he reached for his orange juice he knocked it over. And when his wife, who got up exactly fifteen minutes after him, came out of her bedroom and into the kitchen, she seemed to have stayed with the shift, for she seemed, inexplicably, to be farther away from him. Standing at the counter, making her coffee. She and that whole entire end of the kitchen seemed further to the left, as if the kitchen had elongated.

This sensation continued as he made his way toward his car. If his life had been a series of picture frames neatly stacked one on top of the other, now it was as if that stack had been pushed over and the frames fanned out to the left and the right, and he was left awkwardly stumbling from frame to frame. For somehow he managed to slam his coccyx bone as he pivoted into his car. It took him several tries to fit the key into the ignition, and once in it simply wouldn't turn. Simon's alarm was turning into a full blown panic, but he was a man of great reserves, and he somehow managed to force the lid down over agitated breath, like a manhole cover coming down on a jet of water.

He would take the train, that was all. The train would be just fine. He used to take the train, years ago, when he and his wife first moved out to the suburbs. It had only been in later years that he had graduated to the car, thinking that he now earned enough, and it better suited his professional image to drive to work in his own self-contained unit. But so, today, he would simply take the train. It was merely a switch of routines. By the time he got to work, surely everything would fall back into place.

He was almost completely composed by the time the train arrived. He walked through the doors without any noticeable difficulty and found his seat automatically. There now, he thought, everything is fine. It was just a passing delusion. Perhaps I had a cold during the night and was simply recovering this morning.

Everything was fine—until his collar began to pinch him on the right. He gave it a tug. But minutes later it was pinching him again on the right. Next thing he knew, his pant leg seams were twisting around to the front. Simon began—cautiously—to fidget.

Surreptitiously, he began to scrutinize the other people on the train. Did they feel the shift, or had they moved over also? If they had noticed, how would he be able to tell. If they were at all like he, they wouldn't want anyone to know. He began looking for signs, a gesture, a look, anything that might portray that they shared his shift in position.

All at once his heart seized. The train was going in the wrong direction. Had he somehow gotten on the wrong train? He looked out the window for some landmark, but it all whizzed by anonymously. He reviewed his entrance to the train station in his mind. No, definitely he remembered seeing the signs, and the ticket collector had been by already. He looked around at the other passengers. A middle aged woman with her small son sat across from him. Several men stood in the aisle with briefcases at their feet. No, this *had* to be right. But the direction felt completely wrong. He waited with baited breath for the next stop. And here it was,

Penzington Square. That was absolutely right. Penzington came after Harrisburg. Unless—had they passed Harrisburg? No wait, that wasn't possible, to be going the other way and passing Penzington Square he would have had to have gotten on from his destination. And—he checked his watch nevertheless—it was *definitely* morning and he was *definitely* going *to* work and not *from* work. He sat back, not feeling much comforted. This shift was totally disorienting him.

The woman across from him had fallen into a doze. His gaze flickered over the boy and onto the men standing in the aisle. Certainly no one was looking at him strangely. Except for that boy, perhaps. His eyes slid back to the boy, but the boy quickly looked away.

He went back to scrutinizing people. He began to see more than he wanted to see. That man's tie had caught on the button of his shirt, and he didn't seem to notice. The woman wearing the green dress wore green shoes of a mismatched shade. And she kept tugging at the edge of her blouse as if it were constantly sliding up. There were too many signs. He could not put any order to them. At the next stop two men did a little jig of trying to get around each other as one came in and one came out. The woman across from him got up, brushing his knees with the hem of her skirt as she passed, and moved through the door. The boy did not go with her. That seemed odd.

That boy, Simon thought, his eyes sliding back to him, certainly had big eyes. And he *was* looking at him strangely. The boy caught him looking and smiled a little, leaning forward.

"I've seen you before," the boy said. He couldn't have been more than five years old. Simon looked at the door as the train pulled out of the station.

"Uh, you have?" Simon smiled uncertainly.

"I see you everywhere," said the boy.

Simon was alarmed. "Really?" he said, feeling silly as he tried to consider this possibility. He flipped through his mental files, looking for a face like this.

The boy nodded and leaned closer, "Everywhere I go, there you are, and everywhere you are, I'm there too."

Simon felt a ticklish chill at the back of his neck. The boy's eyes were impossibly large. "No, I'm quite certain that's not possible." Unless, thought Simon, had he? It was possible, he supposed. There were a lot of little boys, and he just didn't pay attention to them.

"I see you *everywhere*," exclaimed the boy, then suddenly serious, rueful, shaking his head slow and wide, eyes like round, polished hematite, infinitely large, "but you don't see me."

Simon looked at the boy's face, and as he looked he felt his entire past beginning to shimmer and shift making room for this new possibility. And he felt suddenly as if he could just see this boy out of the corner of his eye in his past. Yes, perhaps he *had* seen this boy before, and he'd just never fully looked. In a mall perhaps. In the parking lot. Maybe the grocery story. The more he looked at the boy and the more the boy looked at him with his large dark eyes and his slightly inclined face, the more he realized that, *yes*, this boy *had* always been there. It was suddenly coming clear to him. He could just see the faintest image of the boy standing at his bedroom window looking out into the morning when he woke up. And yes, there he had been in the kitchen, the table top meeting his chin, reaching up with his small hands to precariously tip the large orange juice glass toward him. And there he was with his seat belt on in the car, waiting for Simon to get in to drive him to work, with his little lunch satchel on the floor by his little brown leather shoes. And there he was in the park that Simon walked through in the summer to take his lunch, looking over his shoulder at Simon as he was about to throw the blue, white and red-swirled ball back to a playmate. He *had* been there, all along, with every step, every move, every motion, always there. And Simon had just never fully seen him until now.

"Can I kiss you?" said the boy, leaning still closer.

"Why—yes," said Simon, too startled to say otherwise. He leaned down to receive the boy's kiss.

And the boy was leaning closer still, his small arms were reaching up, reaching around Simon's neck, loosely, small hands at the back of his neck, and his small soft, pink face, was coming up, closer, closer, his red lips softly grazing Simon's cheek, and he was whispering something, something soft and barely discernable in his ear so that scent and sound combined to make touch drown memory, and blood to hold its breath in one quiveringly self-conscious moment, like the moment when the hider's breath suddenly roars in ears of total darkness in a closet beyond the seeker's sight.

Then the station was upon them, the doors opening, everyone was rushing toward the door. Simon got up, suddenly breathless with excitement.

"I have to—good-bye I have to tell Mar—" and he rushed off the train, looking back over his shoulder, where he caught that enigmatic smile of the brown-eyed five-year old as he waved good-bye.

He was thinking he had to tell his wife—but what was her name? It had been on the tip of his tongue, he hadn't called her that for years, and now it was lost. He had to go home, he had to catch a train. But suddenly he realized he was at his home station. It didn't matter how it happened, he was too excited to stop and figure out how he could have possibly made a full circle without changing trains, he just began to run toward his home, he felt a new life bursting within him, a new love, a new thrill that he had someone to tell this new discovery, this new revelation.

As he rushed up the stairs to his house he vaguely wondered, hadn't the railing been wood, not wrought iron? And as he pushed into the house, a peripheral part of his brain wondered, hadn't the door been green? And as he opened his mouth to call out joyously, "Honey! I have something to —" the silence of the house struck him hard.

He looked around the house. Yes, this *was* his house, his chairs, his rugs. A gauze curtain ballooned gently inward. A pencil lay slanted on the phone table. The electric kitchen clock clicked as the hands changed. The refrigerator hummed. Everything was just as it had always been, except that he had no wife. She was simply and completely gone. And then it dawned on him that he had never had a wife. He hadn't known or shared his life with anyone. She had never been. And for the first time since he could remember, he felt a very empty place inside himself, and into that opening hole of emptiness he felt the first warm and liquid splash of grief.

WINTER HAWKS

KEN DENBERG

Tumbling over logging roads
in the blue late hours
where snow prairies rolled with corn stubble
to border states, we were looking for winter
hawks fixed mid-motion
like winter stars over a broad-winged
February night sky, the long geography
of loneliness and possibility, a speck
of hope that heads south toward us.

In the silence of coming wings, above ash,
spruce, the certainty of stone walls, a winging up
of wind that turns a head
in the gyre. In a narrow focus of wide eyes,
no hare, field mouse, smaller raptor, escapes
this stare.

Comes, the simple tune invading darkness,
comes, our latitude, spiky notes caught
in the limbs above my reach.
Dozing on the couch of forgetfulness,
wind, snow packs bob and roll,
a dream of shades and no time
smiling on any clock, buds wait to trigger,
the machinery of our bodies clanking on,
a wind's breath distilled by wild signals.

COMMON BIRDS

Little betrayals of winter come on a sparrow's back,
indeterminate, pure, out of season.

We want to name why the earth tilts, why winter
is caused by a deaf god hoarding salted meat.

What marvel still in forty years, gravity, the perfume
of my mistress, canals on Mars.

My stomach falls over my belt, no light escapes
from black holes, Einstein considers.

What other birds do I know, what winds,
was there ever a winter like that?

The hawk's nest, her reed basket, are not subsets.
I am picking apples. I kept your picture.

The city was full of expectations—the metal box
holds tiny rusted screws.

Sometimes we'd scoop up handfuls of snow, toss them
into a black kettle. Sometimes I heard her cry

herself to sleep, in sleep she seems a child, so logical.
Without mercy. Sparrows light in a ditch.

Huge summer days under enormous trees. Snow prairies.
What other birds do I know. He kept feathers in a box.

NOCTURNE

On the porch at night cold comes without warning,
the barn red worn off the steps.
The sunset rises in my neighbor's stream, then stars.
My wife's away in town, the field's dark,
farm machinery cools. Not moving
the whole world goes dark, grows close.
Neither here nor there hour of coy dogs and whip-o-wills.
Crooked iambs of leaves, the garden's muted.
I'm not certain if it's really there.

The loud utter quiet, tv's and newspapers
float up and are gone. The mouth of the world
opens and light steps in. The black cat rolls over,
packed bags of work and muddied boots over the hills.
No moon tonight that I can see, housewood and stones
tick from trapped heat while the elm sheds
its leaves of possibility. The Batten Kill & Hudson
works Hoosick Valley to Vermont with its resurrected
and clanking engines. You can taste fall, its frost,
first snow, trace the outline of my neighbor's stone wall.
Wildflowers have turned the color of my hair,
sweep the soot-colored night from the trees.

CLOUDS & CROWS

Low clouds in a late August valley and crow noise,
nothing but crow noise.

A great lake of ice shatters at once,
heels tapping on the magistrate's endless stone halls.

A stone cutter's chisel. Low clouds full of noise.
Granite, marble, slate: the metamorphic age.

Lark feathers in cool wind and no wind.
Impenetrable. Without passion. Cold trouble.

Chalk over a green blackboard. The silence
of Hannibal's elephants, sleeping barbarians.

One flower opens, one bottle of beer, then many.
She had the complexion of wheat.

A late August valley and crow noise, a murder of crows.
I draw myself lying under you.

Conch, arrow, petrified wood: stone cutting.
The spark of low clouds, a morality play backdrop.

Time and chance, bantam weight, the fifth round.
Her cool fingers on my face.

And now you lie down with the cherry wine of sleep,
all crows settled in a field.

Stones find their joyous gravity,
the mask closed its invisible eyes,

dreams of a lost city of lightness,
the absence of clouds.

BLUEBERRY PIE

A perfect circle, a wolf star in your eye.
Birds are flying on her dress. The limit of all science

is what we know most about history. Goethe's tattered sweater.
In war days we rationed sugar, dark bread.

At night we lie down together like spoons, listen
to what we think is thunder.

What scares you most in this, this tiny universe?
I'd like another slice of pie.

No, I don't pray for anything anymore.
In winter the wind, the wind polishes ice

the ice is the only thing between us and drowning.
My neighbor builds a large boat. A drought for months.

I want to tell her she is my life, but nowadays
that coming from a man is weakness.

I've laid off the clubs for home. I've laid off
all sensation. I've butterflies in my head.

Bag your tools and let's ride, but first,
please, another piece of pie.

AT RISK

MARIANNE GILBERT FINNEGAN

"TAKE YOUR FOOT off the clutch or you won't move."

I tried to do as Walter said, but my left foot felt nailed to the pedal. The motor roared as the small red car lurched forward, then stalled for the third time. After twenty-five years of driving smooth automatic cars on wide American highways, I was struggling to master a two-cylinder, standard shift Citroen on a dirt road in Portugal. My husband, Walter, and I were about to spend three years in the Algarve, Portugal's southern coast, and if I couldn't drive I would be immured in our picturesque but isolated villa. Walter had two weeks to teach me before he left on a month-long business trip.

Every day, I practiced shifting on a secluded dirt road. My hands were OK, but I couldn't coordinate my feet. Whenever I did get as far as third gear, the slightest movement unnerved me: a terra cotta-colored dog running beside the car (most Portuguese dogs are the color of the soil), a stocky Algarvian lady all in black walking beneath a black umbrella to ward off the sun, a motor bike roaring past in dust clouds, a karob pod falling from a roadside tree, and I'd stall the car again. Every lesson ended with me in tears, either sobbing "I can't do it, I'll never learn;" or screaming at Walter, "You don't explain it so I can understand."

He looked very large in the passenger seat with his thick white hair brushing against the roof of the small car, and he was remarkably patient. "After a while you'll know when to shift. You'll feel it." He didn't know I thought I had to downshift through every gear to stop the car, third-second-first, in a mirror image of starting. Imagining an emergency stop requiring this procedure made any driving, even at six inches per hour, seem wildly reckless. "You'll feel it," Walter kept trying to reassure me.

By the time his plane left two weeks later, I still hadn't felt it. I could barely make it home from the airport at Faro, 12 kilometers from our house. Although I had improved on back-country roads, I wasn't ready for bloodsport on the Estrada Nacional 125, the hundred mile long coastal highway. Portugal's record of having "the highest automobile fatality rate in the world" spooked me on the way home as impatient drivers blew horns, flashed lights, glued their cars to my rear bumper, tore loose to pass me on hills and blind curves, and gave me the cross-cultural finger as they sped into oncoming traffic.

Most Portuguese are first generation drivers in love with high speeds. Moreover, they are on first generation highways superimposed on a rural countryside honeycombed with age-old mule tracks and footpaths. Many of these winding narrow roads are edged with cork oaks or stone boundary walls which were easily visible to the walkers or wagon-drivers of old. Now many of these roads are paved and the greater speeds of modern vehicles make their sudden curves and visual obstacles newly dangerous. They cause hundreds of little-noticed rural collisions between cars, motorcycles, wagons, and animals. Added to this toll is the melee on the modern north-south, and east-west superhighways that now bisect the country. These generally have three lanes, the outside lanes for traffic in opposite directions, the middle lane for passing in either direction. Every possible form of transport co-exists (or ceases to exist) on these highways. During a typical auto trip on the 125 for example, you will see Portuguese families crowded onto wooden platforms that have been bolted onto motorcycles; vacationers from northern Europe flashing by in high powered Mercedes; red-tasseled donkeys calmly pulling carts filled with gypsies; drunken young men racing dented Fiats in competitive frenzy; farm women walking with baskets of produce on their heads; lumbering trucks loaded with oranges; huge oil vans; and the local fish peddler in his ancient station wagon, sounding his horn and stopping near intersections to market the day's catch. This mismatched multiple-use transport is enlivened by the Portuguese version of the European male driving code which treats the most casual automotive errand as a combat sport. Portuguese men, genial and slow moving at other times, treat cars as missiles to shoot them ahead of the pack at any cost, even when they have no place special to go. With all these geographic and human complications, even defensive driving in Portugal can feel like a suicide mission.

But I kept at it. Two times a day, while Walter way away, I left the quiet of the villa and made myself drive somewhere. I picked up mail from the post office in Almancil, drove to the Wednesday market in Quarteira, drove to the builders to discuss construction of my bookshop. Twice a day I learned that my little red car could alleviate my boredom by transforming it into terror. Often I came home gasping, but I was mobile.

By the time I met Walter's plane a month later, I collected him and whipped smartly around the airport's ramps and onto the 125. Walter whooped and squeezed my arm in amazement which made me swerve out of my lane, but I was pleased and smug.

Now, though driving in Portugal has become a routine part of my day, it still remains a gripping topic of conversation at many dinner tables. The bad roads, the crazy drivers, the ominous *"Guardia,"* the highway police which doesn't much like *estrangeiros*, all make for many a horror story among our fellow expatriates. But I have come to realize that my women friends and I have driving or non-driving stories that are different from those of men. Many of us women came to Portugal not knowing how to operate a stick-shift car. The technology in our home countries has made automatic transmission customary, and most of us learned to drive in automatic cars. This meant that we were further from competence in a simpler culture than were our auto-wise, tinkering husbands. For them, learning to cope with the unfamiliar Portuguese driving habits was an exciting challenge; for us it was a crisis, a watershed issue that would determine the nature of our lives in this country. At home, we had been free

to go when and where we wanted; suddenly we were restrict-
ed, our mobility depended on someone else's schedule or
largesse. I have seen how five of us women, reacting to our
new helplessness, have made varying decisions.

Former theatre-going Londoner, Vicky, now lives in a picturesque farmhouse, surrounded by almond and lemon trees.
From the terrace she and her husband built, they have a stun-
ning view of villages clustered across the hilly slopes that
lead down to the ocean in the distance. Claiming that she is a
"perfect idjit" with machinery, Vicky has never driven a car
and refuses to begin here in Portugal. She gardens and bakes
delicious lemon tarts while singing Gilbert and Sullivan
songs in a witty British voice. She brings the lemon tarts
when her husband drives her to visit friends on Sundays, but
most of her visits are by note or telephone. When she can get
to my bookshop, Vicky buys note paper and self-help books
on overcoming depression.

An Irish friend, Margaret, paints delicate watercolors of
Algarvian wildflowers on greeting cards which I sell in the
bookshop. The phone lines have not yet reached the isolated
country lane where Margaret lives. Last month, stunned all at
once by the silence, she hastily stuffed some clothing and her
paints into two plastic bags and walked seven kilometers
across scrubby terrain to the nearest phone at a village mini-
market. There she called a taxi to bring her to our house
where she arrived hot and exhausted, asking to spend a few
days. "Just to have a bit of normal life," she kept saying, "just
to have a bit of talk." After a week, she decided that she'd better get home and we drove her back. We keep urging her to
practice driving and she agrees, "I know I must learn, but I'm
so afraid of a crash."

Our sweet-faced Indonesian-Dutch neighbor, Dola van
Riin, is now trying to master shifting. Every Sunday, when
traffic is light, I see her Portuguese-made Ford creeping along
the road with Dola staring straight ahead, clenching the steer-
ing wheel, while her husband, Henk, waves his hands and
gives her instructions. Two years ago, when they decided to
retire to the Algarve, they brought a new automatic car with
them from Holland which Dola drove competently here for

six months. Then the Portuguese government, which discourages importing automobiles, refused the van Riins permission to register theirs. They had to drive it back to Holland and then buy a car within Portugal where automatic transmission is prohibitively expensive. Dola's unfamiliarity with shifting gears made her too nervous to continue driving and, for some months, she rode her bicycle when she wanted to do local errands. But now she has an opportunity to teach at the International School in Porches next fall. For that she'll need to drive. It's going slowly, Dola says after each Sunday driving lesson, but little by little it *is* going. By the fall, she hopes to be ready to commute to her new job.

And then there's my American friend, Carol. She has been living here for four years and learned to shift before I arrived in the Algarve. She guns her jeep up and down the mountain in Santa Barbara de Nexe, where she lives with her elegant British husband, two horses and a Great Dane, to her assignments as a journalist all along the coast. She writes news features for an English language newspaper and also does a column of restaurant reviews. We often meet for lunch at a popular brasserie and when we talk about our doings, we both say that we couldn't imagine life in this near-third-world country without the variety of experiences and the independence that our driving makes possible.

In truth, though, I think that both Carol and I did at one time imagine it. While we knew we were protected from the hard rural lives of traditional Algarvian women, we could easily picture ourselves living here just as Vicky and Margaret now do. Talented women, transplanted from 20th century urban lives, their energies and intelligence are thwarted by their dependence and isolation in a beautiful but rough foreign land; their lives are stalled by a risk not taken, a fear not faced down. And as time goes on, they change. What was once frightening has become more frightening. What they once did easily, they now find impossible to attempt. That vividly imagined picture of a constricted future was for Carol and for me, as American women, even more alarming than our very real and justified fears of the road.

LA CORRIVEAU

Douglas Glover

1

I WAKE UP the next morning in my little rented tourist flat on rue des Ramparts with a really terrible headache and a strange dead man in bed next to me.

First, let me tell you that nothing like this has ever happened to me before.

In bed with a dead man—never.

Often they may have seemed dead. You know—limp, moribund, unimaginative, sleepy or just drunk to the point of oblivion. But till now I have avoided actual morbidity in my lovers.

I resist an initial impulse to interpret his sudden and surprising fatality as an implicit critique of our lovemaking the night before.

To tell the truth I don't remember our lovemaking, but the man and I are naked and the sheets are in wild disarray and I am a bit sore here and there which leads me to draw certain embarrassing conclusions.

Embarrassing because I don't remember any of this and especially his name or anything else about him.

He is clearly dead and naked. And a man. Beyond this I know nothing (although, with his sinewy slimness, protuberant eyes, and thick lips he bears a strong resemblance to Mick Jagger, the man of my dreams).

To tell the truth, it makes me a little panicky being in bed with a corpse (however handsome) and feeling that I might be held responsible for him at some point, when in all honesty I can't say that I have ever seen him before in my life, though our having had intimate relations before, and quite possibly after, his demise seems indubitable.

Briefly, I entertain the sanguine fantasy that this is a joke, that my lover possesses a sick sense of humor which lends itself to overly prolonged impersonations of dead people. Perhaps this is some sort of weird sex game. I laugh light-heartedly and pinch his earlobe as hard as I can—it is cold as ice and stiffish to the touch.

Dead.

I jump out of bed with a shiver of disgust.

At least, I think, he didn't get up and leave in the middle of the night the way most men do.

On the other hand, our breakfast conversation is going to be a little one-sided.

In the bathroom, I pee and splash cold water on my cheeks to promote circulation. I look everywhere for some aspirin, but find none. My hair is a nest of tangles on top of my head and there is something, possibly chewing gum, stuck in the back. (What *did* we do last night?) My breasts look bruised and tiny—androgynous is one word for my chest. I am so tall I have to stoop to see my face in the mirror above the sink. Once a man told me I had the figure of a Yugoslavian volleyball star. I don't think it was the man in the bed, but it might have been.

When I return to the bedroom, he is still there (I had had hopes he would disappear, that I had been dreaming or hal-lucinating).

I think, a girl comes to Quebec for a little winter carnival fun and the next thing she knows a dead man gets into bed with her and ruins her vacation. I should complain to the Ministry of Tourism—anonymously, of course, and from home when I get there.

His eyes are open, little brown gelid globes. I have a weakness for brown eyes and men with accents. I realize now he must be French and am briefly fearful of the constitution-al implications, me being English-speaking and from Toronto; I can see the headlines: ANGLO TOURIST SLAYS

INNOCENT QUÉBECOIS FAMILY MAN IN FATAL SEX ORGY.

The French are so sensitive these days.

I recall his name suddenly—Robert. Not actually *recall*, but there is a workshirt draped over the chair, one of the kind garage mechanics and delivery men wear, with their first names stitched above the breast pocket, and the name over the pocket is Robert.

Poor Robert.

Dead for love. Heart attack, I think, or anaphylactic shock brought on by eating shellfish. (Had we eaten shellfish before making love? I make a mental note to look in the kitchen trash).

But then I notice the dark stain on the sheet beneath him, the spillage on the fire carpet next to the bed, and the Swiss Army pocket knife (mine, I am forced to admit—a gift from a former lover obsessed with outdoor pursuits) protruding from his ribs just beneath his shoulder blade.

My headache is suddenly worse, possibly the penumbral overture to a fullblown migraine. Also, suddenly I am extremely irritated with Robert for inflicting his personal problems on me like this, first thing in the morning before my shower and a cup of coffee. I make up my mind then and there not to let this spoil the rest of my time in Quebec (a mere three-day weekend, a third of which is already gone).

Briskly, I form a plan and put it into action, grasping Robert by his ankles (slim handsome ankles, unlike my unfeminine tree trunks) and dragging him out to the tiny balcony overlooking the river and Lévis on the far shore (shrouded in a brilliant icy mist).

I recall reading in a tourist brochure how drovers once herded cattle across the frozen river to the abattoirs of Quebec and how, if you see a man's severed head upon the ice, it is a sign you will shortly die. Had Robert seen a head upon the ice? If so, I don't believe he mentioned it to me.

(On the whole, I find it disturbing that the people who write these brochures seem to think that tourists will be interested in such bloody and lugubrious bits of information.

How strange, dark, and tortured the Québecois mind seems when you begin to examine it closely, how obsessed with death, separation, the loss of memory—they have that motto *Je me souviens* which I translate loosely as "I remember myself"—and hydroelectric power. I leave you with this thought free of charge for what it's worth.)

I arrange my silent lover in a plastic deckchair, with his arms crossed on the balcony railing and his chin nestled against his forearms, and drape his shoulders with a blanket, so that he looks like a man enjoying the view.

Then I strip the soiled sheets and replace them with fresh ones, and bathe and dress in jeans and mukluks and an over-sized duffel coat which must have been Robert's, for I neglected myself to bring anything so eminently suited to the climate.

I trudge through the fresh accumulation of snow along rue Port-Dauphin past many stately and historic buildings made of gray stone, thinking a propos of nothing that the tourist's lot is a lonely one, and also about Hélène Boullé (also lonely, also a sort of tourist) who married Samuel Champlain, founder of Quebec, in 1610 when he was forty and she was twelve. How jolly for him, I think, somewhat acerbically.

She came to Canada in 1620 but had a difficult time adjusting to life in the New World and returned to France four years later. When her husband died in 1635, she entered a convent under the name of Sister Hélène de Saint-Augustin.

This is a sad little story which reminds me of my own—like Hélène Boullé, I have had a difficult time adjusting to life in Canada, though, unlike her, I have nowhere else to go.

This present contretemps—Robert, clearly a victim of murder, showing up indiscreetly in my bed—is merely another instance of a bizarre and insidious synchronicity that has dogged me from the beginning.

I am thirty-seven years old (Hélène Boullé-Champlain's age when she entered the convent) a poet and office temp, unmarried (unless you count my twelve-year affair with an already-attached CBC radio producer named Edward, now aging and paunchy), and desperate. Also prone to fainting, blackouts, syncopes, and blinding migraines—I have been advised to take stress-management instruction.

Oh yes, I have given everything for my art, just as Robert has given everything, including his jacket, for love, just as Hélène Champlain-de Saint-Augustin, née Boullé, gave everything for God. (Or have I missed something?)

We are people of extremes, a nation within a nation, without language or identity.

At a bookstore called Librairie Garneau in Place d'Armes, I buy a book of Quebec military history (more death and defeat—whatever you say about them, they are a people of poetry) and two newspapers (in French—unreadable). Then I slip through an alley to a cafe overlooking Parc des Gouverneurs, where I sit next to a window and order a croissant and a cappuccino.

It occurs to me that someone ought to be alerted to Robert's condition, that an investigation should take place. But then I think of the bother, the questions, the searching interrogations, which might reveal—what?—more than I care to say about myself. For example, my dismal poetry career, my love for Mick Jagger, certain bizarre sexual preferences which point to childhood abuse (of which I have no memory).

I have surprisingly little curiosity about the actual events of the previous night, suspecting, perhaps with reason, that it was all too, too humiliating for words.

Across from me, in the little park, there are snow and ice sculptures representing mythological and folkloric figures, figures of dream or nightmare. But no severed heads or death-driven cattle. No statue to Hélène Boullé, perhaps the first woman to speak her mind in Canadian history.

(One can imagine the scene: Dead of winter, wind howling through the chinks in the log walls, a miserly fire glowing on the hearth, Hélène wrapped in coarse wool and animal skins, sneezing and coughing between sentences.

Hélène: M. Champlain, I don't like it here.

Samuel: But it's lovely. And the savages are really nice once you get to know them. And why do you keep calling me M. Champlain?

Hélène: I hate it. No one ever asked me if I wanted to

come. I was playing with my dolly, Jehan, and they told me I was to be married. And then I was married and you went away for ten years. And now look, you're very old and I'm not having fun.)

I feel suddenly claustrophobic—as if I have wakened to find myself immured behind the stone walls of a convent. (Do I hear police sirens in the distance, trailing along the walls of this medieval city, founded first for greed and then for God—poor Jacques Cartier, when he got back to France and discovered his diamonds were quartz). My mind is wandering. My headache . . . well.

Suddenly, I recall horses and a carriage and a nighttime ride with a man who seemed, with his horsewhip, duffel coat and French accent, the very image of romance, a Boreal Mick Jagger.

But what did we do with the horse? (Now I *do* detect a distinctive equine odor on my coat.)

I believe things are coming back to me.

This leads me to rush off, leaving my coffee cold (as Robert), my croissant untouched, my newspapers unread (what could possibly be new?). Movement seems imperative to ward off the flood of memories which just might possibly prove unpleasant if not actually inculpatory.

There are still few people about on account of the extremely low temperature and the generally threatening nature of the weather. The place is as hospitable to human habitation as Mars. (Oh Canada, our home and alien land.)

No wonder Hélène Boullé hated it.

Then I have a jarring thought. What if history *is* a male lie? What if she actually loved Canada, and Samuel sent her back because he was envious? What if she was having too good a time, the Indians loved her, she found the savage religions appealing, she was beginning to take their side in beaver trade disputes?

Perhaps she never got to speak her mind, do what she wanted to do.

And when Samuel died, and she went meekly like a lamb into the convent, did she even know what she thought?

Did she remember?

Je me souviens is a difficult motto to live up to; I myself remember nothing.

I circle back past the funicular, following the city walls again, till I stand just opposite my darling little flat (with kitchenette and sitting room and Sacred Heart bleeding above the bedstead, all for an extremely reasonable price). Robert, a.k.a. Mick, is still peering out at the steaming river and the ice-rimed, smoking buildings of Lévis on the far shore, though the snow is beginning to drift a little behind him and he has an odd-looking triangular cap upon his head.

What do his dead eyes see? I ask myself. Figures of ice and floating heads?

Does he hear the lurid song of La Corriveau, the Siren of Quebec (see those tourist brochures), who murdered her husband and was hanged and exposed in an iron cage above a crossroads till her body rotted? (Later the cage became a minor exhibit in Mr. Barnum's circus—you can make whatever you want of this outré fact.)

Did I dream this, or did Robert? A naked woman running, slipping in the snow. La Corriveau, to be sure. Calling for help, calling the men of the city to their deaths.

(This is the legend at any rate—that she returns from time to time, attracts men with her pitiable lamentations, then slaughters them. To my mind, she is just crabby, just a little premenstrual, if you know what I mean, because the whole thing was such a mess what with the cage being built too short and her having to crouch even after they hanged her, a victim of incompetent male technocrats. Ugh!)

I think of the great and saintly Bishop Laval who died here three hundred years ago after suffering frostbite on his bare feet doing penance in the snow.

Oh Quebec (as a poet, I am an aficionado of the rhetorical device called apostrophe), death-driven, poetical, and strange. (The obsession with hydroelectric power, dams, and rivers seems symptomatic of a mother complex—in the throes of passion, did not dear Robert call out for his church and for his mother, or possibly his horse? Am I making this up? Or am I merely, like all English Canadians, obsessed with dissecting my French other—my mother calls them Kew-beckers?)

2

I am writing my confession down—I might as well let you know—under the gray stare of a police detective who tells me his name is Gilbert and who has once or twice interrupted my narrative to tell me amusing anecdotes about his children and his wife, whom he insists on calling "ma blonde."

He resembles Mick Jagger somewhat, though perhaps it is only the black leather bomber jacket he wears which gives me this impression.

Gilbert particularly wants me to explain the presence of my Swiss Army knife in the interstices of Robert's ribs. He calls this knife "the cause of death," a summary designation which I find reductive and unpoetical.

If Robert had not been born, he surely would not have died, I say, remembering (as usual) nothing, feeling the iron bars of the cage squeezing inward on my brain. Yes, my headache has not abated.

The police found the horse, it seems, wandering in the streets before dawn, dragging its empty carriage, suffering frostbite and loneliness.

From time to time, she would lift her head and whinny plaintively for Robert to take her home.

Her name is Nellie, and she is now in police custody.

When Gilbert tells me this story, I break down and weep.

I have seduced a man into betraying his horse.

(With this, I remember again my solitary midnight ride among the ice sculptures, the fantastic, contorted shapes, all lit up and glowing. I recall Robert, duffel-coated and masterful, wrapping me in blankets and guiding the horse with clucks of his tongue.)

Gilbert peers over my shoulder and clucks his tongue sympathetically. Perhaps I would like a cup of coffee, he says. Perhaps some other refreshment, a change of air.

His English is only adequate, I think. But charming. His eyes are brown. When we stand, his head reaches to my shoulder, but I feel certain he has enough self-esteem not to be bothered by the physical discrepancy.

Even so I crouch a little as we walk.

He takes me to a cafe a block from the police station and orders a cappuccino and a brioche.

I tell him of my memory lapses (a common Anglo-Canadian complaint), my language problems, my blackouts, and my inability to find a publisher for my poetry.

Somewhat irritatingly, he keeps trying to steer the conversation back to Robert, who is a dead letter as far as I am concerned, a character to be written out of the story.

I tell Gilbert he reminds me of Mick Jagger.

He smiles and lights a cigarette and tells me I too remind him of someone, a woman he saw in a dream.

Uh-oh, I think.

I say, I suppose you assume I'm the sort of girl who travels around preying on French-Canadian caleche drivers named Robert.

He gives a throaty, Mick Jaggerish chuckle, and I can see right away that we have established a relationship that goes beyond the purely professional, that he sees me as someone other than the run-of-the-mill murderess, someone who perhaps needs a protecting arm.

A tiny muscle in my neck begins to pulse like a second heart.

There are snow-covered statues at either end of the street, resembling the icy sculptures in the Old Town, tortured, demonic creatures, visions of some frigid Hell.

My headache is worse, a virtual blazing light of pain, as though my skull were caught in the bars of a cage.

I realize suddenly that my infatuation with Mick Jagger is merely an extension of English Canada's pernicious Anglophilia—substitute the Queen for Mick and I am like anyone else from Saskatoon or Victoria.

To cover my discomfiture, I tell Gilbert the story (culled from inane and ubiquitous tourist brochures) of Marie de l'Incarnation, an early religious pioneer in New France, who (like me) had visions, was married twice and who is 1631 entered the Ursuline convent at Tours despite the pleadings of her only son who stood outside the doors, screaming, "Give me back my mother."

On the whole, I think, French-Canadian history is littered with dysfunctional families. It is difficult to know what to make of this fact.

Gilbert has a tear in his eye. I have touched him with my little tale. He understands, as any member of his race would, that all life is either metonymic or synecdochic. The policeman in him is at war with the poet. It is refreshing to see such passion in a public servant.

We warm to each other in the humid little cafe, despite the cold front descending on the city beyond the windows. People walking in the streets take on the aspect of ice statues. Ice statues begin to resemble ordinary tourists, shoppers, and dead caleche drivers.

Night is falling, despite my impression that day just dawned moments ago.

Gilbert says that at first they thought Robert had frozen to death. Only after he thawed out did they discover the knife wound.

I remember nothing, I say.

They found me at the city zoo which specializes in native species now extinct in southern Ontario where I live. (There are, for example, cages full of Native Americans, Anglo poets, Entirely Free Women, Liberated Men and Innocent Children.)

I think how I long for the time when the black bear and moose will return to the tepid streets of Toronto.

Gilbert leans forward, his face pregnant with pity and empathy, and touches my wrist with the tips of his fingers. He wishes to tell me that he is not a projection of my dreams, that he is himself, separate and whole, and that he will help me if I let him.

I remember nothing, I say.

But his gentleness disarms me. All at once, I begin to weep. It is clear that I have gotten off on the wrong foot with this man, that there is still gum in my hair, that when I left the flat this morning I put on the same clothes I wore the day before, that killing Robert was a monumental faux pas. (My constant reference to loss of memory in the foregoing is clearly a case of reaction formation—we all try to put our worst crimes in the best light possible.)

All I can say in my defense is that homicide is totally out of character for me—most days.

Gilbert suggests a caleche ride. Perhaps we might attempt to recapitulate the events of the evening before so as to jog my memory.

Meekly, I assent.

(I think, soon now my lifelong fantasy of being hung above a crossroads to rot, in full public view, will become a reality.)

Through the testimony of witnesses who saw me in Robert's carriage, the police have been able to reconstruct much of our route.

The driver is a non-French-speaking Irish exchange student named Reilly.

The horse's name is Retribution. (I mention this, though quite possibly it is an unimportant detail.)

In moments we emerge from the Porte Saint-Louis and turn down Avenue George VI into the former battlefield (now rolling park land). A gusty wind drives swirls of ice particles round the lampposts and into our faces. Gilbert and I huddle together, wrapped in a five-point Hudson Bay trade blanket.

Here, as everywhere else, city officials have erected myriad ice statues commemorating significant events in the nation's history. Behind us, the city walls are illuminated, shrieks from revelers and bobsled riders pierce the night air, the funicular rises and falls like breath. But here, Iroquois warriors stalk unwary habitants, Jacques Cartier is mining diamonds along the river shore, Abraham is herding his cows and planting cabbages, and a sickly Wolfe is climbing a narrow path, surrounded by his intrepid, kilted soldiers, with death in his heart.

At the center of the park, we reach the place of memory (where I believe Robert kissed me for the first time).

I can see by the horrified look on Gilbert's face that he can see what I see—the ice statues come alive, wounded soldiers piled in heaps, dying generals, weeping savages, fatherless children, widows touching themselves in ecstasies of loneliness.

I say to him, I am guilty. Of everything. I wanted to sleep

with my father. I poured boiling water into the goldfish bowl when I was eight. I began to masturbate at twelve. I killed Robert the caleche driver (though I fully believe that after an evening with me, he wanted to die).

I do not say that any of this is trivial, but I shall plead extenuating circumstances. I shall blame history, lurid tourist brochures, and love gone wrong.

This time I'll get off, I say. You'll see.

I do not think he hears me.

FOREIGN AID—PART II

Amy Godine

IF THE ISLAND of St. Tiggs was a dromedary on its knees, then the village called Sampsons nested snug between the humps, an old cozy hamlet of bright-trimmed bungalows and pecking hens, with a frame church under an almond tree where Ivy could talk freely, or so Drinkwater had assured her on the phone.

Drinkwater was a minister, a jittery old man in flapping clothes, bald and shiny as an eggplant and possessed of the kind of grin that can seem to rule a face with the fixity of scars. By the time he got around to writing Mercy, the strike was over, long since lost, but there were still a half dozen union members behind bars. What struck Ivy was the specificity of their complaint: not the usual long-overdue harangue about poor wages, hellish working conditions, lack of benefits, long hours, but something so modest, so benign, it verged on the absurd.

They wanted shit. Literally. As it stood, only growers able to produce a ton or more of bananas per quarter got a share of U.S. AID-subsidized fertilizer. Small farmers, owners, say, of less than two, three acres, were barred from this entitlement—no great problem for the European sellers since plus-nine-tenths of all bananas to leave St. Tiggs came from the grand estates, but the pocket farmer, the barefoot yeoman of the rheumy eye and the one keen cutlass, made up two-thirds the growers on the island.

Drinkwater recapitulated. "Soon the big plantations the last farms left. Small-time cultivator, if he wish to keep on farming, he must go every year more high into the hills, and what is dere for he? The rain forest up dere, you know. Some dem old trees so high and mighty it give a vision just to stand beneath. But the trouble with banana, she nothing but a plahnt, you know. She don't *make* no kind of proper root. She sittin' on the dirt just like a chair. So small farmer, he cuttin' down the real tree, he choppin' out the root, the root come out, the dirt come free, soon come the hurricane, and nothing left!" Drinkwater let fly a bitter cackle. "Island finish! It blow into the sea!"

Ivy touched his arm. "We'll get your fellows out of jail, Reverend. Have faith."

From the paneless windows of the church, she had a good view of the six boys straggling toward them along the track that separated the village from the wide planted fields lifting into mist behind. It was the same track that ringed the entire island like a charm bracelet, the charms being, Ivy guessed, those armless windmills from back before the rise of beets and corn, back when sugarcane was king. Hal lived in one of those abandoned windmills. Drinkwater could have told her which, but she'd decided early on she wouldn't ask. Best let the old man think it was his letter brought her.

"Are these my interviews?" she asked.

"Dese is some."

Some kids wore red handkerchieves around their necks, PLO style: had Drinkwater told them they'd be on American TV? Sources said all kinds of things to get people to talk. Offered cash, promised visas, booze—they thought they were doing you a favor.

"And all these kids went to jail for belonging to the union."

"Maybe all. Maybe some it happen only to the father or the brother. But all cahn tell you something."

"Nice work, Reverend."

"I try to get the lawyer, too, you know, but such short notice . . ."

She shook her head. "Kids are perfect."

"Shall I ahsk them . . . ?"

"One at a time, please. If you don't mind."

Fear made ninnies out of One and Two. They sipped their Tings and made determined studies of their shoes. Three was more relaxed, but bland, withholding, she couldn't crack the nut. Four got sick of waiting and bailed out before his turn, and Five kept craning around while she was talking to observe a girl washing her hair in a tin tub in the yard next door.

Then came Eldred. Ivy perked. He was a thick sullen boy with a rope to cinch his trousers where the zipper stopped halfway, but his big hands held the fine tremor of palmetto leaves before a gale, and Ivy, who knew the signs, bore down.

"I tellin' she in Queen plain English. Somet'in matter wit' she ears?"

Drinkwater leaned in. "She knows this, Eldred. She is appreciating your good effort here."

"Appreciate?" Eldred cut Drinkwater a wink. "Appreciate me take her through de night, mahn. She have all night for Eldred?"

"You were going to tell me about jail," Ivy said.

"Me see dem here from New York City, Pahm Beach, Mee-ahmi Beach. Dem t'ink dey visitin' a stud farm," Eldred groused.

"Shall we turn the tape off?" Ivy said.

He yawned. "Me need a beer."

"Do you think I came here to watch you drink?" she asked cheerfully.

"You nuh like fe watch me drink? You come back my house, show you somet'in' bettah."

"Next time, maybe."

"Hyir dis," Eldred said to Drinkwater. "Next time, she say. I say dere is no next time fe she. She step her shoe upon de plane, she fah-get all about we."

Drinkwater jerked forward on his knees, his grin taut and anxious. "It tough, Eldred. She know it tough," he murmured, deftly bringing on the patois: Ivy was impressed.

"She nuh know."

"I *don't* know," said Ivy evenly. "Tough is what happened to those schoolteachers in Grenada. Or that Haitian, the calypso king—"

"Haiti no place fe calypsonian," Eldred scoffed. "All de power calypsonian from St. Tiggs. Dis a truth. Ahsk anyone."

Ivy sipped her can of juice. "In Haiti, I hear the prison rats are as big as small pigs."

Eldred's glare took on a gold gleam. "Here dey hogs, mahn. You go to sleep, dey bite away you *foot*."

Ivy shrugged. "In Haiti, they use leather whips."

"Here, electric cable."

She affected a small yawn.

"You nuh believe me?"

Peeling off his shirt in one stroke, he dropped it on the pew, and turned. Drinkwater rose slowly, his huge grin tight as a gag across his face, and went outside. All through the shoot they heard him retching, a dry tearing sound, like someone ripping long strips of bark off trees.

Ivy took one roll with the flash and one without. All slides. He was something, all right. A real showstopper. During the close-ups she had to breathe through her mouth— and it wasn't just his back. When he sat with his elbows on his knees, she saw how it went below, the leak of pus through the thin seat of his slacks. He sat with his thighs parted and his forearms clamped close between, everything low down, not moving, tight, like something frozen in the high hot head-lights of a truck, nothing but the flinch of muscle when she had turn him slightly, here and there, for light. Her touch was firm, even brusque. She didn't want to agitate him, offend him with a pity he'd only know how to despise, though in the end, she knew, he'd hate her anyway. Always happened. Nothing you could do.

Ivy declaimed. Words called calmly one to the next, they did their job. She told him how the pictures would be used, and why he should be very proud, and what he had to do if he meant to heal.

"You'll get maggots, Eldred. It's no joke." While the film rewound, Ivy put away her lenses. "Reverend said he gave you pills. Are you taking them?"

The boy was shivering.

"Anyway, it's over. Put your shirt on. You were great."

He rose. "Mahn wit' your name living hyir. Live up Frenchman Cove."

Well, here we go, thought Ivy, startled. Here it comes.

"Your name, your face, your voice exahck. And pretty like you, too. Maybe he more pretty." Eldred smoothed his slacks.

"It's a fairly common name," she said.

"That's all right, El." Drinkwater was coming down the aisle.

"He drivin' one of Santy Mini-Mokes. You know it Santy when you see on de side, it written, 'RastaSafari Mountain Tours.' " Eldred's voice was scrupulously neutral, but he had her, she could see it in his eyes, the bitter triumph, the scoring kick. "Tourist girl come skippin' off the cruise ship, she got she Thomas Cook traveler check, she got she head full of an idea, she just *must* have she a true-life Cahribbean ahdventure." He blinked. "And so she do, mahn. So she do."

Ivy'd read about the outlaw rastamen who hid out in the hills, not the millionaire recording artists, the toasters, the emcees, but the real article, the rooty-headed Nattys, crazy, bold as jays, such artful farmers you could be nose-to-nose with a thousand-dollar plant and think you were looking at a fern. She sighed.

"So what is it, Eldred? This fella Santy and his RastaSafari Tours do a little extralegal cultivating on the side?"

He didn't smile. "Do I say dis?"

"Boy, you fixin' to make me vex?" Drinkwater inquired.

"I hopin' wake she up a little, she go mek sport of me. Woman *simple*, mahn."

Ivy said, "Oh, heck."

"De white boy eye exahck, mahn. I amaze dey let she off de plane." Eldred flapped a careless palm at Ivy's face.

Drinkwater grinned. "Woman only wish to help you and you tellin' she dis shit. She nuh *kyeer*. Y'understahnd? Get out."

So he knew about Hal, too, thought Ivy. Everybody knew. One look at her and it was evidently obvious, whatever Hal was doing, or had done. And now they had her, bastards, the bud of fear was in her throat, thickening, pinching up her breath.

Drinkwater had a bottlecap. He jigged it in his hand.

Across the street, lashed to a tire, a muddy sow strained toward a banana peel. When a girl came up beside the sow and started taking down the flat rounds of cassava dough from a clothesline, the sow slumped back on its haunches and sank its snout between its knuckles with a groan.

"He not a bahd boy, you know." Drinkwater was keeping Ivy company while she waited for a cab. "I don't know why he give you such a dusty time."

"He belongs in a hospital. He's putrefying," she said.

He chuckled. "Now you say this. Ahfter you get all the picture."

She was tired. "Would you like them, Reverend?"

"What?"

"Because you can have them. We can stop this thing right here."

"So dahm tough."

"Not so tough."

A flatbed truck with shirtless laborers in back went by. On the doors a slogan gleamed. *Don't make no fuss. Revolution is a must.* Ivy stared out at the cane fields tilting steeply toward the hills. Skeins of mist twisted high along the green, here dragon-humped, there loose as napkins raveled into shreds. She wished Drinkwater would go away.

"Was it eight years ago, the famous hurricane?" she offered brightly.

"Seven year, two month, six day."

"I remember watching it on television. All the volunteers, the airlift, everybody chipping in from all over. It made quite an impression on me."

Drinkwater grunted. "That dahm airlift. One crate, it landed in my own yard, you know."

"Really?"

"Smack in the button tree." He nodded. "Me son Evan, he fetch it down on his own bahck. So much excitement. Everybody makin' haste to see this thing, you know. Everybody mashin' close to see."

Ivy prodded. "And?"

"Frostbite medecine."

She stared. "They gave you medicine for frostbite on St. Tiggs?"

Drinkwater rubbed his face, his grin as fixed and huge as ever. "My neighbor get a sky box, too. All the way from Germany. Sixteen blow-up igloo."

"Stop."

"White man come up in a truck, give him seven dollar fe fetch them out. Good riddance to bad rubbish, I say. Then last month I visitin' me auntie, and right there in she yard dis dahm *t'ing*. I cahn't believe my eyes. Since when you fix your mind on turning Eskimo? I ask her. Say she gwan use it for a chicken coop. Ten dollar she pay out on dat t'ing. And don't you know she chicken never lay one egg. Not one."

It's the kind of story Ray would love, thought Ivy. Her husband was a great collector of horror stories about foreign aid. He hated it himself. Time to stop playing Papa to the world, was his line on it. Give him the choice, he'd stop it all, the subsidies, the pseudo-loans, even Peace Corps. Let the kids out of the crib, let em scrape their knees and catch their colds and bump their pointy little heads—they're going to break our hearts eventually, he said. Sooner we get used to the idea, the better. Ivy used to argue that he missed the point, which had occurred to her one time in Cairo when she heard an English hippie bitching about cabfare to the Pyramids. "Three times wot they charge the locals," the lad had grumbled. "Ask me, it ain't ethical. Do I look like a millionaire to you?" What he'd looked, of course, was beggarly, but what kind of beggar moseys halfway around the world to claim his alms? Never mind the cold sores and serape, his very presence was imperial. The sheer fact of his being there at all implied a privilege so freakish, so extreme, it was a wonder he wasn't handcuffed on the spot.

"You call it charity," she'd told Ray, "but maybe it's more like a tax. Like hush money, if you see. The penalty we pay for being suffered the capacity to pay at all."

"Taxes give you back something," he'd shot back. "Roads, libraries, Poets in the Schools. What's the last thing Togo did for you?"

Ivy smiled. "Maybe the point is what they *don't* do."

Ray got a big kick out of that. "So we owe them for not wasting us. They're doing us a favor. Thank you, Egypt. Thank you, Chad. Thank you all for being such good sports about what *pigs* we are."

He was one cool customer, her husband. He once admitted if Mercy hadn't got him first, he might have joined the CIA. But back to Drinkwater, a man of God, a man with news. Ivy put it to him.

"Who's Santy, Reverend?"

The old man paused. "This is bahd bunch you asking me about, Miss Glover."

"I don't doubt that Hal Glover is many things you don't approve of, sir, but if you know him, you know he's not bad."

Drinkwater ran his thumb along the edge of the bottlecap and flipped it high, his grin hitched tight. "You takin' him bahck home?"

"I thought this was his home."

He lobbed the bottlecap at the sow. "You will help a boy like Eldred, boy you never met, but this other, your own true blood, your face *exahct*—"

"Is that a cab?" she broke in, squinting. When it slowed, she turned to shake Drinkwater's hand. He held on to it as if it were a bird about whose navigational ability he had grave doubts.

"You think I speakin' out of turn."

"Forget about it. Just make Eldred take his pills."

His grin was wide. "Charity begin at home, Miss Glover."

"Helping Eldred isn't charity. And my home is in New York."

THE BAT

BARRY GOLDENSOHN

On the stump of a torn wing
it planted itself in the driveway
and screeched to keep me away
from doing the merciful thing
and crushing it under my foot.
I scooped it up in my cap
and hid it away in a yew
to save it from the cat.
It would starve in a day or two.
I once heard a chipmunk scream
for hours in the slow jaws
of a king snake under the house.
Gradual death is hell
but the human terrified dream
in the beast face of that thing
made me unable to kill
as it lingered in suffering.
Don't test me on anything close.

REUNION
A fragment

Through stone door and brass ring, the hive
opened downward and a crossed escalator
sank and rose. I sank just as The Five

Hot Spots rose to the top step with their
stage smile and broke into "The Musk-
rat Ramble," weaving the high throaty then clear

horn into the crunch of the rest. In neon dusk
I followed the rich smell seeking heat,
the smell of body in its own heat. A husk

of old Prez rose, his love-me grin in sweet
pink, trying a samba on a cramped step
with a propeller hat and flip-flops on his feet.

On my side, descending, a tense rope
of humorless comedians, rational men about
their daylight lives, on that slow moving slope

keeping a sense of balance, sensible doubt,
ironic about repression. . . .

*****

each door will open on an inner city,
theaters, bookstores, vast museums on
boulevards, music everywhere and free.

Mozart relieves himself and everyone,
Brahms forswears opera and marriage,
Stravinsky blows his horn, and Beethoven

unknots his face with musical carnage.
On the ascending stair a Griffin rose
and rubbed its downy breasts and ghastly visage

against a lion who slavers, licks and blows
the iridescent feathers on her neck.
She coos. He purrs. He rubs his nose

into her beak. . . .

******

In the great
circle of its wings the Phoenix sighs
as flames lick their edges and they vibrate

with pleasure. Janus rises, making eyes
at the woman on each arm, and steps two ways
at once, tumbles down laughing, tries

in a stumbling group to climb with grace,
and his whole soul is seen in that double face.

REDISCOVERING WONDER
Santa Cruz Mts, California, 1989

I struggle to see these hills with a new wonder,
now I am slower, harder to rouse, no longer
possessing the eyes of the boyish lover who floated
and dove through here engraving them in mind
and in my first camera, a small point-and-shoot thing,
trying to hold this world by grabbing, snatching,
with the body's faith in that sudden spurt of vision.

Now the unwieldy mounting on a tripod,
composing slowly on the ground glass
of an old view camera, no more fast work
but to see the great curves, delicate ferns
in the deep shadow and each tree precisely,
backlit by fog and set free of background,
clear in the air of its proper distance,
not leaf masses only and the mess of green.
Now the meditative timeless play
with light and the discrimination of planes,
the sodden leaf clinging to pebbles in a clear pool,
and another leaf floating on its surface
along with bright dust and the sky quivering
in ripples through the reflected trees
and trees shadows.
                    Now to walk with eyes open
and keep them open, not drift inward
with the strong tide that pulls and pulls.

I climbed for the wide view of the slope to the sea,
its lines voluptuous, fragmented, with the faint gold
wash of ripe grass grain that waves over the deep green,

and set the camera up to stop the passionate
advance of the hills' curves on one another
as I climbed, where the hill above had raised its bulk
over the lower, nearer hill that lay
like the back and buttocks of someone at hand.
And the steep hills no longer plunged and dove
around me (how else could I see
but by stopping to compose with slow control,
when the world races in a dream of one green passion
one fertile surface covering everything?)
the whole body lying naked and open
beneath me inviting wonder with a fierce buzz
at every move I made that seemed to come
from my own ears—no cars, no planes—just me
breathless from climbing. "My heart! my heart!" I thought
but it was not inside me and I saw a nervous cloud
of flies rise in alarm from their platter of fresh cow dung
whose rich odor encompassed us all.

A red tailed hawk swung above me and I turned
the camera to the cliff's edge to wait
till he dove to the place he belonged on the glass,
before the warm body of the land and the glare
of the sea. Oh, Love, this patience with the world,
the black draped seclusion as light gathered
on ground glass, sky down, hills
with each intricate tree and the sea above—
easing into focus as the back and lens
tilt and swing and the blue-eyed grass comes clear,
then the dolphin's back as it sinks for air into light,
as the loved body rises from her depths in my mind,
and enters the world to be seen with open eyes
who could so easily blind me with her touch.

THELONIUS MONK DANCING

What might this figure of great force do
Or not do? Seeming uncontrolled he hit
and poked at the piano without error
then rose and wandered off around the floor

doing a march time heavy footed non-dance
dance, slow turns, clown twirls, arm flaps, he cowed
us, massive, dazed and full of drunk
menace and disdain for the college crowd

at the Vanguard. His deep control relaxed
and grew perilous, crazy, a wounded bear
mugging at the dates of pretty girls. I
was confused and frightened for him and for

myself—what humiliation would I be called
to witness or undergo, what fall or fight,
with this genius drinking himself to greater
distance, building distraction or rage—how could

any of us tell? The waiters kept his whiskey glass
on the piano filled, fuelling the veering
circuit that ignored then threatened
but did not destroy us out of love for

something more important than ourselves.
Helpless, polite, white, we disappeared
behind his music, then Ray Copeland's singing
horn brought him round and the drums calmed him

and recalled him to play the piece that had run
through so many variations on the vibes,
sax, horn and drums that only one who could take
a phrase in four directions at once could make it end

as music. He steered his mocking shuffle back to the piano
to sit and let his feet fly, free of all that weight.
The keys, played and not played, turned the room—
terrorized, confused—into our richest, most perilous music.

SONG TO A PORCUPINE
IN MATING SEASON

Knowing from the way I wave my arms
when talking to you that I mean no harm
you consent to walk me down the middle
of our dirt road, your fierce quills
relax and swish faintly, full of charm

as you feel, serene, invulnerable,
circled with weapons, with your deep, settled,
companionable, unwary habit of mind.
The longest of your black daggers end
gravely in white, and your solemn, steady waddle

makes me think you're stable, old, older,
in a disciplined, domestic sexual order,
an adult balance befitting and so on, yet
you scream with lust in the middle of the night
in mating season like a lost child in terror

deep in the woods, as if your leg was gripped
and torn to the bone by the teeth of a steel trap—
or like a man young as my son chained to a post
in fire, who strains for air, knows he's lost,
and screams to his own sons to cover their eyes.

SARATOGA BALLET

Lorrie Goldensohn

Ohhhhhhhh—I've forgotten the tickets!
A cry of distress rises in the blue Honda
plodding over a two-lane New Hampshire highway,
wedged between the curves of the road
and the hard curves of the RV's
refusing to move their metal bulk aside.
We're halfway there but it would be
hours to go home again. No matter.

We tell our story everywhere,
a friend moves in on the case, finally,
in the starlit spaces of their amphitheater, the ushers
close in over a handwritten pass, the captain
herself marches at the head of our column.
Militant with hope, I am
just ahead of my mother's cane:
look everybody, here we all are,
in the front of the house.

In the wide cement aisles
my husband chats up a colleague.
A patron wreathed in insect repellent
flashes behind us in the hot
July rustle of her bare-backed silk;
waiting, I hear my own heartbeat,
pure fish in a perfect water,
nearly the last night, high summer
and then the season ends.

At the intersection of now
and always they are dancing. Or rather,
preparing to dance, the heavy curtain lifting
to bare the first tableau: against the cobalt
glow of the backdrop, a solid stone of light,
the delicate crispness of these figures,
their limbs disposed in something so astrally human
it leaves the rest of us behind. Beautiful,

the delicate looping and twisting
with the long paws of their satin shoes—
plock-plock, as each wooden tip
speaks to the wooden stage.
And then the partnering, and then the
severance from partnering, exuberant male,
his straightlegged sideways leap
like scissors kissing, and then
the slow, slow, weaving and bucking
of his lady's arms, intimately, as legs and arms
slide with such light perception,
brushing each other's private parts.

And then the ensemble swings into motion.
Within a Bach accelerando, people flutter like cloth;
in panels of soft gleaming color
they wave and ripple, spread on their breasts
the glittering sequins—bright spores,
glad tears. Look at the aging child's body

of the prima ballerina: in the Stravinsky
the bikini brief clapped over her leotard
looks like a black diaper. In swift
turns her profiled torso
rests the slight sill of her bosom
above a faintly protuberant belly, the muscles
contract, and the figure vanishes.

                                    The theater,
ringing with bravos, is half-empty;
between the orchestra pit and the outer curtain
a bat flies in ever-larger arcs;
only a crust of the spectators stand.
Still half-dazed to be here
I struggle to my feet and clap
so hard my palms hurt—their stinging
softness slapping against my own
unmelting bone: for an hour of fleeting
access, you offer your gallant comedy,
and trust us to rise and enter.

L'ESPRIT DE L'ESCALIER

During the evening itself
I was fine and gay, I used my hands a lot.
I could feel them going up,
darting, shaping, and pleading.

Pleading with the others to be recognized.
Telling my stories, trying
to pull back, honest,
to let other people have a chance to speak.
But of course that didn't work too well.
I talked on and on.

And then later—
always after to feel my own
strange, prickly, greedy intensity.
Inwardly. In the infinite regress
which is the self's
miserable conversation with the self,
I want you all to see
another little person in my skull
holding its head with two hands,
banging it from side to side, oh, oh,

why can't we both be different?
The one who speaks,
and afterwards,
the twin who listens.

ANESTHESIA

When the resident asked me what I remembered—
the question lifting from her mouth,
like a light glove pulled from the fingers
and lying between us,
a thing of breath and catechism—
I answered as best I could:

As if I were blind, I said.
A hurt so deep and drugged it was only awkwardness,
seeing in curtains of grey, feeling
your presences surround me, asking
what easement was it I wanted. Kindly.
Wasn't that evident, I,
shivering so violently,
half rising from the table under your hands?
Wet and naked, words
withheld from me, trembling
in the cold operating room, its temperature
lowered, antiseptic, the wrapped doctors
and the wrapped attendants above an absent body
no longer needing a temperature.

Put my body back on, I tried to say.

I wanted to leave the soul. Poor
wispy thing, incapable of standing,
transferred from state to state
by powers so contemptuous of the rich body.

We were lifting you, the resident said,
from the operating table onto the gurney.

And yet both of us knew,
tilting between the blind edges of speech,
that lifting is not what the mind remembers;
reaching traveller, lonely for the flesh,
absent from it, looking back
from the next place where it doesn't dare to go.

BALD EAGLE WITH A
SIX-FOOT WINGSPAN

Fog lifts from the grass.
Late October, I watch from the farmhouse window
where Gilda guards the garden,
laying her muzzle down on the forepaws
stretched in readiness before her.
A white enamel chamberpot
leans against the outhouse,
its chipped lid propped alongside.

Beyond us the Bay of Machias
splints the outer reaches
of the Nelson's ground,

and you,

        walking up the field
        from the shore, up
        towards the Bald Eagle
        in that second in which he
        alights on a branch
        of spruce, his body hidden
        by the trunk of the tree,
        on either skinny side of which
        can be seen
        the wide, flapping wings;

you are not what you seem.
Balding, your glasses slipping
forward, you peer

down into your brown bag
which you have filled
with freshly-picked mushrooms

your body now in line
with the tree,
your wings, black—ragged—
spread hugely from the center of your spine.

CLEAR WATER

From the windows above East Long Pond
I can look down into the transparent water
through to his arms breaststroking,
his legs frogkicking.
I can scout them
through the silky film of the pond water,
as the pale flesh of his bent knees,
his lifting elbows and turning shoulders,
flash through the grating
of the green and brown light,
taking up color from the green and brown bottom.

Everywhere clear water bears him up. . .

As if I could see straight through
to the end of his life—
the swimming, shifting field of his flesh
bringing my eyes
to the constant whorl and spin of it,
and the water that glazes him
no bar to my sight:

a man moving through water
and detachable from it.

As if in the meat, bone, and blood
of his body on land
he were not the Zen abbot's
famous junction point: a machine

for the transmission of food,
over a lifetime, converting twenty tons
of vegetable and mineral mass to shit.

If in the medium of pond water
I see the body's finish,
and if on land
nothing but the opacity of stages,
with neither nobility nor vital conclusion—

Well then. This morning
near Walter Bothfeld's, our little car
appeared to leave the ground,
crested, then slowed at the hilltop farm,
maple syrup for sale,
cows and machinery
erratically crossing the road
from field to barn and shed,
and we let them pass,

pausing, in the rising of those
deep animal airs, up there
where the stench and the view are strongest.

Off on the downslope
the other bony-rumped, great-bellied
Holsteins bunched,
their noses pressed to the cropped green,
just below the peaks of the Woodbury mountains
layering and lacing the broad canvas
of our descent.

Maybe I should have stayed
here by the window.
Seeing the friendly water:
pine, beech, and maple
lying upside-down in the flat glass, their leaves
reflecting the current, a swimmer

amusing himself—
my hand at the glass,
his hand at the water,
here and there,
depth and shore, water and air—

everything simply itself.
East Long Pond, a man
turning, translucent in pond water.

NOTHING NEW

ELAINE HANDLEY

No corpses have bobbed up,
no letters corked in bottles.
I still can't swim.
My face remains sorry in its shape
and greed comes in the safety of baths.
Listening to the plinking of water
talking to itself and listening
for the quick death of bubbles (the only perfect
entities in the universe), I realize
water can be
as still
and blank
as ever.

Lovesick, seasick.
I contemplate this, you,
and the rush of sharks.

PENANCE

Three times a week she makes her way
past the vacant lot where her house had stood.
She stoops to pick among the perennial
roses blooming in the old garden and always
counts the crows on the wires above
the small church.
It is there she sweeps the floor
removing the deep hush
restocks the vigil candles
and plucks dead blossoms
from the altar—
always genuflecting before the crucifix.

Walking home
her arms are blessed
with long altar cloths and priestly robes
to mend, wash, and iron—
a litany she was taught young.

Every week
smoothing the pure stiff linen with arthritic hands
she hangs the vestments white and breathless
and leaves the church
waiting for grace.

SECRETS AND SINS

The trees outside the window
are sculpted blue
and fragile as blown glass.
They darken
to gentle stirrings
in the black spring night.
The earth that clutches us
in the morning is closing
in upon itself
and our lovers
have found other people.

At this moment
nothing holds us.

I think of things
I might say
self-conscious and breathless
as a seven year old
making her first
confession
afraid
of her own whisper
afraid
of the voice
that will escape
and tell all.

It is in the arms
of such dark
secrets and sins

are lost.
Our wine glasses hold
a glint of light
a gift to see by—
for mysteries
will give way
and soon
it will be night
all through us.

TEN SPEED

I live in my knees.
They are Sirens singing
blood and heat.
Lost in pedals and spokes,
I have become simply legs
craving motion,
demanding distance.

At the top of the hill
the glister of sweat
talks to the dew.
In light fractured by clouds,
air and breath collide.

Beneath me
the world sings
meadow, woods, and tiny houses,
with the road echoing through.

Perched for an instant
between where I've been
and might be,
letting the must of scents
tune me,
the knees choose
surrender again.

A push off
and I'm launched in sparrowy
downdraft,
honeyed songs
in my limbs.

WEATHER

I want to speak of everyday occurrences:
of stirring soup, smelling snow
before it arrives, the reveries of the dish pan,
the flash
of a redwinged blackbird.

I ask the hills
what about the power
of my brain?
the hot circuit of my womb?
the windfall, the weather of me,
the refuge?

Was it forsythia
backlit by a fevered sunset
Moses spoke to?
You cannot have what you cannot see.

What happens is made to happen—
the pattern of leaves rustled by one
season to another, the scorch of frost on marigolds,
sadness rimming a mouth.
I want to speak
of everyday occurrences—
solar winds,
faithful
as loneliness.

SELFSAME SONGS

WILLIAM HATHAWAY

I know the song O-ka-*lee*
of the redwing blackbird
flitting from cattail to fencepost,
but I can't whistle it
like the bird pedant bossing
the nature walk does. Another call
is a cry that I can't even duplicate
resembling the slurred squeal
of squashed air and grating steel
when a hydraulic woodsplitter
wedges wet elm. My father
read Ruskin and taught me to look
and listen, and he meant too
for me to learn to label. Too bad—
what a shame it's all for naught,
and so on . . . Anyway, I stood
one morning by a ditch dug
for pleasure craft off the Napa River,
which is a sort of fairy land
forlorn if you're from New York,
and I heard a redwing call
a call I'd never heard before.

Tinka-tinka-tinka.

It clung sideways to a weedstalk
swaying in the breeze, one foot
overhand, the other underhand,

the way my father tried to show
me how to pole vault. Its beak
gaped wide so I saw a lewd stub
of tongue in silhouette.
Certainly such notes must beseech
meanings in lost Indian lingos?
Sounding dead names the blackbird
never knew it sang, and still sings
for no ears that know to care.
But this tinka-tinka-tinka
I'd heard before. The father
of a friend of mine would clink
the edge of his knife against
the side of his waterglass whenever
children relaxed into happiness
at his dinner table. This memory
was an overgrown path and I seemed
to see it afresh—I think
he thought children should dress
like church to eat and sit
so stiffly because failure awaits
the weak with cunning patience.

A man sat fishing in a lawnchair
by the open doors of his van
and some words on his bumper
caused me to pause and chat
about our higher power
while the sun gathered force
and lit up flaxen greens along
the mudbank as if from within.
O-ka-*lee* sang the redwing,
as everyone's heard its song
before and not listening
felt some distant thought
well out. One key for countless
doors. His name was Robert,
my boyhood friend, and a scar

like a gray nickel on the back
of his hand marked where his father
had crushed a cigar to punish
playing with food. What a cry
he must have mashed inside himself!
I remember my astonishment still,
for I could not imagine my father
doing such a furious thing.
"Want some," the fisherman said
offering his coffee thermos,
"it's premium hightest." I did,
and thinking how right the words
pleasure craft go thrown together
thus, I took the day within me
then—fresh for its cacophony
of usual signs and wonders.

MIRTH

On one stair as you grope down
to feast in the midnight solitude
of an arctic blast of light
is a football. Such is life; a thing
of tears. Upsy-Daisy! Airborne,
afloat in a slowed moment
which always accompanies catastrophe,
you resemble the moon-pale fetus
asleep in formaldehyde that rose
and sank with the weather
under the dust of a science exhibit
called "Freaks of Nature."
Your instep still feels the curve
of this world, how it spun away
under you, and now time drags
to let you ponder how disagreeable
a real freedom feels. There's
your life: "flashing by"
in colored frames like a comic book.
A truculent gust tosses up curtains
and snatches calendar pages end
over end out the window where
they flitter as winged dollar bills
among flowers that zoom up
to bloom, droop, shrivel and drop
all in one instant forever.
Like the grasping hands of the dead
pushing up daisies from the dark
boxes. As they say the wizened Sybil
floated between heaven and earth
in a gray, thumbsucking Serenity.

Always somewhere on the stairs
is a football and so a wise heart
should surely dwell with mirth
in a house that is always mourning.

GUILLOTINE

Thirsty from croquet, we rollicked up
the veranda steps where a golden sun
had cooked our sorbets to a purple soup,
sticky in silver bowls. But I drank mine.

Quick! Before nurse could see. And winced,
the raspberries had gone so lickerish wild
in the heat, the bowl's bitter metal mixed
with sugary sweet. As if our trifle spoiled

to ferment a new delight. When I fell
from my pony Polichinelle and struck my head
those same tastes rose up my throat to fill
my mouth as balls of light burst blue and red.

Honey, nail rust, vinegar wine. Like a clown
head on a ribboned stick, Vieux Jean's bloodless
face bounced past as they rode us into town.
"Adieu, adieu!" Crushed in Maman's embrace,

again my mouth floods with sun and soil.
A red ball clicks into the blue, sour yeast
sweetens a cold dew. Frost blazes into boil,
a soft breath blooms lights with wild tastes.

THE TEXACO OPERA

Saturday afternoon 1952;
Mr. Mintz washes his Hudson
in front of his crackerbox
duplex where he's at 12
o'clock and we're at 3
in the Project's cul-de-sac.
Like every Saturday,
which isn't his sabbath—
though neither's Sunday.
Always, everyday he wears
a bowtie and knit vest
yet his sleeves are rolled
and he's got rubbers on,
arcing silver dollops out
of the hose over the Hudson,
and always I strain to see
the pale green numbers
like a smudge on his forearm
as he rubs the sun into
the hood with a "shammy."

A man alone, quiet, neat,
a face that never lent
nor borrowed. Throughout
all the Project's chartered
streets and circles, other
men splash their cars
together. Laughing loud,
spraying swarms of kids
and whooping like a stadium
at the ballgame, they bum

in faded green fatigues.
V-8 engines rev from dusk
to dawn and from each lawn
a whirr and clash rises
from their joyous mowing.

But I sit on his curb
with my head on my hands
cupping my knees, watching
Mr. Mintz. Inside the Hudson,
Faust bellows farewell
to Margarite. A cloud
darkens the sun and leaves
riffling on the elm turn
color. An ancient tragedy
is charging the air; I just
know it. But Mr. Mintz
gives no sign, shaking out
a rag. A fine white mist
hovers for an instant, then
melts away in clamoring sun.

THE LAST COWBOY

Bang, he said and only the sun
centering the sky's milky dome
wobbled in the puddle
he strutted through. Nothing
seen stirred. Ker-pow, ker-pow,
he cried and a hitherto
inaudible stillness, the sound
of the light gripping row
after row of lawns, the sound
of all emptinesses otherwise
left everywhere untaken,
took his small chirps into
itself as effortlessly as mist
envelopes a pair of lights
in the night and darkness grows
more evident in aftermath.
It occurred to a watcher,
who stood unseen behind one
black pane witnessing a square
of suburb waver in liquid sun,
and only saw the boy say bang
and blow an invisible stream
of blue smoke off the hole,
how small old Priam had looked,
head bowed, lurching grief-mad
from side to side, muttering
over the field of dead. No,
neither this cowboy swinging
bowlegged over the saddle
of his purple plastic bigwheel
to go grinding off in a glare

of blinding light, nor
his witness, sipping absently
in reflective shadow before
an empty frame of history,
heard the rising hymn of closure—
O do not forsake me on this day. . .
Yet, no proof exists such song
did not stun the light
on some other wave of air.

WINTER SCENES*

Bruce Hiscock

At the top of a small hill on the tundra an Arctic ground squirrel stopped and sniffed the wind. It was a blustery day in September, and the ground squirrel's whiskers quivered in the gusts of cold air. The wind smelled of snow, but it smelled clean and safe. There was no scent of fox or wolf nearby. Cautiously, the ground squirrel sat up and looked around. It inspected the rocks and lichens covering the hill and then looked out across the tundra. The ground squirrel could see a long way, for there was not a single tree to block its view.

A series of broad, marshy meadows stretched out from the ground squirrel's hill. The meadows were dotted with small lakes and ponds. Low, stony hills ran through the meadows, dividing them and breaking up the flatness of the land. A few weeks ago the meadows were green and bright. Now they had turned brown, and the wind tugged at the clumps of dry grass. In the distance the ground sloped up into a long ridge. During the night the dark ridge had been dusted white with a covering of snow. Only a patch of dwarf spruce remained green.

The ground squirrel looked carefully at everything, but it saw no animals moving.

Even the Canada geese that had nested by the lakes were gone now. One cold morning when the water was covered with a thin layer of ice, they rose into the air forming a great vee-shaped pattern against the sky. The geese had circled the hill and then headed south, honking noisily.

---

*from *Tundra the Arctic Land*.

Since then the skies above the tundra had been gray and empty. No ravens or owls had been seen for several days.

The ground squirrel looked around once more and then went back to gathering seeds. Big flakes of wet snow began to fall. A flock of ptarmigan cackled faintly from a distant hill. The animal paid no attention to these things. When its cheeks were stuffed with seeds, the ground squirrel hurried down the hill and disappeared into a burrow in the sandy soil.

As the autumn days passed, the ground squirrel continued to eat and collect seeds. Beneath its tan fur a thick layer of fat was forming. The time of hibernation was drawing near.

One morning in early October, the ground squirrel emerged to find the earth frozen hard and a cold, dry snow blowing across the tundra. Already the wind was building little drifts behind each rock on the hill. The ground squirrel blinked the flakes away and twitched its tail.

Suddenly there was a slight vibration, a rumbling in the ground. At the top of the hill a thousand antlered heads appeared. The caribou were coming, migrating toward their winter feeding grounds. The herd trotted quickly down the slope and out onto the meadow. They made a clicking sound as they passed. The caribou streamed across the frozen tundra, and then the main body of the herd was lost from sight as they went up and over another hill.

It began snowing harder as the wind picked up its pace. Out in the meadow a few straggling caribou were running, trying to catch up with the herd. Tiny white flakes clung to their gray fur. In the growing storm two pale wolves began to close in on a caribou that was limping badly. The ground squirrel ducked back into its burrow as the wolves and caribou vanished in a thick swirl of white.

Underground, the animal crept down a long tunnel to a chamber lined with grass. It munched a few seeds and curled up in its nest. The ground squirrel would not see the meadows and sky again until spring. Hibernation had begun.

All around the top of the world, ground squirrels seek their burrows when the cold and snow come to the tundra. This is the land of the far north, the open land beyond the trees. There, winter is the long season, and it begins very early.

By October the tundra is covered with snow. The days are short and the sun stays low in the sky. Each day it shines a little less, and each day the air grows colder. As winter deepens, the days become so short that the sun just flickers above the horizon before it sets again. Finally, over much of the tundra, the time comes when the sun does not rise at all.

In the darkness the sky is often clear. Northern lights shine overhead and the big dipper makes circle after circle around the north star. On the ground, the wind packs the snow into hard drifts, creating strange sculptured shapes. The hilltops, however, are bare. The wind strips the snow from the high places and sends it rushing across the flat lands like wisps of smoke. Hardly any new snow falls in the coldest part of winter for the air is very dry. Underneath the drifts, hardy plants lie frozen, waiting for the sun to return.

Yet even in the dark of winter there is life on the tundra. A herd of muskoxen roams a ridge, looking for plants exposed by the wind. Their long coats swish about their ankles.

At the edge of a bog, lemmings are busy in a network of tunnels beneath the snow. Dozens of these small, furry creatures move about, nibbling on the roots and stems of plants. Not far away an Arctic fox trots silently on the surface of the snow. A thick white coat protects it from the cold, but the fox is hungry, for the hunting has been poor.

As the fox approaches the bog, it stops, sensing the hidden lemmings close by. The fox moves slowly forward, then suddenly rears up and pounces, breaking through the crust into the lemming's runway. With flashing feet the fox digs along the tunnel, biting and scratching, while a lemming scurries ahead. This time the fox is lucky, and it kills the lemming with one clean snap of its jaws. The fox finishes its meal and, satisfied for now, moves off into the night. The snow sparkles brightly beneath the starlit sky.

There are other kinds of life on the winter tundra as well. Near the Arctic coast a cluster of small houses stands out against the treeless landscape. From each chimney a thin plume of smoke rises in the cold air. Electric lights brighten the windows of every house, casting yellow patterns across the snow. Behind one house a husky dog lies sleeping, curled tightly against the cold. From across the tundra comes the whine of snowmobiles. The dog wakes and pulls at its chain. A father and his sons are returning from their traplines far out on the land. They are bringing home the carcasses of a dozen Arctic fox. As they pass the village store, a group of boys and girls wearing parkas and jeans come out to admire the catch.

In another place on the tundra a different sort of hunter is at work. Bright floodlights chase away the darkness and bull-dozers scrape the frozen ground. In a cleared area a crew of men and women begin erecting a drilling rig. These hunters are searching for oil beneath the tundra. They are dressed in heavy clothing and the work goes slowly in the cold.

Men and animals alike face a long, bitterly cold winter on the tundra. The season begins with the first snows of September and lasts until sometime in May. During the coldest months the temperature remains far below zero and the chill wind can be felt through the thickest parka or fur. The Arctic climate has kept the tundra isolated for centuries. Most of the land remains a vast wilderness, untouched and beautiful, where animals wander as they choose. But as the oil and minerals of the warmer lands are used up, development is moving northward despite the Arctic cold.

BUT MY FATHER DANCES

Kay Hogan

IT IS SUNDAY, one of those "gather the people together" Sundays. My mother stirs up the quiet as she calls out and bustles through the rooms.

Her voice is melodic and lilting as she reaches for the string light.

"It's time, it's time for lights."

Twilight has passed and Con Edison, for now, recedes as the enemy. So much of their time passes in near darkness as the dread of gas and light bills hangs over them, but today is Sunday. "They'll be here soon," she says and pats down the yellowed doilies that line the couch.

I watch her as she unrolls the three metal curlers from her hair. Tilting her head slightly, she dusts her face with powder, then streaks pink rouge across her cheeks. She pulls her stockings tightly, defiantly knotting them just below the knees.

Slowly my father comes from behind the newspaper. Always he is behind something. Always he is on the edge of anger. But now, he stretches tall, reaches for his leather strap and methodically strokes the razor up and down. There is a smile just starting at the corners of his mouth.

Uncle Ned is the first to arrive. He is a tall man and his laughter fills the doorway as he lumbers through with his accordion tucked under his arm.

"Sweet Jesus. This house is like a wake. We need a bit of music, a bit of song."

"Go, get your Aunt Margaret," my mother says "and Bridie, too."

Neighbors, hearing the music, drift in. Voices call to one another across the yards, and soon the apartment fills with people and is alive with pealing laughter.

Uncle Ned sits on the edge of the overstuffed chair. The sweat slides down as he balances the accordion on one knee while the other foot stamps to time. Someone always says, "Doesn't he look like Tyrone Power?" Ned smiles and throws his head back, the straight, thick, black hair falls freely, and his eyes roll back in time to dreams and songs of his youth and his father's dreams before him. The timeless balm of music makes them all seem young, and they laugh, and hum and sing in unison.

Food appears mysteriously from the once empty icebox, food brought in with a "Hello, God Bless, here's a bit of something." Ham sandwiches pile up on trays along with salad, soda bread, and melting ice cream for the kids. I can't recall where my brothers were in that scene peopled with laughing adults, except when one or the other took turns to wind the victrola.

"Give us a step, Johnny," someone calls out. He hesitates for a moment, but then rises slowly, shyly.

"Give them a hornpipe, Johnny, show them," my mother cries.

He winces slightly, but then pulls himself tall. How brave he is, I think, as he pushes out from behind himself, from behind the shyness. The dance is a blend of speed and power, of beauty and sweeping steps. I watch his face; the worry lines that held to him like a tightly-closed net give way. My mother beams, smooths her dress, jiggles her shoulders a bit and keeps throwing her chin out. Yes, he is mine, the movements say.

"Again," Ned cries, and they begin again, rocking the floors, the music bouncing off the walls. The windows open out to the yard, spilling light, as the curtains billow across the dancers, until my mother shouts above the music.

"Close the windows; a child may fall."

It was a waltz. I remember that. Before he came across the room, I had been, "Kathleen, get some more chairs from next door." Or, "Kathleen, go borrow some ice." But then he walked across that room and said, "Kathleen, why don't you and I give it a go?"

At first, my body tightens, and my hands go hot, then cold with sweat. I wonder if rings have formed under my arms. Will it show? Will I stumble? Trip over him? But he is relaxed, not drunk, calm and casual and that soothes me. I remembered then the straight-lipped tightness, the unbending tilt to his chin, the clipped guttural sprays of conversation and I think all of it will carry over to his dancing. But his smoothness and rhythm steady me, and gradually I let my body listen, sense the music, feel it sway in tune and in time.

"You are doing fine, just fine," he says. I stay quiet, afraid words may clash, interrupting this new world of harmony. I stare into his face and wonder, *Have his eyes always been that blue?* He smells different from my mother, a clean, sharp salty smell, mixed with Lava soap and pipe tobacco. I wish I could touch his hair, feel the brown curls. He twirls and swings me between the adults, laughing.

"You are good, Kathleen, really good." People turn and watch.

"She's all grown up," one says.

"Looks like you, Mary, don't you think? When you were young."

"Kathleen, we need some more soda," my mother calls.

"Not now, we're dancing," my father smiles as he pulls me back up to the fast-pitched sounds of the "Stack of Barley," a driving polka.

"All grown up," the words form a feeling and I straighten and stretch my body. "I'll never get this," I laugh.

"You will; just follow me and listen to yourself. The rhythm, it comes from inside."

We dance that as easily as the waltz, and whatever Ned plays. I seem to know them all. I want the evening to go on forever, to stave off the silence of tomorrow. The twilight days. But the pace slows, and the accordion comes to a wheezing whine. Then stops.

"Oh, it's tired I am," and Ned brushes the sweat from his eyes and reaches for the foamy beer.

"Just one more, please, Ned, one more," my mother pleads. She seems nervous and moves her hands up and down her broad hips. "Go get another sandwich for your uncle, Kathleen." I want to say "No," and I stand watching for a while. I want to say, "No, it's changed. It's different, I'm part of the dancing now."

Uncle Ned, renewed by the beer, swings the accordion back in place. My mother stands ready to dance. Her hands are pumping, as she pushes forward on her thick legs.

"Slow down, slow down," my father says. "It's a waltz, not a race."

"Of course it is. I know that." My mother's voice is small.

"You know, it's amazing, it truly is. The way that Kathleen picked up the dancing." I smile back at him and watch my mother. Her head is bobbing up and down, out of sync with the music. For a fleeting moment I glimpse the hurt locked into her eyes. Then I turn away.

SECOND LANGUAGE

Dennis Loy Johnson

SOMEONE SENT ME their heart in the mail. It came on Valentine's Day, and it was anonymous, but for a brief moment—*ah!*—I thought it might be from my not-yet-officially-ex-husband; then I gave myself a reality check. Even after this, though, noticing the D.C. postmark was a bit of a let-down. It meant that this thing—it was a simple cut-out of a red heart—had local origins, and must have been from one of the lonely men I'd suddenly found myself surrounded by since Dan left: the middle-aged bachelor neighbor I'd given a ride to the auto mechanic's, one of my divorced or philandering colleagues, one of my dark-eyed students. The thing that should have brightened my day just made me sad. Mystery and wonder were no longer happy things for me.

Still, I stared long and hard at it, trying to figure out who it was from. "I love you very much," it said. "You are a good person." The handwriting was somewhere between print and cursive. The envelope was plain, of rough paper that looked almost hand-made, and there was no return address. The stamp was upside-down.

I got absolutely nothing done for the rest of the day. I mooned around my new apartment, drinking coffee and poking through the boxes of books I hadn't been able to bring myself to unpack for weeks now. I kept going back to that heart, lying on the card table that I ate off in the kitchen. It was warmer in the kitchen, I told myself.

One thing I knew. There was no way it was from Dan. "A clean break," he'd said. "It's the only way."

My first strong suspicion was that it was from the bachelor neighbor. His wife had left him a year before and he had, as far as I could make out, gone to pieces and even lost his job. When I'd taken him to the car repair shop, he told me all about it. He remembered dates, he knew times. Entire conversations verbatim. I couldn't get a word in edgewise. When I pulled up in front of the garage, he lingered for a moment with his hand on the door. "You're a good, ah . . ." he said, " . . . listener." Get a job, I wanted to say. "Thank you," I said instead, "I have to go now."

No, it wasn't him; he wore his heart on his sleeve, he wouldn't be anonymous. As for my colleagues in the English department—all married—there, too, further reflection ruled out any possibilities. They were a preoccupied lot. I don't think many of them even realized my situation. And for the ones who were going to play around, marriage had never been a boundary, although they were more apt to go after young students.

Oh, Lord, I thought, that's all that's left. I picked up the card. One of my students. I'd explained Valentine's Day to them in our last class.

I took attendance in my mind.

Esteban? Esteban, eager yet young and lost-looking, always hovered near my desk after class as I gathered up my material. He always seemed to want to talk, but never really said anything. "*Cafe?*" he'd tried once. "Coffee," I'd corrected him. "Oh," he said. "Thank you a large amount." "Thank you very much," I'd corrected again. "*De nada,*" he said, then backed out of the room with a series of smiles and half-bows and nods. Only later did I realize he'd wanted me to go out for coffee with him.

Niloo, my favorite Persian? After all, the heart didn't necessarily have to come from a man. And Niloo seemed to like me. She was young, too, but very sure of herself, and any attention from her seemed to be some sort of earned respect. She'd once told me I was not "normal," by which I think she meant "normal American," by which I think she meant a compliment. I also liked that she was always careful to ask for the author's name of whatever I read to the class. "Please to spell," she would ask, keeping her hand raised so that I would say nothing more until she'd diligently written down the name, as if it was of the utmost importance, as if she were going straight to the library after class.

Seiji? He was forever asking me to run drills on the letter L. In particular, he was clear on wanting to learn the proper pronunciation of the word "love." That was the word he kept coming back to. "I need much help on this," he said.

At about 5:00 that afternoon—right after the rates went down—my mother called. I was still in the kitchen at the card table, going through student mug shots in my mind. "I've been thinking about the multitudes," my mother said.

"So have I," I told her.

"Have you got a new one? Because I have a new one," she said. "Listen: a *business* of ferrets."

"Precisely," I said.

"What?" she asked.

"I said, that's a good one, Mom. A *business* of ferrets." Actually, I already knew that one, but I didn't want to tell her that. "Have you heard of a *murmuration* of starlings?" I'd been saving that one for her.

"Oh, that's beautiful!" she said. "Yours are always so much more beautiful than mine! 'A *murmuration* of starlings'!"

There was a click as my father picked up the extension. "A *shitload* of trouble," he said.

"Joe!" my mother said.

"Hello, Dad," I said. "What's up?"

"A *whole lot* of nothing," he said.

"We're going shopping," my mother chimed.

"And you know what that means," my father said. "Your mother's going to spend a *pile* of money."

"And that's enough out of you," my mother said. I could just picture her, scowling at the wall between them. And then turning to me. "Do you need anything?" she asked. My parents thought it was easier for them to drive twenty miles to the giant new shopping mall that had taken over the old fairgrounds, buy something and send it 400 miles to me parcel post, than it was for me to find what I needed where I lived, in one of the world's largest cities.

"No no," I told her, "I'm fine."

"You settled in yet?" my father asked. "Got those books unpacked?" I looked off through the doorway at the stacks of boxes filling the next room. My parents were getting psychic in their old age.

"Oh yes," I lied, "the books are all unpacked."

"All those books!" my mother said.

"A *shitload* of books," my father said.

"A *shortage* of brains!" my mother said. I could hear her scowling at the wall again. Then she said, "That reminds me. What was the one about the ravens?"

"An *unkindness* of ravens," I told her.

"Oh, right," she said. "I love that one. Wait'll I tell these to little Elizabeth." Elizabeth is my brother's child. My mother had taken to telling her the multitudes as if they were bedtime stories. "It must be like your poetry," she'd explained. "I don't exactly understand it, but they're so pretty, it's like the words mean something else."

"Let's go," my father said, "you kept her busy long enough now."

"*I'm* keeping her busy?" my mother said. "Who keeps putting his dirty old nose in here?"

They could go on for days, but they did it partly just to keep me on the line. The multitudes had become a thing with them, an excuse to call more often and check up on me. I wanted them to stay on the line, too, wanted to find a way to tell them that I was all right. I thought for a moment of telling them about the heart. It would make them think that I was beginning to socialize again. But the fact that it wasn't clear to me who would send me a valentine suddenly struck me as embarrassingly sad.

"Is everything really okay, Dee?" my mother's voice was asking. Psychic, I tell you.

"Yes," I told her.

"What about the car?" my father asked. I hadn't told them yet that Dan took it.

"Just had it oiled," I told him.

"Oiled?" he said. "You mean, you had the oil changed?"

"Yes," I said.

"Changed or filled?"

"Right," I said. "Changed. I mean, it's definitely different oil now."

"What," he said, "has it been using a lot of oil? How long since the last time you changed it?"

"No," I said, "I mean, not too long. Long enough. It's fine. But I better let you two get to the mall."

"Well . . ." my mother said.

"You don't mean lubricated, do you, you had it lubricated?" my father persisted.

"No. No, it's changed. It's all changed."

"You're sure?" he said.

"Yes."

There is a moment's silence and the line is so clear it's as if there were no distance at all between us.

"Well," my mother said again, "as long as you're okay . . . I guess we'd better let you go."

"Okay," I said.

"We love you," she said.

"A *thousand* goodbyes," my father said.

I put down the phone and picked up my heart. It made me ache, almost, that my parents were being so kind, the way they'd put aside all their normal qualms about my life—that I lived in the city, for example, or that all I knew was poetry. My father no longer made jokes about how useful poetry was to him when it came time to hoe the back forty. Instead, they said things like, "Throw yourself into your work."

My work. I drifted off once more, back to trying to figure out which of my students might have a crush on me, which made me realize that it was nearly time to go to class, which made me realize that I had nothing prepared.

Not that it was a class I'd been putting a lot of effort into. All I'd been doing was reading poetry to them, pretending I was what I'd set out to be: a professor teaching a literature course in a major university, instead of an instructor at a community college with a night class in English as a second language. Intermediate Conversation. There was no text, they all spoke different languages: Spanish, Haitian-French, Japanese, Persian. There were two Sikhs, a Greek, some Slovaks. Representatives, all, of the swarm that is Washington. Or, as my father put it, "a *bunch* of foreigners."

I'd been directed to give the students exercises in role playing. In the first class, I took one straight from my handbook. "You're in an airport," I read out. "You want to buy a ticket from me to go to Argentina. You need a round-trip ticket for your mother-in-law, one-way for yourself." I'd chosen the most sullen student, a middle-aged man named Alejandro, because he was from Argentina. He looked at me crossly, then stared at the floor. "I will never return to Argentina," he said. "*Nunca.*" Surprised into immediate sympathy, I'd said, "Don't you miss it?" Alejandro would not look at me. "No," he said. "Is better here." Without raising his eyes, he'd simply returned to his seat. I'd looked down into the handbook and, completely at a loss, gone on to the next exercise. "You're in a grocery store and your child is choking." I closed the book.

So, instead of exercises in role playing, I'd taken to reading to them from my Norton Anthology. "Yeats," I would announce, or "Whitman," and begin: "*A sudden blow: the great wings beating still/Above the staggering girl. . . .*" I told myself that they needed to have a fuller sense of my language's sound, its rhythm. . . . "Can you hear the emotion?" I would ask them afterwards. "Was that happy, or sad? Can you hear what it was about?" Sometimes—and it would make my heart swell—they did guess; most often, they did not.

After this I would pick out random lines and have my students repeat them. Actually, they were so starved for conversation—the thing they were paying for—they would repeat nearly anything I said. During the readings, they would practically hold their breath—they sensed these were something to savor—but everything else was fair game. Their sullen looks (was it me, or the fact that life was forcing them to rearticulate and rearticulate?) would evaporate, given a certain opportunity. As soon as I walked into the room, for example, "Hello, everyone," led to a resounding, "HELLO EVERYONE!" One night, I looked down and saw that I'd spilled some coffee on my dress. "Oh, damn," I muttered. "HO! DAMN!" intoned the group.

And it wasn't just me; they would repeat each other, too. "HELLO!" one Sikh would call to the other across the arc of the room as they settled in at the beginning of the night. The entire class would turn in delighted surprise and bellow back, "HE-LOOO!"

One evening, just before the handwriting on the wall suddenly snapped into focus, Dan had tapped on the door in his polite way, stuck his head in and said, "I have to talk to you." "I HAVE TO TALK TO YOU!" the class boomed, stirring and smiling at this new tactic in pedagogy. Dan did a double-take and took a step back. "No, not you," he mumbled, perplexed. His obvious discomfort made them laugh. "NO, NOT YOU!" they belted out. "Wha—? Wha—? Oh, never mind," Dan said, leaving. "WHA WHA HO!" the class resounded, "NEVER MIND!" The two sikhs smirked and gave each other high fives.

At first, this tendency of theirs had been a problem, especially in the period right after Dan had found the words to tell me he was leaving me. "It's not anything you do in particular," he'd said. "I just don't . . . love you anymore." It was just a few days after he'd come to my classroom, and when he had gone I thought, my god, he was going to say this to me in front of my whole class! But in any case, it was too late. There is no recovering when someone tells you they don't love you anymore. It left me a shell-shocked, manic-depressive wreck; I wanted to stand up there saying things like, "Son of a bitch," and "Bastard." And worse. I imagined those words going round and round the room, bouncing off the walls, swelling like a pipe organ. Most nights, though, I realized how much I loved Dan and wanted to say words like, "Please," or "Forgive," or "Sorrow," to let those be the words filling me, to let those be the words of volume. Over and over, a resonant murmuring, tumbling slowly around the bottom of that cavernous lecture room like a velvet fog, like a Gregorian chant . . . . Somehow, though, I managed not to give in to either urge, and I read the poems and then fell silent, unable to think of what words were important enough for them to repeat out of context.

I felt guilty about my lackluster performance, but I'd gotten used to feeling guilty about everything. I told myself that because I loved the poems so much, what I was exposing my students to was not totally without value. I told myself that I would get better as we went along. I told myself I was doing all I could do. Ultimately, I became half-convinced that I was something different, but perhaps okay: a language teacher who no longer believed simply in the face value of words.

Which, I guess, is part of what disturbed me so about getting an anonymous declaration of love: I had nothing but the face value of some free-floating words. Were they words of romance? Mockery? Simple human compassion? It was impossible to tell without a face. You would think that if someone actually showed you their heart you would instantly and profoundly recognize them. But I knew now, after all I'd been through, that having a heart was not enough. You had to stand behind it.

It's a funny thing about a broken heart: it both believes in true love and distrusts that true love really exists, both at the same time. You get all involved in trying to understand not only the person that broke your heart but yourself. But you find out that your own heart—just like everyone else's—is wearing a pair of glasses with a fake nose and mustache.

Another thing about a broken heart—it's exhausting. Everything in the world suddenly seems relevant and in need of examination. By the time I was able to re-gather what was left of my wits and leave for class, what I wanted most was to not think about any of it, in any of its million possible refractions, anymore. The mystery of this valentine had worn me out. I felt like I'd been up all night, feeling lonely and sorry for myself, mainlining not just coffee, but espresso.

It revitalized me somewhat to be outside, on my new street, in the open, under a deep blue bowl of night sky. There'd been a light rain earlier and there was the smell of spring in the air—the famous cherry blossoms would be in bloom in just a few more weeks. Not much, but something to look forward to. The street was dark, that's something else I like about Washington; it can feel small and dark and cozy sometimes. A city you can hide in without feeling over-whelmed. Buildings are not allowed to be taller than monu-ments. (By today's standards, that's not very tall; in other words, the monuments aren't as tall as they used to be.) Streetlights are few and far between. Except for the federal buildings, bright in their security, there is not a lot of glare and false shine bouncing around. On nights when the moon is full, like it was that night, it gives the white stone monuments a kind of natural glow, as if they are in a lush nighttime field. I stood for a moment in the shadow of my building and looked off at the moon hanging low over the Potomac.

I had a lovely moment, then, of thinking everything was going to be all right. I had the sensation of being in a secure place, a place of good hope. I was still relatively young, I had a job. As my mother had taken to saying lately, "a *world* of pos-sibilities." "Yeah," my father usually put in, "a *shitload* of pos-sibilities."

I started off down the sidewalk toward school. There were people on the street, I felt part of something. Normally, I would have taken the subway, but Washington's system is confusing, you have to pay when you get off, the amount varying with how far you've travelled. In my recent distract-ed state, I was always getting on without enough money to get off. I'd developed an unnatural fear of being trapped beneath our nation's capital, of coursing through those sub-terranean arteries for the rest of my life.

But tonight was different. I would take some control, I would walk. I patted the pocket of my raincoat where I nor-mally stuffed the thick Norton and told myself that should anyone accost me I would simply brain them with the weight of world literature. I've always believed poetry can save your life.

Except that there was no Norton in my pocket. I was so preoccupied I'd picked up the heart it its place. Great, I thought, I'll just whip this out and hold it up to my mugger, like a crucifix to a vampire, and love will out.

I looked at that heart and thought, I can't get away from this damn thing.

Something went out of me and, defeated, I hailed a cab. I suddenly felt I could not bear to pass any happily fascinated tourists, tromping along hand in hand, kids on a leash. A *herd* of elephants, a *plague* of locusts. No concerned Democrats, no determined Republicans. No carefree teenagers or settled senior citizens. No displaced minorities, wounded veterans or intellectual malcontents. I did not want to come upon any tragic souls—no blind men, no cripples—whose problems, I knew, actually dwarfed mine. Most of all, I did not want to pass any loving couples strolling along the Mall, clutching at each other in the monumental moonlight.

Still, even after I'd managed to hail a cab, plop into it and pull the door closed behind me with a kiss of suction like I was being sealed into an isolation tank, even after we were hissing along the wet avenue, something came to me that seemed worse than all that. It was as we swept around Lafayette Park and swung past the White House, which was lit up beautifully, as always. Spotlights dotted the long drive and lengthened the columns of the portico and filled the bare trees with light. It looked like a distant painted backdrop, almost, like a picture. And I had to look away, because somehow it summoned up in me the memory of the first time I'd ever seen the White House—I was uprooted, new to town, newly married and excited—and what had been on the sidewalk in front of it: a man, his back against the tall black-iron fence, huddling under a lean-to of canvas. The canvas draped just over him like a pair of limp, dingy wings; he was camped over a small flame licking up at him out of a coffee can. On either side of him was a badly lettered placard reading, "Mr. President, Have a Heart. . . ." Dan had been driving too fast for me to read the fine, desperate scrawl covering the rest of the signs, or to see that man's face.

When I finally got the nerve to look up, there was my class before me, scattered, rising in gradual increments over my head, off toward the hall's distant rear, which, in my nearsightedness, I sometimes took to be fog-enshrouded: students *ad infinitum*. It was a large semi-circular room, with seats that folded up like in a movie theater. Each one had arms that swung up into writing surfaces. There were tall, narrow windows through which I imagined the gauzy daytime sunlight beaming in, sparkling with gently floating dust motes, enlightening and warming the room full of lecture-lulled freshmen. At night, though, the sputtering fluorescents seemed far overhead, and with the sparse population of my class, an echo bounced off the walls and the concrete floor. I did not use the podium or the microphone.

Not that it was a small class. I actually had quite a few students—42, to be exact; six over the class limit—and, unlike most Americans I'd taught, these people were positively religious about attendance. Often, they brought relatives. Even so, they did not come close to filling that place.

Still, there they were: forty-something faces staring at me, scowling in concentration or impatience, a few of them smiling. One of these looks, I realized, was a look of love, although that was not a recognizable look to me anymore. Dark skin, light skin. Round faces, narrow faces. Sandals with socks. The two Sikhs wore turbans. There were saris and dashikis.

I stood there in my trench coat, examining them, my hands buried in my pockets. I don't know how long I stood like this before I realized that I must have looked like a crazy person to them.

My knees actually buckled then. What could I possibly say to these people? Where was my poetry when I needed it? I had no text. My husband had left me. I was unsure of love.

I took off my raincoat and tried to regain my concentration. I could have recited to them any number of the poems I knew by heart. I could have said, *"One that is ever kind said yesterday: / 'Your well-beloved's hair has threads of gray. . .'"* (. . . mornings when I would wake early and look across the pillow at Dan's tousled hair). Or, I could have told them, *"Low hangs the moon, it rose late, / It is lagging—O I think it is heavy with love, with love. . . ."* (. . . standing quiet on the front porch looking at the moon hanging low over the river . . .)

The fog began rolling into the back of the room then. I could see it curling around the chairs at the end of the aisles. I was losing it.

"Oh, Dan," I muttered.

It washed over me like a wave. "HO!" they yelled. "DAMN!" I'd forgotten the similarity to what had become one of their favorite words.

My laugh of surprise felt like a moment of relief, and I swung my eyes around the room at the spread of suddenly smiling faces. And one of them loved me. One student, two parents. These things multiply, I told myself.

"Multitudes . . ." I said out loud, to confirm it.

"MULTITUDES!" they called back.

I looked up at them and for some reason thought of something my mother had noticed—that most of the multitudes were of various kinds of birds.

"We are not alone," I told the class. "We are a dissimulation of birds."

"A DISSIMULATION OF BIRDS!" came the reply.

I thought first of people who paraded, who weren't in love with each other so much as with love itself. "An ostentation of peacocks," I said.

"AN OSTENTATION OF PEACOCKS!" they said.

I thought of people who were too scared to do anything about love. "A peep of chickens," I told them.

"PEEP!" they chirped.

Niloo was trying to scribble these things down in her notebook, but I continued without pause, thinking next about people who had so much self confidence that loving someone was merely another way to love themselves. "A deceit of lapwings," I said.

Then I thought of what was actually more common and rushed to get it out: people who genuinely count on love, but sometimes stumble. "A crash of dodos," I said, "a tumble of penguins." How they want others to witness love, and in that way share it. "A mustering of storks, an offering of loons." How, within the chest of someone in love, compassion swells "A pitying of turtledoves, a tender of swans." How realizing love makes you want to sing. "An exaltation of larks."

The class was with me on each one. Sometimes, what they managed to blurt out was nowhere near the words I'd actually said, but they never once missed the beat, or the tone, and they spoke with an earnestness that seemed nearly deadly. This was no role playing. It got to where the words didn't matter much. They were all smiling, face after face off toward the back of the class, where my vision blurred.

There seemed to be so many of them. It was as if they had multiplied, like the bread and the fishes. It occurred to me that I might never know which one of them had sent me the heart.

I paused for a moment. "Take poetry where you can find it," I told them. And then I went on with the multitudes.

AFFIRMATION

NATON LESLIE

When I rise in the morning,
lean against the nearest wall
and then careen like the near blossom
on a stem to the sun
days and the lesser days of no
real shadow, all light
hidden in a smoked glass
sky, I think of only such
shadows

and the corporeal feel
of plaster, the no
saint that guards those
like me. No one, not
a voice quaking, commanding.

> *Don't go out with a tie*
> and do not have more than five,
> ten dollars for the hand
> ready in the pocket.

That is the first rule, the last
you never learn. Left alone,
my nature repopulates like ragweed
on the unwanted places of the earth.

I am exhaust. When the telephone
rings I get answers,
give answers. It is easy
then, only my breath
saying *yes, yes.*

CHARLES DICKENS TRAVELS TO CLEVELAND

"It soon became too dark however,
even for this amusement."
American Notes, 1842

Maybe he saw the necks of smokestacks
in the flats of Youngstown, Steubenville,
young and ingrown. And probably tophats.
Of course, great iron tophats,
stiff and honorable with names.

Boz found his way on a new macadam road
through the wide spaces
of clear-cut Ohio forest.
He had left the prairie day and now
saw in stumps of the great woods,
by muted dusk, from a seat in an open,
clattering four-horse coach, the old woman figure,
the poised, blank back of a bear, the terrible
hunchbacks of his many minds. And then in a last
broad slap of western light, a lost father
found, the head of a Scottish stag
drowning in moor, horns formed in a hydra
of new growth on an oak stump. It thrashed
in the bog water, tongue lolling in stiff mud grass.

THE DARKER EXCURSIONS

I want someone to tell them
lies provide nothing

but themselves, when you die
your name does not appear

on the credits. And those
you kill with these weapons

survive as lonesome chunks of flesh,
once living together, still moving,

a single hole not made,
not allowing last words.

And your friends can die, yes,
and they can cause their own

deaths as provable theorems.
The dead beget themselves,

a necessity. Understand
the heart is mathematical,

that machines can be as vicious
as wild animals, and we can sell

and sell and sell and enter
contracts we don't realize,

that when the body is rudely opened,
life, the organs, slip out

like children after midnight
without permission.

MERCY

The neighbors have noticed me once
I decide upon another town.
They are seldom outside, the side
walls of their houses give desperate

ignorance. I hear that the man
I talk to upstairs, another neighbor,
is a known idiot, that the wideness
of the world is clueless. So I walk

in short bursts to the corner
gas station, buy supplies
as though in an outback. The point
of the man's narrative is simply

beyond me. What he says
is out of line with the polar push
of days. And he doesn't believe
I should move away.

*

They stole your cap, you say,
after Anzio Beach. You were beaten
badly in your memory now
in Italy, on the mountain street

standing against four men from town,
as young as you. When they carried
you off senseless, you counted ten over
and over, hands in front of your face.

Having your memory is like carrying
furniture up twisting stairways.
Let your end down slowly, as I just might
drop mine, the pine-dead weight

of sixty years and of words revolved
and recounted ready to drive me
through the bannister as passengers
in cars wave tired limbs.

LATE FREEZE

This is casual weather,
it does not take
a stand. The cold is so temporary
a piece of clothing hangs
loose about the shoulders,
a full-length sign of adoption.

No one runs through this naked,
the iced air, the drink of lungs
which have no real desire
for change. You cannot change
the mind of an image
that has reached a final solid.

So I have to stop for everything
fragile, the impenetrable crust
of the banks that must wash
in new moving weather. Those who stop
on the bank feel the knuckles of late
winter wind and water, a vertigo
that does not make you fall
but has the back of your shoulders climb
up in chill, over the ears.

I live with the careful
flat light of a bulb. I live
in the cold
we call love of the world
spread among others like frozen food.

I want to walk today,
with the people in *El Nino's*
dry breath, the tan grasses,
the dull gasp of sweatless herds.

BREAD

F. R. Lewis

So THERE IT WAS and there it was.

First it was please, please, please; it was we want you; it was we need you; it was leave where you've been; it was come with us. Then, almost before there was time to digest, it was a glass of wine, dry white, and a plate of red clam sauce on angel hair (they haven't made a pasta too thin for me) and it was thanks and it was good-bye, all at the restaurant of my choice. It was one afternoon on the phone to the Yugoslav movie-maker and it was the next morning queued up for unemployment.

"No good deed goes unpunished," Leonard my husband said, reading the saying off his saying-of-the-day desk calendar. Everyone has an opinion.

The first six months or so after, it was doing my paperwork and getting a check, like a regular State worker, every second Thursday. For the bi-weekly bread it was perusing the classifieds and pursuing all that applied. It was keeping track on a form: addresses and phone numbers and names and what, on the other end, they did, the names. Half of half a salary extended, it was possible, by occasional employment. From occasional employment yielding occasional pay, it was taking away here, adding on there until, between one thing and another, the checks, the getting of the checks, may have been closer in months to seven, or maybe even eight, than to six.

For me, the occasion was restaurant reviews, the writing of them.

It was the morning after, standing in the "E" line (whatever that meant), because at unemployment the "E" line was the only line working, except for the white line that a sign and the clerk told us we should stand to the rear of.

"No Social Security card?" the clerk said when I stepped over the line, sounding as if she thought someone in July dressed in nylons and a pin-stripe should know enough to carry the card.

"Lost," I said. "Sorry."

"You have thirty days to produce one." She pointed a finger to her right. "In there," she said.

In there, it was a woman sitting next to wire baskets holding forms. They all held forms, the woman and the wire baskets.

"Take from the back, return to the front," the woman said. I wondered was this like being mustered, then thought that wasn't quite the word.

In the room, a small room, close, it was the sound of pencils, short ones with no erasers, like from miniature golf, scratching line to line along page after page of forms, front and back. Men and women, all of us recording our where did you works and how longs and what are you qualified to do's and how far to get a job will you go's, finishing rapidly, racing to the basket, jockeying in the only way we can.

It was the in-there woman skimming my forms from the basket in their turns and her saying, "I don't see your Social Security card."

Frizz-haired and wizened, the woman wore a vest of granny squares, raspberry and lemon and lime, crocheted, and chocolate brown polyester-knit pants. In her room it was that much of a refrigerator.

"Lost for years," I said.

"Bring it here in thirty days. If you don't produce . . . ," she paused to gaze sympathetically at her nails, bitten-to-below-finger-tips, then shook her head, ". . . you're in the soup."

"Sit out there," she said, stretching thin lips into what I decided to take as a smile. "You'll be called."

Out there, it was one of those glass and painted over-and-over metal partitions stopping a couple of feet short of the ceiling, that separated whoever they were from us. Among us, it was constant stirring: one woman much younger than I, knitting; men in jeans talking car repair and baseball; this one, then that, disappearing behind the partition, new ones filling the "E" line.

Behind the partition, at a green metal desk, a kind of office version of lean Danish-modern that was all the rage in the sixties, it was a man who didn't tell me his name folding the forms I'd filled in the other room, reducing them to fit, reaching down to a bottom drawer, extracting "and what did you earn" forms that he completed as I answered. He Xeroxed or Canoned or Sharped or maybe even Mita-ed my W-2, my sample payment stub, asked after my Social Security card, explained how on this orange record-keeper I should do my day-by-days, recording **Y** for have or **N** for haven't blended with the work force and on these legal-length Pepto Bismal pink sheets how to list what he called my contacts.

It was the nameless man reading my forms. It was the nameless man saying, "Employment history," and, "I don't know what to tell you."

It was the momentary chill, fearing the nameless man would send me for re-training to the Job Service where I'd overheard the unemployed ahead of me in the filling-out room being sent, and then his saying instead, "With all your experience, I would not count on securing a position."

Almost twenty years, not counting time off for nature and nurture, and only three employers, I thought maybe it was not experience he meant.

"I have an interview," I said. "This afternoon."

"Good for you," he said, patting the air just above my shoulder. "Sign here. Come back next week."

Weeks beyond having to pink-list them, it was answering classifieds.

It was filing responses in files labeled "Kiss-Offs, Immediate" and "Kiss-Offs, Ultimate." It was some of the time believing I would land a job, and not just any job, but a position in my field, even though during the interviews all my experience harvested it was having nothing meaty occur to me to say, not until the interview ended, sometimes while I gathered my things or worked my arms into a coat, not until it was barely polite smiles, raised-eye-brow glances. In my history, it had always been the job seeking me.

It was every morning coffee first thing and the delivered-to-my-doorstep daily turned to the back of the back section, then adding Sunday's *Times*, and then, for good measure, magazines that when they asked me to subscribe called themselves "professional journals."

For the employment recipe it was only my Social Security card and rooting out jobs in my field(s).

For my restaurant reviews, on the other hand, it was what the editor called a "nice mix": pricey and cheap and all the range between.

For my restaurant reviews it was once a week ordering as many courses as I could stomach and every Tuesday setting on the editor's plate a supply of food-and-drink words, served up under stars. It was the editor promising two meals and fifty clams every review and my name among the listed staff and on a mail slot.

It was the editor saying, "We don't pay for wine, just review the list," and it was me breathing a sigh. What, after all, did I know of wine?

It was studying restaurant reviews, their presentations, ingesting vocabulary, sniffiness of tone.

It was choosing brunch and lunch and breakfast and sup-per and companions for the supper, Mary and Eugene, afi-cionados of review, to aid my rise to the occasion.

It was matters of taste: caps or crowns, which would dis-tort most? And aromas. Since the concussion, even with the car crash being a dozen years previous, did I get them right, the aromas? Or even enough. This restaurant reviewing, it was not the simple matter it had at first blush appeared.

It was being sure that Mimi Sheraton, when she ate for prof-it, what she ate was not her friends, even when her friends were in the pot by choice. Their choice. Really.

It was the day I interviewed for energetic part-time

writer-editor excellent communications skills, able to work
with a variety of people in local BOCES that would have kept
me in the pension plan but offered not over-time but comp-
time, of which a good deal could be expected, if not taken,
that night Leonard and I taking our first dinner with Mary
and Eugene.

The first-dinner restaurant, it was located just down the
road from the BOCES, in a motel owned by Asian Indians, in
a room furnished in brass-footed Danish-modern tables and
chairs of Chinese red and black, with specials printed on a
blackboard that wasn't black but one of those white, shiny
things where you use markers.

It was the waitress saying she's only Tuesday, Wednesday
and Thursday, her nights, with a State job days and weekends
with her husband in the VA. To most of the others she just said
food; we must have looked as though we wouldn't eat her.

About food it was the waitress saying, "Forget the appetizers. Forget the dessert. Trust me," and placing before us
course after course that came:

*smorgasbord of pickled herring in sour cream and
cucumber in mint and yogurt and chick-pea salad with
chopped onion and green peppers and cranberry-orange rel-
ish and Swedish meatballs served in a glass-and-silver Lazy
Susan, the double of those that, newly-wed, or maybe
-engaged, Mary and Eugene and Leonard and I had received;

*linguini in well-garlicked Marinara (they haven't made a
sauce with too much garlic for me);

*house-salad of iceberg and tomatoes that tasted home-
grown;

*two filets mignon because Mary and Leonard, they don't
get it at home, and two salmons;

*corn fritters that Leonard says the maple syrup is real,
and baked potatoes and fresh zucchini in Marina more onion
that garlic;

*apples, Macintosh and Delicious, two each, fried dough
dusted with confectioner's sugar, after-dinner mints.

It was Eugene saying, "Reminds me of places we eat in
the Adirondacks, on vacation," and me saying, "No antlers,
no birch bark furniture, not one stick," and Eugene summing

up, "Heart, quality, the best of intentions—and absolutely no sophistication, not one whit."

It was Eugene saying and me writing what he said. Exactly.

Funny, they said that time, after their reading, Mary and Eugene.

Things went on.

It was an all-day grilling by committees and sub-committees to hire top-notch college publications editor-coordinator, experienced, ambitious, creative thinker, excellent marketing and communication skills, no job-line, no budget, then Mary and Eugene and Leonard and I, in an authentic early-nineteenth century farm house complete with planked floors and stone fireplaces and homespun curtains and flowered wallpapers and stamped-tin ceilings, celebrating the fall that arrived on the coat-tails of a hurricane.

It was a nervous-seeming and giggly waitress saying when we asked, Mary and Eugene, Leonard and I, what's this? what's that? "But don't you want wine?"

"In addition to our regular entrees, we have specials," she said, waving her pen in the direction of one of the chalk-written regular-menu blackboards-on-easels sitting here and there in farm-house rooms. "But I don't remember what they are."

It was her describing a preparation—*maison*—as "one of those cream sauces with mushrooms and shallots and some kind of wine. Don't you want wine?"

We sent her off to re-discover the specials, which by the time she got back to us if she found them out, she had again forgotten. So, for us, menu items it was.

"You won't be sorry," the waitress said, looking, we thought, relieved.

"Perhaps, she is new," we said.

"I would describe the menu as thoughtful and eclectic," Eugene said. "Oh yes," Mary said, "thoughtful and eclectic."

Our waitress re-appeared, looking once again, troubled. "You forgot to order wine," she said.

Eugene ordered the feature-of-the-week wine, something from California. Long enough later for us to have been served out appetizers, the waitress returned.

"The wine," she said. "We don't have . . . It never arrived."

"Try here," she said, thrusting wine-notebook at Eugene. Eugene selected a second California something. The waitress carried away the burgundy-colored notebook clutched to her breast.

"An interesting list, but not intimidating," Eugene said.

"Interesting but not intimidating," Mary said, sounding entranced.

When the waitress showed up with the bottle, she splashed a sip for Eugene, awaiting his nod, bottle on hip, then filled Leonard's glass, then Mary's glass, then mine, then turned to leave us again.

"A glass for Eugene," we called after her. "Our bottle."

Plaudits for appetizers and soups. My cream of broccoli, steamy hot, light-textured and tasty, even with the broccoli no doubt having been some previous day's, or even days', *vegetable du jour.*

"I always puree," Mary said. "No chunks, no mush, no problem."

In Mary's delightful salmon tortellini with satin-smooth salmon cream, the smoked salmon contrasted nicely with pasta and sauce, that's what Mary said. Eugene savored every morsel of his artichoke hearts lavishly filled with a cream cheese, honey and walnut mixture, and Leonard his snails laced with a honey-sweetened tomato sauce.

Harold's and Eugene's crisp garden salads came topped by the loaded-with plump-blueberries vinaigrette, Mary's and mine by the almost-tangy Dijon.

While we awaited our entrees, it was Leonard at our table saying how his taste buds were hyper-aware, his palate elegant, and it was in the service alcove, in direct view of our table, the restaurant owner saying, "Look at the spider. Look at the spider. You afraid of spiders?" to our already giddy waitress.

It was the waitress shrieking, "Get it away. Oh-oh. Get it away," while the owner laughed and didn't leave off with his teasing.

"What a jerk," I said.

"Well put," they said together, Mary and Eugene.

The "half-roasted" ducks, Leonard's and Mary's, came de-boned and de-fatted in a lingonberry sauce the chef said over the phone several days after was just one of the many and various fruit sauces with which he "just loved" to serve his sautéed dishes.

Eugene found his catfish in Louisiana-style walnut butter firm, sweet and, so he said, "as fresh as can be without jumping directly from pond to plate."

"Pond to plate," said Mary.

The *maison* topping off my cooked-to-perfection *tournedos maison* turned out a Madiera so sweet as to startle.

With each dish came tiny boiled red potatoes and strips of summer squash and zucchini with a hint of red pepper and onion sautéed, what every restaurant we ate in, except for breakfast, called that year "garden medley." Leonard adored summer squash and red potatoes; harvests of each were abundant.

For reasons the more-or-less fresh-out-of-culinary-school chef was later that same week during that same phone call unable to account, our dinners arrived post-hot. "Unless the waitress didn't pick them up right away," he said. "What can I say? I mean the heat lamp, it's new. I just upgraded."

Not wishing to over-stuff, it was two desserts, not four, both of them fresh-tasting, light-as-air lemon souffles that betrayed not the tiniest hint of lemon.

"The chef," Eugene said, "is not assertive on the tart side."

It was a blast of hurricane slapping rain and Crimson-King maple leaves against the panes of window through which we looked out on the farm house's porch and it was Mary saying, "Not assertive on the tart side. How lovely."

It was what they said. What they said, just the way they said it, was exactly what I wrote.

In the end it was the end.

It was the man for whom I used to work saying, "You write reviews for people like me," and it was me saying, "I'm giving it up." It was him looking startled and me rushing on to explain the newspaper's apparent no-pay, that's-how-it-goes policy, its series of bouncing checks-in-the-mail.

It was unemployment, the benefits running out, and it was small claims court to recover twenty weeks at fifty per and something for my one exotic-fish cookbook for Christmas-giving review and a list of the year's ten best. And, of course, the bounced-check bank fees.

It was knowing, or being, at least, pretty sure, that no restaurant, not even the ones we really liked, except maybe the pot roast with still-crisp carrots and genuine mashed potatoes served in a real diner setting (set in a real diner), would blow up and hang up, behind plastic, my dining tales, or quote them, my food words, in their ads.

It was having to dine alone. Leonard. Me.

It was Leonard being able to choose almost as soon as he opened the menus and it was me not being any longer able to discriminate between mushroom beignets, with or without garlic cream-sauce, and rabbit fritters.

It was one hundred and twenty-three cover letters and one hundred and twenty-three resumés and nineteen interviews, one of them with the woman who when they started high school together had been our oldest son's first major flame.

It was "we were impressed by your credentials, but . . ." and it was "we've offered the position to someone who more closely matches . . ." and it was "we'll keep your resumé on file should something more appropriate . . ."

It was taking the job with the ad that told me, "You can count," at least temporarily, and it was Mary and Eugene eating out with us again, Leonard and me, once the reviewing stopped and they would not, they said, find their words in print, making them feel, they said, like fools.

It was all in all imagining how different things could be if every now and then, just once in a while, just sometimes, I could maybe get myself in toward the middle, after the choices, every one of the choices, had already been made.

ON THE SECOND TIME LOOKING INTO CAESAR'S GALLIC WAR

George Liaskos

There are low lying, wet fields and woods
In the ancient land of the Oneidas.
Sometimes as the sun sets
And the darkness settles down
The mist strands spiral up, up,
Whispering up from the heavy ground.
Clouds descend, to come to rest
Upon the roads and the deep cow pastures.
From an auto window peering
There's a visual quiet unnerving.
The headlights slice a sparkling path.
The hardtop-rubber whirr announces
A sanity to every new thirteen feet;
To a weird world where reality quivers
At that oft spoken fine line.

Watching along the edge
Where the fields meet the wood
I espied two young deer
On a twilight such as this.
I stopped my vehicle up off the road,
To witness them frolic in the mist.
They broke the misty, spiral strands
With the kick and twist and jump
Of their wiry forms.
The scattered pieces of fog,
Still airy borne, tickled their noses. . .

I know they did.
I smiled to see their mouths in a laugh.
I strained to hear the sound
Of what no man has heard before;
And I think it was this
That made me leave my car.

Ears cocked, straining to hear,
I stumbled across the clodded earth.
Earlier on, a quick clumping of a machine
Had thrown the ground about
In the noise of an afternoon.
Now, in the quiet of a field,
The laughter of deer trying to hear,
My shoes sloughed through the puddled mire.
So strange my busy approach
Stopped not their wonderful play.
Even at a distance to touch
They heeded not my presence.
Oh, what joy this spectre self
To stand so near them.
I wouldn't touch but oh, to see
The browny coat, their twitching ears,
Those lovely eyes and graceful frame,
And the upturned mouths;
Still the laughter not heard
But yet so near to me!?

And the moment next
Of how can I explain?!
That shudder of the earth,
The splitting of the ground
That froze us three still
As the trees behind us.

The deer, they bolted,
But still there alone I stood,
To see that strange glow

At the end of the crevice
A ways off in the wood.

Approaching and not knowing
How my feet brought me there,
To a glow of a pool in a bubbly forming
From the deep, deep depths.

There came to me thoughts
Quiet but sure, unquestionable
As to their truth,
That I looked upon the Histral Pool;
The place where centuries upon centuries
Have tossed and tumbled together,
Where space and time by the chance
Of an out of sync galaxy motion
Has taken a tear
And spilled forth a something past,
To exist as flesh and words in the present.

From the depths appeared a finger
And then a hand;
I fell, kneeling at the edge
And grasped it hard;
It rose to the elbow
And no farther could go.
My body strained, I shifted my weight
To hold the position.
Its grasp was tight and so strong.
The hand was rough and I knew
It to be so from the work of sword
And the battle axe and the hoe.
"Oh, Histral Pool," I cried,
"Why this night? Why this grasp,
Water wet and muddy slimed?
What is this here I hold
And what story need it tell?"
The gurgled name arose

As bubbles to the surface
And breaking, popping,
Announced—Vercingetorix.

"Vercingetorix, yes," I said,
"Surely you're here."
His voice became as a geyser,
Spilling up, up into the trees,
All around as wavering thunder,
Up amongst the leaves.
"Surely, yes, Vercingetorix,"
It was said.
"Here, now, finally a time
Breaking through with this tear,
With this pool, into your empire capital;
A few words born of the woods and fields,
So much as our beloved Gaul.
And yes, so much more
Than the thousand upon another thousand
Words enfolded cozily
In the libraries of the world;
The small, inky entrapment of thoughts
Of the mind of the Regal Roman Runt.
How fitting for his honour,
How cozily, warm and snug
He spent the winters of his 'campaigns.'
Oh, wonderful military travelogue
Of how he so nicely took hostages,
As honorable as their way of war:
Clank, clank formations of armour,
Bang, bang, bang, build another machine,
Dig, dig another trench, another moat.
Not a man among them standing tall
To fight you as a warrior
And test the spirit of the force
Behind the weapon;
Just a slobbering clump of engineers
Not caring how they'd kill a Gaul:

Crunch under the armoured phalanx,
Crush with a flying stone,
Drown us in a moat;
It's all the same thing—
Gone, another enemy of Rome.
The life of the spirit
Lost to their way of being.
And now, to this day's inheritance—
Deadening of the arteries and veins
Of the living, breathing earth.
Their state of things
As dead in life as the stone
Of their encolumned buildings.
Your inheritance this Roman state of things.
Acquire the last death—
The earth made a tottering rock in space—
If not the tribal feel remembered.
Refreshed blood chemicals handed down
Will spirit life of earth renew,
The ancient mysteries brought forth in time
To guide the life as once we knew.

But quick my words and scant
In this unnatural freak of time.
In this short life I live
I take one last Roman Runt."
His arm flexed hard and pulled.
My body prone became
And slid into the pool.
My words announced as bubbles,
"No, no, a Roman not I,
I am a Greek.
Ici not Rome Italia,
Ici a Rome de L'Amerique."
And it was then I drown.
No. Yes. . .
I know I did.

WHERE MORNING FINDS YOU

Ron MacLean

"ANY SIGN of him? He turn up yet?"

My sister has answered the phone on the fourth ring. I was afraid she wasn't home at all. We had arranged the time that I would call, and I had to search frantically for a pay phone, to gauge my drive time to make it to an offramp, then find a pay phone outside a convenience store, at exactly 2:00 a.m. The desert breeze is still warm.

"No," she says. "Nothing." I can hear Spanish radio playing in the background, the music loud enough to be distracting. I wonder why she doesn't turn it down. I wonder when she began listening to Spanish radio. "Where are you?" she asks.

I look around before I answer, though I already know, by the words on the road sign that led me off of Interstate 15. "Yermo. Outside a Circle K." Inside the store a middle-aged man in an orange smock watches me talk on a pay phone, talk to my only sister about our missing father. "Where have you been looking?"

"Fanning out in expanding circles from the supermarket." My sister was a math whiz in college. Very analytical. I don't know how she ended up a sous chef at a steak house in North Las Vegas. But then there are a lot of things I don't know. "Then expanding circles from home."

Traces of sand graze my skin, carried on the warm air. I don't even ask about the police. I learned years ago, from movies, that they don't consider someone missing until they've been gone at least twenty-four hours. What I do ask her is about the music. Why she doesn't turn it down. That it's so loud now I can't even hear her. I'm on a fucking pay phone, I say. Consider the circumstances.

"There," she says. "I'm in the kitchen now. Is that better?" And it is. The lilt of samba now serves as background to our meandering urgency. "It's usually better in the kitchen. I try to keep walking around to find the spot where it's quietest."

"Why don't you just turn it down?"

"How can I turn it down?"

"You know, the little volume knob on the radio?"

She laughs. "Since when do I listen to Spanish radio? It comes over the phone line. You haven't noticed it before?"

I tell her I haven't. When I call her from my home, I don't notice it. A ballad takes over from the samba. The man in the convenience store still watches me, through his black-rimmed eyeglasses, through the glass of the storefront, through my own glasses, our eyes meet for a moment and I'm reminded of my father.

"I'm going back out there," my sister says. "Call me in two hours."

Interstate 15 carves its way through the southern Mojave Desert, connecting Los Angeles to Las Vegas. Five hours from Santa Monica. I left my house at midnight, right after the call from my sister, telling me that my father, at 67 a relatively young man who has lately been subject to occasional spells of disorientation and forgetfulness, had apparently wandered out of the grocery store where she'd taken him to buy some milk, after they'd had dinner together and before she was going to drive him home. She'd spent a few hours looking for him, first in and around the market, then figuring that he must have gone home, before calling me. My mother, his partner for thirty-eight years, died several months ago. He's been depressed. Frustrated that he can't just pick up the pieces and get on with it. Part of a generation and an Irish heritage that resists emotion. Considers it something to be wrestled into submission. Defeat grief. But life doesn't neces-sarily cooperate. Forced retirement and the death of a spouse within six months. No wonder he's a little disoriented. Still, it's hard not to think that it might be something else. Something even less easily worked through. This isn't like him.

I think of a couple of times I've heard him say he doesn't see any point in going on. That there's nothing for him. But those are thoughts of a tired mind emotionally overwrought. I don't know what to think. Then I find myself thinking about the last time I was driving frantically in the middle of the night, this same road, this same time, this same knot in the middle of my stomach, after the same kind of phone call from my sister. My father only started using the phone after my mother died. Back then, that last time, my sister called to tell me that my mother's heart was failing. That it didn't look like she could last more than a couple of hours. And I hung up the phone and drove, faster than I dared think about, yet feeling like the car was moving through water, no way to shorten the five hours, the three hundred and fourteen miles between myself and the hospital where my mother lay, no way to stop the brain from thinking that I should have gone earlier, should have been there when I first heard there was trouble, two days earlier, when I first heard of the most recent heart attack. That I knew the signs weren't good, that she couldn't keep fighting much longer, that her heart wouldn't take many more of these eruptions. But she had seemed so confident of pulling through. She had sounded determined on the phone. Had said, "Come up when you can. In a couple of weeks. I'll be home then."

Deciding that this could go on indefinitely, that I could confront this decision several times a year forever. Wondering is this the time that it's serious, the time that I should be there? Deciding that I couldn't keep making the drive time after time. That this wasn't likely to be it. That I had factors to consider. Work deadlines. A wife. But then being in the car, racing so impossibly slowly without knowing, racing against the morning and the information it would bring, the drive interminable and yet evaporating so that the moment of getting out of the car at the hospital seemed almost concurrent with the phone call, like a taut tv drama that had merely paused for a commercial.

I didn't make it. Ten minutes, my sister told me. The body lay on the bed behind my sister, hands folded across the stomach, quiet, my father standing over it. Ten minutes ago, my sister told me. Ten minutes ago, she was still here, my sister said. I can't believe it.

So I'm driving again in the middle of the night, although everything is probably fine, and I've got a knot in my stomach although there's probably nothing to worry about, and I turn on the radio this time to keep my mind from racing, from playing back the eerie similarities. I hit the scan button, and when the scanning stops the speakers play Spanish pop music and I don't change the station.

At 4:00 in the morning, I'm waiting to use a pay phone.

I'm parked in front of the Mohawk Cafe in Nipton, California and I'm a few minutes late because I had to go a ways off the interstate to find a phone. I don't want to try to find another one, so I decide I'll wait it out. The phone is being used by a girl in her late teens, a white sleeveless cotton blouse, blue jeans. Long, dark hair being blown around by the still, hot wind. She's arguing with someone on the phone, moving and twisting her body to the minimal extent the short metal phone cord allows. She's trying to convince the person on the other end of something. I'm looking at the facade, a pink stucco with large letters painted in black that say MOHAWK CAFE, NIPTON, CALIF. POP. 380 and I'm thinking that's a funny thing to put on a sign, but then it's funny that the bar is open at 4:00 a.m. in this desolate town and that I'm waiting to use the pay phone.

The wind blows dust in swirls across the entrance, an aluminum screen door that is the only hole in the front of the building. Behind the cafe, the desert is big. The girl slams the receiver in place and spins into the bar. For a minute, I can't remember my sister's phone number. I never write phone numbers down. I have an amazing capacity for remembering them. It's a gift, I tell people.

"You're late," she says, accompanied by what I think is the voice of Linda Ronstadt doing a song from her Mexican album.

"Had to wait for a phone," I say.

"Where are you?"

"Mohawk Cafe. Nipton, California. Population 380."

"You're a strange person," she says. The probable Linda Ronstadt fades out, replaced by a mariachi tune.

"Well?"

"Nothing," she says. "Nada."

"What next?"

"I don't know. I'm running out of ideas." Music fills the silence. It's like being on hold and having a conversation, all at once. "Do you think he's okay? I mean, this isn't like him."

I think for a minute, mostly about how honest I want to be. "No," I say. "I don't think he's okay. But he needs to decide to get on with his life. We can't do that for him." Suddenly I feel like Phil Donohue.

"I mean now. Tonight. Do you think he's alright?"

"I don't know. I don't want to think about it. I just want to get there." We're an east coast family. We're a little uncomfortable in the desert. We prefer smaller spaces.

"How much longer?"

"Less than two hours." this has become the standard unit of measuring time. "You going back out?"

"Yeah. I'm going to try the parks. He sometimes likes to walk in the park in the evenings." She must not be in the kitchen. The music has gotten louder. She has an antique stove in her kitchen, given to her by a man she lived with for eight years, a man she kicked out last year, right before my mom died, a man who very much wants to get back together. She's not sure what she wants. She says right now it's a matter of choosing not to run. Of waking up each day and choosing not to run. Learning to live with an empty place inside. She's told me before what keeps her going is Katie, her daughter, who tells her every morning, "I love you, Mom. 24–7." Every hour, every day. That's what she means.

"You're not in the kitchen, are you?"

She laughs. "It's been like this for a few weeks. Driving me crazy."

"Have you called the phone company?"

"They insist it's not the line. That it's not their problem."

"So where's it coming from?"

"That's what I said. They said that's not for them to figure out. They said there was a part I could get at Radio Shack. The guy at Radio Shack said he'd sell it to me, but it wouldn't fix the problem. He said it was a question of hounding the phone company into submission."

Something about that makes me feel sad, as though all our efforts are merely distractions to take our attention away from the fact that people vanish every day. People die. "Maybe it's something you could get used to," I say, in a hurry again. "I'll see you soon."

The last time I saw my father we had one of our rare conversations. I had been offered a full-time job writing advertising copy, and I was trying to decide between the security of that offer and the freedom of the freelance life. His first reaction was to get mad. He said where did I get off complaining about a choice of well-paying jobs when he couldn't even find part-time work. We were sitting in a coffee shop. Dark wood beams ran above the counter, the vinyl of the booths was a rich burgundy and his voice was loud enough to make me a little uncomfortable. I could see his point, but still. This is my life, I said. What do you want me to do about that? Then his face softened a little.

"I wouldn't want to be young today," he told me then. "We didn't have so many choices—at least I didn't—but we knew where we fit. Who we were." His voice trailed off, sad. I remember thinking at that moment how ironic it all was. For years, I'd tried to get my dad to talk, to open up a little, and now that he was, it made me uncomfortable. Part of me wished he'd stop. I find now, with a complicated life of my own, that I can't blame him as I'd like to for the distance that's separated us all these years. For the silence. After all, I have my own limitations.

After less than a year, I have difficulty remembering things about my mother. I remember vague, general things—she was small and she didn't have much hair and she was a child in so many ways—but I don't remember moments. Incidents. I sometimes focus on her face, just to hold it in my memory, just to make sure I don't lose it. And I practice remembering moments, reconstructing pieces of her life, of our lives together. I practice with other people, too. As a hedge against loss. I concentrate on picturing my father's face. My wife's. My sister's.

*   *   *

Reaching Las Vegas in the dim, early morning is disorienting. Driving for hours through desert, in darkness, in quiet, with only the illumination of your own headlights. Then lights flickering in the distance, the twinkling of a little community that might be a mirage. Then you're in the midst of it, dizzying, driving through neon, bulbs flashing, beckoning, shouting each other down to get your attention. The eyes don't focus. They try to shut out all the activity. Sensory overload.

It's six a.m. and I can't find my sister's house. She gives lousy directions. We communicate very differently, she and I. I can't tell if I'm in the right neighborhood, or on the wrong side of town.

I am not ready for my father to die, because I cannot, still, picture his face when I close my eyes, or conjure the sound of his voice. I keep hoping to see him by the side of the road. To turn a corner and see him walking along, watching the sun rise.

I imagine that I will stop at a pay phone outside a Circle K and I will call my sister, and the man in the orange smock who works at the store will watch me through the window, and the Spanish music will make it hard to hear, and my sister will answer the phone.

He's here, she'll say. He's alright. Do you want to talk to him?

And she'll put him on the phone, and there'll be sheepish hellos and then he'll tell me that he went to a hotel bar and got a little drunk, then sat on a bench at the park and talked to himself about his life. It's time to get on with it, he'll say, then he'll pause a little and he'll say, I miss her. Then, after a minute, my sister will get back on the phone and I'll joke with her about her bad directions, and then she'll get me there, in time for breakfast.

THE SEARCH BEGINS*

SHIRLEY NELSON

THREE YEARS after Olive Mills was raised from the dead, my father's family moved to Shiloh—he, his parents, and his three sisters. He was twelve years old. My mother was already there, her family in fragments. She was fifteen.

That was in 1902. Nine years had gone by since Frank Weston Sandford had launched his movement in southern Maine, and five since he had laid the foundation for the first towering building on the Douglas sandhill just off the River Road in the town of Durham. It would be eighteen months until his first manslaughter trial, and another nine years until the second.

The world was fairly quiet in 1902, if we discount the concluding skirmishes of the Boer War, an earthquake in Russian Turkestan, and the explosion of Mt. Pelee in the West Indies. By the same dubious standard things were quiet at Shiloh as well—clear through to the middle of December, when the smallpox broke out. Even so, we must move across a snowy New Year and include the whole winter of 1903 before events take on their true significance. And then they do so only in distant retrospect, for not one of the four hundred persons living at Shiloh during those months could have identified that time then for what it really was—the Black Winter, the year when things began to go wrong. The people who told me Shiloh stories were not historians. Dates were seldom given, if remembered at all. The past was

---

*from *Fair Clear and Terrible:*
The Story of Shiloh, Maine.

recorded much as it is in the Old Testament: "In the year that King Uzziah died. . . ." In the year that Olive Mills did not.

Long before Shiloh was a reality in my life it was a sound, a word that began with a hush. Even now it echoes back into the depths of pre-memory, carrying the overtones of many other Scriptural names—Manasseh, Shechem, Baal Shalisha—war cries hidden in their soft syllables. In time I learned that the sound was a place, and then that there were other places in the world called Shiloh. My Shiloh was somewhere in the state of Maine. Yet at the same time it was nowhere. It was less a place than a thing that had happened, like a private volcano in the vague past, its ashes, decades later, still sifting down.

That was how it came to me, in fact, a speck at a time, isolated stories told as the occasion arose. More often than not, these were stories of hunger or cold: scores of families with nothing to eat for days on end, or only carrots, or only cornbread; my father splitting green wood in the snow; my mother washing down six flights of stairs in an unheated building; and a laundry of overwhelming proportions—underwear, sheets, and shirts turning to ice even as they were hung on the line, flapping like cardboard in the wind.

My brain held no spaces for these scenes to settle into. I could not imagine a house that could hold so many people. They jammed themselves around the table in our own small dining room and slept in layers on our beds. I had never seen six flights of stairs. In my mind's eye they shot right out through the rooftop into a wintry sky, and my mother was up there crying, her hands so cold she could scarcely wring out the rag.

Yet there were the "good times," my mother insisted, invariably describing the gingerbread as evidence, great sheets of it—"as big as this table," she would say—served warm from the enormous brick ovens. So the images gathered, full of odd surprises. In the midst of hunger two matched trotting horses pulled a gold and white "chariot" over country roads, a luxury yacht sailed around the world, and—dinner or not—my father played a horn at sunset from the window of a tower, the notes echoing brightly over the valley of the river.

The river was the Androscoggin, the tower "David's." There were other towers as well, and buildings with graceful, feminine names like Olivet and Bethesda. Bethesda was a hospital, minus doctors and medication. Sickness also pervaded Shiloh stories, sometimes in detail. Yet on the whole, references to dying were rueful and brief. My mother spoke of her brother's death almost cryptically. His name was Leander. He died of diphtheria at age fourteen. Diphtheria, to me, was one of the things you got a needle for in the second grade. It left a red-hot welt on your upper arm. No one explained that Leander had been the focus of one of the more anomalous court trials in the country. I never heard my grandmother talk about her son or so much as say his name, though she lived with us for months in New England.

We moved north from New Jersey when I was six, in 1931. I had no idea we were moving geographically closer to Shiloh, and certainly that was not the intention. We rented an old farmhouse on Underwood Street in Holliston, Massachusetts. The house was heated by a wood range and a parlor stove. There was no electricity. All our water came from a pump in the iron kitchen sink. I learned how to prime that pump, how to light a kerosene lamp, and how to carry a load of wood heaped up to just under my eyes.

If I was proud of all that, I was also worried. The move seemed to have replanted us in an earlier time, as if we had slipped backwards. Our house in New Jersey had been "modern." But it was not just the kitchen pump that troubled me, nor the fact that we were quite suddenly and obviously poor. It was people, relatives and old friends of my parents whom I had now begun to meet, and their unmistakable threads to an earlier generation and place. They had all been "there."

Furthermore, our Grammy Bartlett, my mother's mother, who had only visited before, was now an integral part of each day, sometimes as an extra adult, sometimes as a petulant child. She prayed in her bedroom, a hanky (produced from her bosom) on her head, kneeling on a little cushion that smelled of balsam. That kneeling pad was all she owned, along with her Bible and a magnifying glass to read it by. I think I have never since known anyone so free of possessions and human bonds. A sister in New Hampshire and her daughter, my mother, were her only family, all that anchored her safely to earth. God provided for her needs from day to day, she told us cheerfully. I have a strong memory of the sense of magic her declaration provoked in me—that people could actually live that way, their ties held loosely, or not at all, without ownership or income.

I loved her, there was no question of that. She was affectionate and brave, but she was a road that led directly into the past, and the past, I had learned, meant trouble. At supper time amazing words flew across the table. A tool of the devil, Grammy called my father one night—a traitor and a quitter. He, the mildest of men, grew red and dismissed her from the dining room. She left, with a parting shot. "God will strike you dead!" she whispered fiercely at the door. "You see if He don't!"

By now I had begun to realize that there were people who were still "in" Shiloh and those who were "out." Grammy Bartlett was in. My parents were out. Some who were out were really still in, and some who were out were *actively* out—that is, being out was the centrality of their lives. My father was in a class by himself. He was *aggressively* out. He was so out he was out with most of the others who were out.

To confuse matters more, the White grandparents, on my father's side, seemed neither to be in nor wholly out. Our real reason for moving to New England was to be close to them in their aging years. They lived in Framingham, along with some cousins and aunts, about a block from the Dennison factory, a neighborhood of Italians and Jews and Irish—from whom my relatives held themselves distinctly apart.

They needn't have gone to the trouble. Their apartness was unavoidably clear. It showed in their speech, their clothing, and their habits. They did not approve of movies, danc-

ing, permanent waves, playing cards, or too much skin showing anywhere.

What was I to do about this? I saw myself in their faces.
Their freckles were mine, their extravagant grins, and the
way they walked, swinging their arms and bent on duty.
They welcomed us, the young tribe of Whites, kissed us hard
on the mouth, and laughed when we showed off. I wanted to
belong to them, but the present was too alluring. I had just
found out about nail polish and Hollywood. Our three-holed
backhouse had been papered by a former tenant with old
rotogravure photos of movie stars, and Douglas Fairbanks,
omniscient in eye-makeup, watched me pee.

The local movie theatre was in Framingham. We slipped
in and out of the matinee, then stopped to see the relatives on
Freeman Street. That house, soot-gray and ugly, was the only
place I ever knew as home to my grandparents, yet I could
tell it was not their real home. It was an outpost between life
and death. They had come to Framingham after Shiloh, pen-
niless and in their mid-sixties. The purchase of the ugly house
was an economic triumph I could not appreciate, and the fru-
gality of their lives within it merely strange. If we arrived
after dark, we would find them sitting in an unlighted living
room, saving electricity. Two of the rooms were shut off in the
winter, the shade-drawn bedroom cold and musty, a place to
collapse in at the end of the day.

The steely rod of principle that ran down their lives—owe
no man anything and share all you can—set them off from
Grammy Bartlett, who was dependent on other people for
her very survival. Yet she and they both, in their opposite
ways, represented what I understood of Shiloh. There was a
hard reality to their religion which repelled me. If you gave
yourself to it an inch, it would take all of you. Yet that very
quality was magnetic.

Over the years we lived in five different houses in
Holliston, and in each the words about Shiloh increased, for
my father had begun a book about the place and the more he
wrote, the more he seemed to talk—the more everyone
talked, all those relatives and old friends. Children were

snared into hearing this by the simple requirement of being polite to adults. Whole days of vacation might erode away while people talked. Plans could be cancelled, dinner postponed unbearably. We would stand in somebody's front hall, itchy in coats and scarves, while hope vanished that a last goodbye would ever be spoken. The Talk, we called it, tyranny in an otherwise happy and free existence, the ambiguities of those Shiloh years examined again and again, the name Frank Sandford slipping in and out, never neutrally spoken, always in tones of either bitterness or adoration. He was hated or he was loved. And where was he now, people asked each other. In hiding? Still alive? He was responsible for the deaths of many people, someone said, but he himself was not supposed to die. Did I hear that right? It didn't matter. He had nothing to do with me.

I was eighteen when I visited Shiloh—the place where it had been, that is—for the first time. Let me locate it specifically. The Androscoggin River, plunging out of the Teutonic Range of the White Mountains, hooks north just short of the Atlantic and joins the Kennebec in the waters above Casco Bay. The land between the rivers is hill country. The Androscoggin, rock-strewn, breaking often into falls and rapids and other burly business, offers water power for the mills of the towns that crowd its edges: Lewiston and Auburn, Brunswick and Topsham. Durham, quite in the middle of these, untouched by industry, spreads out just across the river from Lisbon Falls. Here Shiloh settled and grew until its "Scattering" in 1920.

Following that event, close relatives of my family stayed on to farm Durham's sandy soil and harvest its woodlands. So in the natural course of things I had been to Shiloh at least once before the visit I refer to, which to me was the first with any meaning. Only mildly interested in going, once there I was captured by a familiarity that seemed to entail more than memory. Though the whole back portion of that enormous structure had become a sagging shell, two levels of veranda wrapped around it like loose string, I had no trouble imagining it as it once had been, a giant triple-decker river boat caught on a lofty sandbar, flags snapping from its turrets, people moving back and forth across the stretches of sandy waste between the buildings. And there was my mother (so I imagined) on her way from Olivet with her friends, toeing out like the good nineteenth-century girl she was, her dark ankle-length skirt blowing in the wind.

But that moment of intrigue was short-lived. For a long time yet I would struggle to keep the place a safe distance behind me. Let my father write his book if he must, or rather, the first chapter, the introduction, the prologue, epilogue, and summaries that he seemed to be rewriting again and again, fiddling with file-folders under tortuous labels ("Mythical Nonsense Foisted Upon Modern Believers"). I was still not asking the most basic questions—how it could happen, why people went there and why they stayed, why it took a war to release my father, or why my mother had to leave twice before she was really gone.

It was two decades before I saw the place once more. By that time the "river boat" had disappeared altogether and Olivet was a hollow of granite. Bethesda's upstairs floors lay crumpled in its cellar, the ground outside scattered with veranda spokes and bricks. Shiloh Proper, the original building, was the only remaining structure, its golden crown still perched at the top of its tower.

I walked with my father down to the private cemetery, on a trapezoid of land between two dry river gullies. There, two hundred graves were sprawled with no apparent plan, most of them designated by wooden or cement slabs. Some of these bore touching and dignified tributes: "Papa Dear," "Marjorie—A White Heart," and "More Than A Conqueror." Leander, my mother's brother, was buried at the back, so closely bound by others there seemed scarcely room enough for him to lie. Perhaps there wasn't. He had been buried in a hurry and graves are hard to dig by hand in the dead of winter. There was nothing on his marker except his name and the dates. "He had planned to run away," said my father.

I had heard that before, but no one had ever explained what it meant. Now, out of the dozens of questions still unanswered and unasked, it was essential to know one thing—why this boy had died. So it was for Leander that the search first began.

I found him with surprising ease—in the basement of the Bowdoin College library, at the end of a mile of microfilm. His story hit the screen like a clap of thunder on the front page of the six o'clock edition of the *Lewiston Saturday Journal*, January 23, 1904: THE CHARGE IS MANSLAUGHTER! To the left of the page a Bath schooner tilted into the Atlantic, the *Augustus Hunt* wrecked in a storm, and on the right flames raged at the windows of the Masonic Temple in Chicago. Between them sat a well-groomed gentleman with a short beard and intelligent eyes which looked directly into mine. This was Frank Sandford. It was he who had been charged in the death of the boy, and he—though he had nothing to do with me—who had pervaded and shaped my own life.

For almost two weeks the *Journal* carried the entire proceedings of the trial at the courthouse in Auburn, Maine. On February 5, the headline announced that the mother of Leander Bartlett, in sworn testimony, had given "important evidence for the defense." My grandmother. For an instant I thought her picture had been included. In a nearby column a sketch of a buxom woman looked just like her. Instead it was an ad, a "prominent society woman" of Boston with her own sworn testimony, cured within twenty-four hours by TO-NI-TA, which would "heal any case of grippe or influenza if taken as ordered, as well as catarrh of the head, throat, lungs, stomach, kidneys, bladder and female organs."

Back at my cousin's farmhouse in Durham I scanned the microfilm prints again, then escaped outdoors to work in the garden, in my ignorance hoeing a crop gone by. Kittens crouched, watching, while brown hens sat in a square of sunlight on the shed floor, wary of my presence.

I needed to see the place again, I thought, to come upon it suddenly and with surprise. I set out walking toward the village of Lisbon Falls, two miles on the other side of the river, waiting to be startled by the first glimmer of the Shiloh dome and crown through the trees. There it was, a flash of light in that rural context, then gone. At the entrance to the River Road I could see it again.

The road had been graded and surfaced, and new little houses with lawns and straight driveways occupied its edges, where once there had been open fields. But it was still the same road. This was where you walked, to and from Shiloh. If you ran away, this is where you turned, at this corner, on the way to Lisbon Falls, while over your right shoulder—where you might frequently glance—the gold crown appeared and reappeared between the houses and the trees.

Charles Lindbergh, I had been told, flying over Durham in 1927, saw the gold dome below him and thought it was the capitol of Maine. How long did it take him, I wondered, to catch on? How many second looks did he need to realize that the city of Augusta was not there, and that farmland encompassed the imposing white structure below him for acres and acres, save for the red brick mills of Lisbon Falls?

Imagined from above like that, the story took on new breadth. It was clear to me now why my father had grown paralyzed, standing at the end of his first chapter like a stunt man at the tip of an airplane wing, staring into that beguiling vista. For fully as important as the event of Shiloh itself was the wider world that contained it and made it possible, from a nineteenth-century sky clear of machinery—clear of anything but crows and circling hawks—down to chickens in sunlight on a shed floor and that society woman in Boston who was cured of all that ailed her by a dose of TO-NI-TA.

It was the danger that took your breath away. I had never really seen it. It was hard to see, so softly focused in the background of safety and innocence and heroic intentions. It must have been now that I recognized the story (and the danger) as my inheritance, and knew that equal to it or not, when the time was right I would go after it.

Not that I nurtured any illusions of ownership—not then or now. The Shiloh story has always belonged to many people, a thousand stories in one. It belongs to Frank Sandford, above all. Without him there would be no story, and his becomes everyone else's. But for me, the story belongs first to the members of my family who lived it—to my grandparents, my mother and Leander, and to my father, surely, who completed his memoirs after all, and saw them published. My relatives were not among the principals in the wider sweep of the Shiloh drama, or even witnesses to all that took place, but they are my authentic access to the history. More, they help to tell it, whenever they have lent their eyes and ears and voices.

THE CRAB

PAUL PINES

ON THURSDAY of Easter Week, the *Maya Queen* took fourteen hours to make the eight hour run from Manioc City to Cashew Beach. The Captain left the pier with only thirty gallons of oil on a voyage that required two hundred and thirty. As often happened in Manioc, the oil shipment he was expecting never arrived and the Captain found himself stuck with a full boat. On deck below, close to a hundred and fifty passengers waited. Most of them were people who had come North for jobs going back on their holiday visit with the proofs of their success: radios, tape recorders, clothes, tents, bags of sweet oranges, rum and baggies full of marijuana. Girdled between the rails, passengers uncorked the rum, starting smoking reefer. By two, the singing and chatter had become pandemonium. The Captain did what he had to do—gave the order to cast off.

Twenty minutes out of Manioc City, the muddy waters turned sky blue. An hour and a half after that, the Captain announced to the floating fiesta that they were low on oil and would approach the rig beyond Long Boat Cay. Hopefully, he'd be able to buy enough fuel there to bring them safely to their destination.

He neglected to say what he'd do if the rig had nothing to sell him. Alone in the wheel house, the Captain cursed the high cost of running his old submarine chaser. They limped toward Long Boat Cay on one of the *Maya Queen's* two engines until a tug came to meet them.

In an hour they'd taken on enough fuel to continue the journey.

166

At dusk, the jungle coastline became a black ribbon. Heat from the engine room opened every pore on the boat. As darkness descended, passengers struggled to lie where they stood, sleep where they sat. By the time the *Maya Queen* docked in Cashew Beach early the following morning, it smelled like a garbage pit.

Tachito was the youngest of four children, three of them girls who had helped their mother, Luisa, from childhood. They helped with the laundry, sewing, baking and preparation of tamales which they sold from under a house, hedged with bougainvillea, raised above the sand on posts. The growing demand for tamales and empanades kept them busy. Every Sunday, people from as far away as Soursop and Cashew Point waited patiently on the concrete side walk that ran past their front yard.

Radiance, Tachito's middle sister, had been largely responsible for him. She was his special friend—the one he played with, whispered to, lay against—until recently. As much as he still loved Radiance, Tachito suddenly stopped taking baths with her. Only a short while before, he had laughed as she'd soaped him with well-water. Radiance washed herself beneath a loose t-shirt and shorts, like the other women in Cashew Beach. Lately, he peeked at her from behind the house, wondering what it would be like to soap her body as she had soaped his. The thought disturbed him.

His oldest sister, Lilly, was married and had two boys of her own, one of whom she nursed right in front of him. Every time she did, he felt his cheeks grow hot and turned away.

Musa, barely a year older than Tachito, had begun sprouting breasts and hips, which she allowed him to glimpse by pulling up her shirt, letting her skirt ride up in the hammock. She pretended to be asleep. He knew that she wasn't. And he couldn't rid himself of the suspicion that Musa knew everything, that she could see right through him.

There was nowhere to hide—either from the pictures in his mind, or before his eyes. They were there all the time, the soft skins, scents and voices from which he had once drawn mindless comfort. Now, they were bars he clung to like a caged bird.

And then came the letter from Manioc City. His father would be down for the Easter holiday. Nothing less, Tachito was certain, could have set him free! The cage door opened and he soared on the wings of a less confusing excitement.

At eight p.m. he was seated on the far corner of the town pier waiting for the *Maya Queen*. He remained there until five-thirty the following morning, when the vessel eased in to dump its load.

Norbert Flowers hadn't been home since his visit to Cashew Beach twelve years ago. Then, he'd come down with his new camera to take pictures of his only son. Tachito was starting to walk and Norbert had captured his early faltering steps. For a moment, he had considered remaining. But the thought of bringing up another conch, pulling in another hogfish had been so repugnant that he'd quickly dismissed it. After diving the cays for fourteen years, he had resolved never to make his living that way again.

When he first left Cashew Beach to find work in Manioc City, a few weeks after his twenty-fifth birthday, Norbert promised to send for his wife and children. Luisa realized before Norbert that he never would. The whole family had traveled to Soursop by dory to see him off. With a bag of clothes and thirty Manioc dollars in his pocket, he waved goodbye from the back of a soda truck. Who could have known that in ten years he would become assistant to the Minister of Public Works, sire two more daughters by a nearly white Creole girl and build a concrete home in the Fort Albert section, right on the water!

The pressures of his new life were unimaginable to the man who first arrived in Manioc City with the smell of fish on his hands. Inevitably, the demands of his job and new family made it impossible to visit his first one. But nobody could accuse him of neglecting them. Every month, he sent money and a note to Cashew Beach.

Then why, now, had he been seized by a compulsion to

board the *Maya Queen* when, this time last year, he hadn't found time to go down for Lilly's wedding?

Leaving the question unanswered, he had written Luisa, packed his second wife and kids off to her parents in Lemon Drop and, two days later, found himself on the stern between Caribs with ghetto blasters. Before his mind's eye he saw his son in a series of poses committed to memory from his own snapshots, and those Luisa had sent him. This, he repeated as he gazed at them, was his only son.

2

Tachito stood at the edge of the crowd wondering if he'd be able to identify his father from the old wedding picture taped to Luisa's bedroom mirror. He'd spent countless hours staring at it, trying to determine if he would grow up in his father's image. As the crowd thinned, he saw him—a tall man in brown slacks and a white shirt carrying a leather bag. The man's sandals, also, were leather—and expensive. Nobody in Cashew Beach carried such a bag or wore such sandals, except for white tourists.

His father hadn't noticed him. He almost hoped that it would continue like this. Suddenly, he wanted to be invisible, seeing but unseen. He noted his father's square jaw and straight nose—so like his own. But the muscles beneath the man's linen shirt belonged to one who had spent years diving the cays. Pride swelled Tachito's wiry frame, as if pride alone might produce such a physique.

It wasn't until Norbert noticed the boy staring at him that Tachito felt fear. The boy became aware he didn't know the man. When Norbert stood in front of him, Tachito looked away.

"Son?"

The man was smiling—but there was something remote in his eyes. Tachito wanted to call him 'father,' but the word wouldn't pass his lips. Instead, he nodded. It was not the scene he'd played to himself while waiting for the *Maya Queen*. He had seen himself jumping into his father's arms. Now, he noticed that the man who towered over him was greying at the temples.

"You have a hand for your father, Tachito?"

"Yes, sir."

The boy reached up to grip a palm as hard as bullet-wood.

"Lead the way, son. It's been a long ride."

Norbert allowed Tachito to carry his overnight bag. It proved heavy enough to make him grit his teeth and swear, on pain of death, not to set it down before they reached the house. He wouldn't let his father see him struggle, not even if his arm fell off.

Luisa hadn't spent time grieving for Norbert. It had been clear to her that he couldn't live any longer in Cashew Beach. It was even clearer that she and her children could not live in Manioc City, a crowded place with dirty streets and numerous dangers. The truth was, that she liked the arrangement. Norbert sent her money religiously; in addition to which she did quite well selling tamales and empanadas. Life was simpler without a man in the house. To make sure that no man would change her mind, she put on enough weight to disguise the fact that she had once been as attractive as her daughters.

Her only preparation for Norbert's visit was to put clean sheets on her bed and move into Radiance's room. Musa would sleep in one of the hammocks, next to Tachito.

Norbert had changed little, except for some grey at the temples. If anything, he was handsomer. And he greeted the women who stood on the porch with the smile of a man who knows how to win women's hearts. Lilly ran all the way from the other side of the village to hail him.

Only Musa remained aloof, her nose in the air.

Tachito panicked, afraid the women might make his father uncomfortable and send him running back to Manioc

City. But his mother was an angel, serving her husband spicy fish 'bocitas' and Pelican Beer. Luisa talked with her husband as if he were her brother.

To celebrate Easter, and Norbert's visit, Luisa had bought a butchered pig from the Mayan village of Santa Rosa. Throughout the meal Tachito was aware of Norbert searching his face. At first, this frightened the boy. Then he saw something else—a fear in his father's eyes that mirrored his own. Was it possible that he, Tachito, with arms like sticks and ribs like a washboard, could make a grown man tremble?

"Wake up, Tachito. We're going for a swim."

It was morning. Pink fingers extended from a band of gold on the horizon. Norbert stood over the boy's hammock holding a mask, fins and snorkel.

"These are for you, from Manioc City. Come on. Let's see if I can still find my way. When I was your age I knew every inch of shoal, from Hummingbird Cay to the reef."

It was Ascension Sunday. Last night's revelers lay on the beach where they'd fallen. Tachito hurried behind Norbert's broad back. They sat in the surf to put on their gear, then swam out slowly over old posts, red starfish and beer bottles.

The water was a weave of hot and cold currents. One minute it caressed Tachito like Radiance's soapy hand, the next it numbed him. Norbert swam straight out for about a quarter of a mile, then swung north paralleling the beach. His son, like a pilot-fish, stayed close to his side.

They moved weightlessly through turquoise so clear the sunshafts had sharp edges, even as they spread to carpet the sandy bottom. Needle-fish darted, schools of grunt and yellow-tail parted for the swimmers. Norbert pointed with a gloved hand to a leopard ray baring its spiny tail beneath them, not fifteen feet away. It winged past, slowly, unafraid. Then they were gliding over turtle-grass that rippled the sunbeams. Their patterns hypnotized Tachito. He stopped to watch them shift in time to the sound of his breath in the plastic tube.

Ahead, Norbert veered right and dove into a group of

rust-brown coral heads. A stream of bubbles floated up from his snorkel. Tachito sucked in his breath and went down to where his father explored a space between the heads. Norbert seemed able to stay down forever, feeling his way around the stag horns, red sponge and yellow plume worms.

Tachito had dived these coral heads before. While he didn't know every inch of sea-floor between Cashew Beach and Casava, he did know these rocks were picked clean. Norbert prodded a ledge with his long yellow spear, then pushed on.

Skimming a field of purple fans, they headed toward the reef, to a formation that Tachito didn't know as well. These rocks were maybe ten or fifteen meters down. The depth of the dive made his ears ring. Boys his age seldom went out this far. He rose and hovered on the surface. Everything undulated. The ringing in his ears had turned into the echo of his heartbeat—as though his heart contained the whole watery world. Tachito kicked hard, following his father down. This time, when his ears began to fill, he cleared them.

A family of black angel fish pecked at the coral. Two translucent jellyfish appeared on his right, umbrellas fanned, tentacles trailing as they propelled themselves. The boy swung to avoid them only to find he was surrounded by a school of the creatures. Tiny stings rippled over him. Tachito tried to ignore them. Suddenly, he noticed his father pointing with the spear to an opening in the brain-coral. But his chest was about to explode so he went up for a breath.

"Did you see it?" Norbert asked when he surfaced.

Tachito shook his head.

"A crab."

The boy filled his lungs with oxygen and descended to where his father hovered, one hand, gloved, spread beside a hole in the brain-coral, the other hand, naked, waving the spear. Norbert made way for his son, who lingered at the opening until he saw what appeared to be three sticks of wood. At the end of one, folded neatly into a cleft in the rock, was a large claw. The swimmers nodded and followed their bubbles toward the light.

"He's a giant!" Tachito removed his mask.

"Shall we cook him up?"

"Yes. Let's get him."

The boy felt his blood quicken, but took time to prepare himself for the assault. Norbert was already at the coral-head when he started down. Tachito watched him draw back on the sling until the elastic stretched the length of the yellow spear. At the point of maximum tension, his father steadied, then released it. The spear shot forward. It must have hit its mark. The last thing the boy saw before surfacing was a shudder that ran along the shaft.

"I got him, boy." Norbert spoke slowly, resetting his mask. "Now, we get him outta the hole. He's in pretty tight."

They took turns manipulating the end of the spear sticking out of the hole, twisting it one way, then the other—levering it, pushing and pulling. But the creature refused to come out of its lair. At first, Tachito saw only its leg and claw—until the crab shifted and he watched a huge body emerge from the shadow. It was a pebbly red and had raised eyes like two black beans.

"He's a strong old man." Norbert spit in the water.

"How old?"

"Maybe the oldest crab in the world. Smart, too. He doesn't want to come out of that hole."

"Too old for boilup?"

"Not the way your Mama makes it."

Tachito saw himself walking into the house beside his father holding the giant crab. As it stewed along with the other fish and vegetables, they would recount their battle with the creature, how they had fought with it and won.

"There's only one way. I know how this old man thinks. We have to get a wire around its leg and pull it out. Can you watch the spot while I go back for tools?"

Tachito nodded.

The man started for shore. The boy watched him grow smaller.

3

Alone with the crab, Tachito shivered. The world below seemed to be suddenly filled with danger. What was he afraid of? Certainly not the crab. It was pinned by a spear. He dove and circled the coral-head once to make sure things were as he'd left them. Then, grabbing the shaft, he rolled it, gently, trying to coax the creature into a different position. When that failed, he pushed and pulled until he was tired and aware of a resistance he couldn't break.

He had never considered a crab in terms of age, or that one crab might be stronger and smarter than another. And now, here he was, alone with a creature older, stronger and smarter than himself, with whom he was locked in deadly struggle. If he were no match for the crab, what could he do against a barro who saw him as fish bait, or a shark! Not a nurse or lemon shark, the kind divers teased, even punched in the nose—but one of those which sometimes slipped through the reef? A Great White or a Mako. What if, right now, the crab was sending out a silent message—not in words, perhaps, but in a ripple along the sea-floor?

He scanned the surface. No sign of his father, or any boat. The sky had begun to thicken. There was a veil of dark clouds in the east. He could feel his heart beating and tried to control his panic. If it weren't for his father, he wouldn't have waited this long. What would the old man say if he returned to find Tachito gone? He imagined the look of disgust on his father's face. No. He would wait, had to. How else could he show Norbert that he was his father's son, even if they hardly knew one another.

Adjusting his snorkel, he told himself that the only thing the crab could do was resist—and though it did this with all of its age, power and wisdom, it was doomed.

Below, Tachito discovered that news of the crab's condition had, in fact, spread across the sea-floor; not to the Great Whites and Makos, but the brightly colored coral feeders. Black angels with white lips, red and green parrot fish, and luminous blue tang rushed in and out of the hole to pick at the injured creature. These small mouthed reef fish dazzled the eye but were no better than vultures feeding on a carcass by the roadside.

He chased them from the hole and looked in. The crab had shifted still further out of the shadow and met Tachito's eyes. In that instant, the boy understood what it was to endure on the sea-floor. The creature's eyes, tiny black buttons, burned into him.

Tachito wanted it to be done, finished, over.

He surfaced and dove repeatedly, sometimes maneuvering the shaft—but mostly gazing into the crab's lidless eyes and chasing colored fish from the hole.

Norbert returned carrying a long stick with a looped wire on the end. After briefing his son, they went down. While the man prodded the creature from an opening on the opposite side of its lair, Tachito manipulated the spear. Their objective was to loop a leg with the wire snare. But no matter how his father prodded, the crab remained invulnerable. Norbert tried to hook the claw. The creature withdrew, seemed to melt right into the inner wall. It was hopeless.

No, said Norbert. He had run into old men like this before. It was just a matter of time. The spear had penetrated the crab's shell, and the wound was softening.

His father was right. On his next descent, Tachito felt the shaft sink more deeply into the crab when he tried to wrestle it free. Norbert handed him the snare and began to work the spear. Stopping and starting, Tachito watched his father figure out the crab's resistance. He was not using force anymore. It was more like he was sending and receiving signals—as if they were talking and his father were trying to use persuasion. Finally, the man managed to pull one leg loose. Grabbing the snare from his son, he looped it in one swift motion and gave it a tug. Suddenly, there was a snap. The crab came out of the brain-coral—in two pieces.

Norbert raised his hand in a signal of victory. Half of the crab hung from the snare. The other half, impaled on the spear, lay on the sandy bottom. His father gestured for Tachito to pick it up.

The crab had split on a bias. Norbert's piece held the claw and most of the meat. Tachito's contained both eyes, but was weightless on the end of the spear—almost without substance. He waited for the glow of triumph over a smart and powerful adversary. But it didn't come. Only an emptiness in his chest that stayed with him on the long swim back.

Before dinner, Musa came upon Tachito bathing and joined him uninvited. He didn't protest. When she raised her blouse to soap herself, offering a clear view of her budding breasts, Tachito rinsed off and walked away.

Luisa cooked boilup with yammy, cabbage, onions, snapper, coconut-oil, hot pepper and the crab. Tachito picked at it, but ate only rice and a few vegetables. When Norbert told them all how they had defeated the crab, pointed proudly at his son, without whom he couldn't have done it—the boy managed to smile.

Before bed, Radiance, hugged her brother, holding him for an extra second. The boy let her, clinging as he fought back tears.

The urge to cry dried up as soon as he lay down, but the boy couldn't sleep. Not because his father was leaving the next morning. He was ready to say goodbye to Norbert, wanted things returned to what they'd been before his father came.

But they never would.

No more than he would forget the sound of the crab's shell snapping, its weightlessness on the end of his spear. Its meat had barely flavored the stew. And those eyes, filled with their knowledge of the ocean floor—which now looked out from his own.

HOW WE CAME TO STAND ON THAT SHORE

Jay Rogoff

How we came to stand on that shore
I don't know, but in the failing
light whose particles sank in the sea
like diamonds, my father threw
his arm around me and walked me down
the beach. "This place was gorgeous then,"
he said, waving his free arm at
the shuttered mansions and concession
stands. "I loved your mother then."
Tar and glass cluttered the beach.
A steaming smokestack looked stuck
in the ocean like a lipsticked
cigarette in a coffee cup.

                                        Why

we came to walk on that shore I
don't know except
for him to say, as before, "You
are the best thing I have done."
He'd stopped and stood stopping me.
"I've never told you this." The light
had nearly gone. Waves crept in
like sharkfins, dark against dark.
"When your mother and I vacationed
here, I know that there is where
you got started." I followed
his finger up to the boarded-up
window in the now burned-out hotel.

AESTHETICS

Invisible in her dark lectures
           I'd see my prof's eyes
                      shine like the blues
in saintly Venetian pictures,

but it wasn't Survey where I fell—
           she wore a Yankees cap,
                      halter top,
and cargo shorts, playing softball,

a faculty-family pickup game.
           Crouching behind the plate,
                "Choke the bat,"
she told her son, on the other team,

who scrunched down lower at the plate,
           held the bat at the knob,
                      swung at a lob,
and popped out into his mom's mitt.

When she sprang up I watched the long
           line from behind her knee
                      up her thigh
(to study its sculpture with my tongue!),

and when she batted she poked
           a soft liner past first
                      and burst
out laughing as she joked

with my English prof, who said, "Some
              mother *you* are." Quick laugh.
                  Then she took off
on a deep double and came home.

You can't define it and not say "beauty":
              the pivot at second, the pitch
                  that can catch
the breath like Keats, Klimt, or Stravinsky.

Yet I'd seen only hard-edge lines,
              a cool green right-angle world.
                  A child,
I ran from fiery disciplines,

playing ball with a boy's passion;
              but seeing her on the field
                  with her child
as mother, catcher, second baseman,

feeling a pang as she held hands
              with her husband, I saw
                  felicity
in Passions of the Renaissance

as well as in a double play,
              in the curves of Samothrace
                  or Koufax
or her exquisitely made thigh.

Three years in dark hush I hid:
              my heart thumped—she lectured—
                  our transport
when she'd say, "God, that's a gorgeous slide."

ADIRONDACK SCENIC

The blue-hung clouds dangle, a wavering curtain
above the stage-flat lake, as though a show
were about to start—I have a good seat
on the cabin porch. Offstage a cardinal
rehearses, some birds tune up, and from the trees
a wood thrush flutes an air like Debussy.
Offstage the loon begins an aria—
a *long* note—carrying it out onto the water.
A *long* note, a *long* note—and then it laughs,
it can't recall if this is tragedy
or *opera buffa*. Back and forth it shuttles,
deciding, and before I can call you out
to catch the ending of the second act,
asbestos clouds ring down, and I run
inside, battered with the applauding rain.

TRANSLATIONS

Starts somewhere in a subcutaneous
shudder, somewhere beneath the heart,
gut feelings parsing into syllables
about as easily as I can translate

the chocolate warble of the hermit thrush
fluting through a gauze of trees
like blood through a pinprick or tears through ducts;
its trill erupts—*doutz brais e critz*— You tussle

with German in the bedroom, courting the vampire's
heart, while I ransack the nervous
system. The birdsong charms its listeners,
striking us dumb. What is the meaning of this?

SELTZER

In a glass between my hands I hold the past:
no sand trickling through a choked glass neck
but from a deeper source a bubbling up
like used breath, clear, stony, bitter. All things

come back: seltzer—in polystyrene liters
with screw-caps spraying crazily round the kitchen,
a clear descent from the magisterial
blue-glass siphon that prophesied *Good Health*,

presiding on my grandparents' tablecloth
squat, serene, mysterious as Buddha.
Weekly my hands would blacken with rubbing
Dick Tracy's pointy jaw in the comics

of the exotic *Sunday News*, as *Zaydee*
would stub his Camel out, slick back his hair
with yellow fingers, and bring out the bottle
of yellower pineapple syrup. He'd pour

an unbearably slow dollop
into a tumbler sculpted like lancet windows,
which I'd hold to the gleaming spout. I'd squeeze
the siphon's trigger—*sploosh!*—and transfigure

the rainy day by effervescence, so
the old light arriving through thickening
slabs of kitchen window, though stuttering
through dust-scented lace curtains, would never

fade to dark. The seltzer-bubbles prickle
my nostrils like my pineapple schpritz's,
gushed from the siphon, its bottled power
threatening to burst: the charge of the Czar's

horses' hooves beneath the Russian sun springing
off swords, the trundling of bundles miles
and miles to port. Then sweating in steerage,
my grandmother creeping out, four, seasick,

begging the captain's scraps for her mother,
who ten years later locked in fury the door
against my grandfather, poor, apprenticed,
already affecting a tailor's black.

One day when her mother had gone to market
he took those slender fingers in his callused ones.
They look out through the yet-unwavering glass
at a continent to conquer, a shining sky

(New Lots Avenue, where boys in *payis*
and black fur-felt hats belt a stickball,
their ears opened to the stubborn thunder
of the el exploding overhead),

and they stare together at the siphon
with all its bottled trouble, on the table
standing blue and solid as all time.
My grandfather shoots a jet into a tumbler.

He sips, gulps, and hands the glass to her.
All of fifteen, he asks her hand in marriage.
She stares, all of fourteen, into the glass,
sips, swallows, and turns to present her face to him.

MEANWHILE, WHAT THE OLD WOMEN WERE UP TO:
A Revisitation of "Indian Camp" by Ernest Hemingway

HOLLIS SEAMON

THIS IS ONE OF THE BEST stories my grandmother tells, when I can persuade her to remember the old times. Mostly she says she doesn't want to remember, that the old times were bad times—just like now—but when she gets started, she can't stop. Today, she leans up hard against the card table in my trailer kitchen, looks out the window into the mess of dog roses that grow in the ditch and smell like good times, and taps her coffee spoon against her saucer in tune to her story's rhythms. This story, like so many, makes her mad, so the spoon is really hopping before she's even half-started. I reach out and put my hand on her wrist. "Granny," I say, "slow down. You'll break my plate."

She stops, but only for a minute. "You want to listen, or not?" she says. "You better listen because this one got stolen from me and put in that white boy's book. He took it and then he told it all wrong, the asshole."

"Yeah, but he paid, didn't he, Granny?"

She laughs, her face a net of deep lines. "Yes. We made him pay," she says. "Head for a head; life for life."

I nod. "Tell me, Granny," I say, and the spoon begins to tap. She starts again, where she always starts, for this one:

My oldest sister had been trying to have her baby for two days and her asshole husband wouldn't let the women near her anymore. He was always an impatient man: he thought he could control the time of birth. Well, he learned. Ha. Sitting up there on that high bed with his stinking infected foot rotting because he wouldn't let the women bathe it in the drawing herbs. Said the women were superstitious old fools. Asshole. But he let me stay with my sister because I was small and not important.

I wiped her face with cool cloths and talked to her. She was still strong and she was well-nourished; the old women had been feeding her clear broth and tea, right along, until he threw them out. She wasn't even very tired. It hadn't been hard labor yet. My sister turned on her side to face me as I crouched by her bed and she said, "This child is mean and stubborn, like his father, I can feel it."

I gathered the loose hair from her shoulders and began to re-braid it. "How will you get him out?" I asked. I was very young, remember, and this was my first childbed. I really didn't know what to expect.

She smiled and touched my cheek. "Don't worry, little sister," she said. "When the baby is ready, the woman with the smallest softest hands will reach up inside me and, if he is crooked, turn him around and lead him out. That is how we do it."

I looked at her hair, smooth and neat now. "I have very small hands," I said. "Could I do it, if he won't let the old women come back?"

She started to speak, then just patted my hand, turning toward the wall to groan softly, pulling her knees up against her round hard belly.

But the white men who came had big hard hands. And it was Indian men who went to get them and who brought them to our house when her asshole husband said to: I can't forget that. The women had been kept out all day, except for one, an ancient half-blind useless woman, and even she wasn't allowed to touch my sister and she just stood in the corner, singing softly to herself.

My sister's mouth was dry now, without the broth and tea, and her pains were strong, pulling her belly into a jutting mound. She kept asking for the women but her husband said no. He said he had sent for a real doctor. He sat up there on that bed with his stinking rotten foot and he thought he could fix things. Ha. He'd been to mission school and he thought he knew how things should go: asshole. I did what I could, bringing the wet cloth to her lips and putting my two small fists against her back, where she showed me, and pushing there with all my strength when she groaned.

It was dark when the white men and the boy came into our house. They were loud and they smelled terrible, like whiskey and dead fish and old sweat. My sister's eyes got huge when she saw them and she started to scream. She hadn't screamed once, before that.

The first thing the white doctor did was make the men lift her from the low birthing bed, where I could reach her and where she could sit up and roll around and push her feet against the wall, and they put her on the high table, the one we only use for eating. It was hard and flat and he made them push her down on her back, flat, with her legs straight: the worst way for a woman to labor. Even I knew that and I was small and unimportant. She screamed for real then, when they stretched her out like deer meat on the table and held her arms and legs down. I backed into a corner, into the dark. I don't think they even saw me.

Our own Indian men stayed in that room, watching her scream. I will not forget that. And when she bit the fat white man and he cursed her, our own Indian men laughed. It doesn't matter if they were laughing at the fat man or at her: I will not forgive that.

The young white boy, about my age, he looked at my sister differently, with a little pity, maybe, and he asked the doctor something. I could tell that he was afraid and I could almost have forgiven him, if he had even seen me there in the dark, but he didn't. He never even saw me. And then he took this story and he stole it and put it in his book. He made it seem like this story was about him, like he was the one who got hurt. He didn't even see me. But he paid. Ha.

My grandmother's spoon clangs against the saucer, hard, and she falls silent. She looks tired; she has told this story too many times, maybe, but I don't want her to stop. She hasn't told my favorite part yet.

"Here's fresh coffee, Gran," I say, filling her cup. "Tell the part about what the old women were doing all this time, OK?"

My grandmother grunts, blowing on her hot coffee. She puts her spoon down. "Forget it. This story is too old. I'm sick of this shit. I'm tired."

I touch her arm. "Please, Granny," I say. "This is the only good part."

"Good?" She shakes her head. "All that blood is good?"

"They paid, Gran," I say. "They had to pay."

She smiles. "You're a ghoul, girl," she says. "OK: once more, I'll tell you what the old women were up to." She picks up the spoon and starts tapping:

> There were three old women, only they weren't so damn old, none near as old as I am now: that's another thing that boy got wrong. One was the mother of the laboring woman herself, my own mother. Think about that, girl. That was her own child in there with those filthy white hands all over her, her skirts pulled up above her breasts, way farther than they needed to be, held down on that table like meat. Her own child. My mother couldn't see but she could hear, couldn't she?
>
> And then came the knife: same knife he'd use to gut fish, remember I saw this, that doctor put that same knife into my sister. I saw that. Remember that I saw that: he sliced her belly open like she was a fish and then he dragged that baby up out of her like he had it on a hook. Then he cut off part of that baby's penis. For what? For a prize, I've always thought, to prove he'd done it. And he sewed her up with fishing line and she never even moved. My sister went away that night and she didn't really come back. Not really.

Her eyes get all teary and I say, "But they paid, Gran. Tell me how they paid."

> Yes, they paid. Ha. Because of the three women outside the house, working with the smoke, they paid. My mother, my aunt and my granny. I couldn't see them, of course, because I was still in that room with all that blood, but my granny told me about it later, when I couldn't stop crying. The three women were holding hands around the fire and singing, soft at first, just the old songs to bring the baby right, the songs that he would hear and that would turn him toward the light, and

guide him along the passage. My aunt, she had the smallest hands and she says that her hands kept itching and jumping, straining to go inside my sister's body, gently, and bring that baby right.

But when my sister started to scream, then the three women sang loud. Their voices went high-pitched and their songs joined with my sister's cries for revenge, on the white men and on her husband who brought them. The women didn't ask the spirits for help: they demanded it. My granny was a powerful woman and the spirits knew her well.

Something listened to the women that night even if they didn't get it quite right. Somehow, at least, somehow that asshole husband's throat broke open, just as the white doctor put his big hard hands into my sister's belly and hauled that baby out like a big wet fish. That asshole husband's blood dripped down out of his high bed and it mixed with the birth mess the doctor left right on the floor. Ha.

And didn't that doctor's white face turn whiter, then? Didn't that knock his stuffing out? And didn't that boy, didn't that boy who says he saw it happen but who never saw me, didn't that boy who stole the story and who pretended it was him the story was all about, didn't that boy grow up and go around stealing lots of people's stories, and didn't he, one day, walk outside and shoot his own head off?

Didn't he pay?

Granny's spoon keeps tapping, tapping, after her words stop. I want to sing. "Ha," I say.

HOW I LEARNED TO LIVE
WITHOUT A PAYCHECK

Nancy Seid

BEFORE I QUIT teaching to stay home with my first baby, I thought the hardest part of leaving my job would be losing the money.

I was wrong.

Oh, sure, I can think of a few things we could buy with my salary. Clothes from a store instead of a garage sale. Ben & Jerry's ice cream sundaes. Maybe even a car that doesn't run on rubber bands and prayer.

But the real problem with not earning a paycheck, I found, was keeping up my self-esteem. If I'm not earning a salary, what am I worth? We live in a world where Donald Trump gets instant service and grovelling not because he's a nice guy, not because he's bringing up happy, well-adjusted kids, but because he makes a lot of money. So where does that leave us stay-at-home moms, who work twenty-four hours a day but don't put money in the bank to prove it?

I first discovered this problem a week after Zack was born. I was filling out a form and came to the box marked "occupation." I had never spent more than a split second contemplating this question in the past, but all of a sudden it hit me. "Teacher" wasn't accurate any more. "Writer?" Well, I was aspiring, but everyone I knew had a novel in the attic, and I hadn't yet published anything. That left very few choices. "Housewife?" The word made me gag. I'm not married to the house, I thought, no matter how much time I may spend within its walls. "Mother?" Yes—and proud of it. But is that what they meant by *occupation*?

189

I understood that the question was really asking how I earned my money, not how I spent my time. They weren't interested in how many hours I spent singing lullabies and changing diapers. They weren't even interested in my work for the Literacy Volunteers. They just wanted to know what kind of organization signed my paycheck.

I left the box blank, stymied by the problem of how to define myself without a paid profession. Later that night, I talked to my childless friend Laura about my dilemma, and she didn't understand why it seemed so important to me.

"Nobody even reads these forms," she shrugged. "The whole thing just goes into a computer."

"Hmm. Yeah, you're right," I sighed. "What difference does it make?"

But when I emerged from my new-parent shell and started going to parties again, I found it made a great deal of difference in the way I was treated by the outside world. When strangers asked me what I did and I'd say I was home with my baby, they would smile and talk gently with me about how nice it must be not to have to work. They spoke to me as if I were not quite bright; I must be staying home with my child because I had nothing "better" to return to.

On occasion, instead of saying I was an at-home mom, I would mention that I taught part-time (one night course a week) at a local college. The reaction was very different. People assumed that I must be very well-educated to be able to teach college. I began to realize that the status level of full-time mothers hovers somewhere around the status level of children—nice, but there's not much to talk with them about and they aren't quite up to snuff intellectually.

There were days when I internalized these condescending attitudes. I would hesitate in front of the Price Chopper deli counter, wondering if I was worth the ninety-nine cents I wanted to spend on rice pudding, since I hadn't earned the money myself. I would feel guilty about not having a thrifty but exquisite three-course meal waiting for my husband every night. Though I was on my feet constantly, taking care of our baby and our house, I had a nagging feeling that I should at least be digging my own truffles or concocting Viennese apple strudel from scratch, since by society's standards I wasn't working.

My husband's support and sense of humor helped me through those difficult days. Our decision not to have the kids spend nine hours a day with a babysitter was a mutual one. It's difficult for both of us; his burden is the heavy financial pressure he feels being the sole breadwinner. But we both believe it's worth the cost. And when he feels I'm getting too down on myself, he brings home a quart of rice pudding, a gesture more romantic in our house than flowers.

I've also been lucky enough to find a wonderful group of other at-home mothers who give me great strength and encouragement. These women include an artist, an English teacher, a nurse, an editor, a psychologist, a financial advisor—every one of them capable professionals who've decided they need time more than money right now. Not only do they cheer me up when it's raining again, they also inspire me. Early on, when I wasn't sure staying home was something a smart person would sensibly choose to do, I took a look at the other women around me and realized I was in very good company.

Three years into full-time mothering, I now find that being relatively unpaid still may make a great deal of difference to strangers, but it has little effect on my own self-esteem. My resurgent confidence comes partly from the encouragement of good friends and family, but mainly from the gut certainty that staying home is best for me and my family right now.

This certainty arises not from one glorious epiphany when I suddenly knew I was right, but from a gradual exploration of my values. All my life, I've known I wanted to be a mother. I've always loved kids; that's one reason I became a teacher.

I know "working mothers" (is there any other kind?) love their kids just as much as I love mine, and their kids will grow up happy and well-adjusted too. My sister's son is the most terrific boy I've ever known, next to my own two little guys, and Amy's a full-time computer analyst. I'm glad women have the opportunity to earn money and have stimulating, prestigious careers.

But I grew up reading Louisa May Alcott and believing that the family hearth is the center of the universe. My husband refused a great job offer in California partly because we wanted to stay close to our families on the East Coast. I love being able to spend Tuesday mornings baking muffins with my two-year-old, playing "sooo big" with my six-month-old, and even singing songs with the kids as I change their diapers and smear on the Desitin. When I close my eyes and envision happiness, I see children climbing all over our bed like puppies.

Until recently, I used to wonder whether my friends and I were turning back the clock for women by choosing to stay home with our babies. I've always considered myself a feminist, and when I was in college I remember feeling sure my career would always be an essential part of my life. But now, I see a reconciliation between feminism and being a stay-at-home mother. Because to me, feminism doesn't necessarily mean doing what men traditionally have done; it means allowing women to exercise choices.

I think we'd all be better off if America had more respect for mothering as a profession. In my own private Camelot, being a mom would come with a paycheck, complete with bonuses for toilet teaching and well-handled temper tantrums. And more parents, fathers as well as mothers, would be able to afford staying home with their kids. Instead of passing our weak Family Medical Leave Act, we would have passed legislation that actually encourages parents to take time off from work when they're blessed with a baby. Other countries provide subsidies and free child care to parents; we could, at the very least, have health insurance that wouldn't end with a leave of absence and job-sharing that would include its share of benefits. In my world, pious politicians who spout off about family values but don't support family-friendly workplaces, programs and laws would be shot at dawn, or at least thrown out of office.

But in spite of my disagreement with the short financial and social shrift at-home mothers receive, I have not a single regret about the way I've spent the past few years. Yesterday, my oldest son and I were cuddling before he settled down for a nap. I was just leaving when he sat up.

"Mommy," he whispered, "I have to tell you something first."

"What is it, honey?" I asked, all set for another juice request.

"I want to tell you, you're my sweetheart."

My heart melted on the spot. It might not be money, but the chance to hear that childish voice at noontime is worth a million bucks.

ILLUMINATION

JOANNE SELTZER

no need for chandeliers
or sconces
where art glows like
a divine spark

no need to explain
shadow images
in this observatory
we call
the real world

face to face with God
heaven
teases us with darkness
by stretching
beyond our vision

HALF MOON BEACH
Piseco Lake

I'm under the spell of the moon.
All is quiet except the water
and my surge of tidal blood.
It won't stop, won't stop
until the moon shrivels away.
This is no modern situation:
it's as old as the first dagger
that carved the most primitive rune.
I try to control my anger.
A woman alone on a moonlit beach
is a bird of prey without a mate,
a hawk in the guise of a rock.
Somewhere a mouse scuffles home.
I shriek and soar to follow.

AS THE HUDSON IS SWEPT
THROUGH THE LOCKS

my river
which once boasted
of clean Adirondack waters
has been defiled
while descending
southward to the ocean

my river
is now polluted
by pebbles grated against
a ruthless current

long ago
it left the rarefied air
of the hills
to move within
a middling valley,
soon it will pass
through the final dam
of the barge canal
surging toward the low tide
at sea

a lonely drop
will disappear
into the ocean
with infinite sadness
and no ghost dance
can halt the flow
nor send my river backward
to its source

MOHAWK MUSIC

The river
has always been here.
Long before the ditch was dug
mostly by Irish and Italian labor
fresh mountain water
ambled toward the ocean
through the lands of the Five Nations.
The birds sang in woodland chorus.

Cows came to the fields
brought by the farmers
who settled the valley
where the drums no longer beat.
They lowed to the morning
with the wakening birds
and the farmers heard
a duet of river music.

Mules pulled heavy barges
bearing machinery
lumber and iron ore
along the muddy towpaths.
On chilly mornings in warm-weather months
bargemen blew
the horns of the river
that beckoned the birds and the cows.

When cities broke the lines on maps
the farmers planted houses.
Once at daybreak as the fog rolled deep
I heard a foghorn bellow
like a bovine, protesting,
defining, delimiting
the river.

AMBER

I will find my way to the cradle
of the runic northern word
and comb the beach near Klaipeda
from twilight until dawn
looking for solid sunlight
cast ashore from the Baltic Sea
by dead Lithuanian gods.

Gulls will sweep like ancient tribes
up and down the sky
as I sift the sand for a piece of mist
an antiquarian fern
the tomb of an insect long extinct
to set in an amulet for warmth
against the arctic noon.

JOB

Jordan Smith

He lost all the goods his piety might claim,
Property, a family, the serenity of age.
It's easy enough to make a joke of it:
Patient Job is full of complaint,
And his God is too much a gambler
Ever to bet on a sure thing.
So laughter unsettles the comfort of reasonable men
Who keep their accounts with the Karmic Trust,
And see every sufferer as a sinner in mufti,
Every sorrow as payment in part, in kind.

But what joke can I make today,
When I have learned of the death of my friend's daughter?
What comfort can I offer,
For all my refusal of the need for reasons?

The dogwood tree at the college gate
Is a whirl of splendor, of petals,
And in the wind, it has a voice, which is the wind
Made articulate in the suppleness, the subtlety of its motion.
Yet the voice undoes it, the blossoms
A blaze, a burden of air, as they fall.

Can you span the sorrow of a man, I asked,
Can you encompass it with your voice,
Can you divide its ferocity from the love where it began?
If the rain has a father, the ice a mother,
What forgiveness have you asked of them?

You spend their issue like water.
How should they grant you forgiveness?
I looked at the tree, where the branches were unblossomed,
Where limbs had been lopped and taken off for burning.

I too, the voice said, *cover myself in ashes.*

LILAC

I should take out the lilac beside the house
Before it roots
Into the fieldstone foundation.
But every spring, I say the job will keep
Until after the lilac blooms.

The vanity of the lilac's flowering
Is in the brevity of those white or purple blossoms.
The rest of the year, it is a woody weed,
Dark-leaved, serviceable for a border or a little shade,
A sermon in humble usefulness.
(The saint's severity, Freud said,
Is the proof of desire. And what is greater
Than the pride of the outwardly humble?)

The lilac's bark is tough, and rasps the knuckles.
The sap clings to the saw, and the wood
Is dense, purplish at the heart,
Surprisingly heavy in the hand.
It might bloom all summer, without reproach.

This too is vanity, I thought,
As I took the saw from its nail,
As I ran my fingers over the purple rings of the wood,
Something should be made of this.

TRISTAN

He wanted to be neither here nor there,
The go-between, lost to the sea's continuous
Music of loss,

Not only the gulls and the gullying swells, but
The reedy shoreline, unchanging, gone—
A tedium, like love's

Intoxication with sameness, all depth given
Over to implication, the shadow
Of his hand

On the shadow of her breast, as the ship
Lurched, sluggish, toward the Cornish coast.
Nothing

Held here, except the surfaces—
Texture, tension, treason—not even longing,
That gull's cry, hovered,

Dazzled with the thin gold of her hair,
Splendor like light on water, illusory
But enough,

Enough, a protest at such unsanctioned, un-
Substantiated plenitude.
He wanted

Most of all not to want, yet to have lost nothing.
He wanted a calm, but she was there,
And the wind fell.

THE DREAM OF HORSES

It began with the deer, dead in the water
Just off my parents' dock,
And then there was a procession of horses,
The water churning around their necks
As they struck out for the island,
Circled it, headed back,
And I was in the water with them.

I thought, how clumsy dreams are:
I was taking my kids to a draft horse show the next day,
I knew that cabin on the lake
Was the last dear place
My parents would manage to make for themselves,
And who needs to explain
The beauty and power of horses
Out of their element,
Or in it—that "realm of the mothers,"
The lacustrine trope
Of return.

Maybe it was the passing of my parents
Finally back into my childhood version of them—
Beauty, power—
And maybe it was the stall
I felt in my own life just then,
An unwillingness
To face up to anything beyond a day's routine,
Or just the anticipation
Of a day spent with children
In the large peace of work animals.

But none of this makes sense of what I knew,
Caught in the swirl of water around the dappled shoulders
And lifted heads, the purposeful
Silence of swimming horses.

I knew that my death meant nothing,
Although there were no words to appease my wonder at it.

ON AMBITION

A man may change . . .
—Marvin Bell

Above Blue Barns Road, another hawk
Swung low across the blacktop.
They gather here in willows by the golf course,
Stern, unnecessarily beautiful, predators
Who by nature prefer an unequal contest.
In the owl's headdress, the blazer-blue
Striations of the jay,
What is there to praise
But their rapture of patience, of calculation?

I might change, I thought, and this
Have nothing to do with my will,
Which is the principle I've made of hunger,
The elegant, particular insistence
Of the raptor's flight.

I was on my way to fish
On Opening Day, a gesture,
Really, of mere determination
Because the early creek's too high and fast.
And though I could make a sort of minor
Quest of my streamside walk
(Tangles of brush, fox scat, a snake
Grown supple in a lattice of sunlight),

I was just tired. I sat on a boulder,
One of those red-brown, rounded

Adirondack erratics that hold
The winter chill of bone on bone,
Took out my fly box and watched the stream,
Scanning, I thought, for the shape,
Compact, hungry, of what I hoped to grasp.

I stared at the water, each little whirlwind
Between rocks where I knew the trout might lie.
I didn't choose my fly. I didn't cast.
I was waiting, I knew then, waiting for the words to come,
Words that were more than an occasion of my will.

I was waiting to learn what I was worthy to speak.

—for William Hathaway

PICNIC IN BODH GAYA

MARILYN STABLEIN

OUTSIDE OUR HOTEL ROOM chickens crisscross the courtyard turf and peck dirt. There is no food on the ground: no grass, no grain, no crumbs. Still the competition is fierce. Indian crows, mongrels, pigeons, even paper-eating cows are all contenders. Scavenging is a way of life. Chickens poke at twigs and pebbles as if the choice required careful consideration—eventually they consume both. Gobble everything in sight before a crow steals it.

Today we're resting because mother has dysentery after the train ride from Delhi. She sleeps and I look out the windows and watch the chickens. No TVs here in Gaya. Not in this hotel. At home on vacations we camped to save money. Mother says hotels in India are cheaper than campgrounds in America.

Everyday the chickens peck the same turf. They're free-runners—every one of them. And scrawny. They don't sit around chicken coops getting fat. No hormones, no pesticides. What is more appetizing: India dirt or American pesticides? No baby chicks in incubators to sell to kids at Easter. No incubators in India. No Easter, either. It's dry and dusty here. People don't get enough to eat.

We're the only guests here. Gaya is off the tourist route except for Buddhists who travel to Bodh Gaya to see the famous tree. That's where we're headed—by tonga tomorrow morning. It's a seven mile ride by horse and cart.

There are two of us and five hotel staff. Their families live in a compound behind the hotel. The staff do not have much to do. Mostly they stand around and watch us. When I carried my pack from the rickshaw, two butt in to help.

"It's good to give them jobs," Mother said. "Makes them feel useful. It must be off season."

After four days in India, I feel useful. There are hundreds of jobs I create just by walking down the street. "Rickshaw, memsahib?" "Shoe polish, memsahib?" And I'm wearing tennis shoes. Get serious. "Guide boy, memsahib? Sweets, cigarettes . . . change money?"

We came halfway around the world to see a tree. Last summer we visited the petrified ginko forest in the eastern part of Washington state. Before that the saguaros in Arizona. Mother sketches trees. She carries a sketch pad and fills page after page with trees. She has a portfolio of sketches now, but she's never sold one or had a show. After the divorce Mother took up sketching. I was five then; I'm eleven now. One day my father left for a business trip to California to sell ties. He never came back. Mother says she doesn't miss him and that it wasn't a real business trip since he never earned any money. Sometimes I wonder if I would recognize him if I saw him.

Once I hid in the branches of the magnolia tree out front. Mother and Father were inside arguing over money. Then Father came out. He opened his car door and was about to get in when a scruffy old man, walked up and said something. Father dug in his pocket and gave him a dime. The man saluted like a general.

Back home in Palo Alto, we have an almond tree in the backyard that I climb. I sit in the branches and keep to myself. I collect walnuts; I press leaves into scrapbooks. I swipe apples and lemons from the trees down the alley. I like trees, too.

We breakfast in the dining room. There are no chandeliers but there are white linen tablecloths and an overhead fan. On the train I ordered soft-boiled eggs. I got hard-boiled instead. To play it safe, today I order scrambled. Scrambled are hard to botch up. Tea is served in a white pot.

"I feel better," Mother says. "Today we'll picnic at the bodhi tree. Would you like that, honey?"

"I guess."

Mother packs her charcoal and sketch book while I check the kitchen. The cook has packaged food in a tower of tin bowls that fit snuggly on top of each other. A handle loops through a slot on the side of each bowl, keeping them in place. For the picnic he made chapatis, now cold, hard boiled eggs and a dry potato curry that looks like brown potato salad. Roasted peanuts in shells fill the bottom tin.

"Dessert," he says, handing me some branches.

I squinch my nose. "What is this?"

"Lichee, memsahib."

"Lichee? What's lichee?"

He nods as if in agreement.

The branches hold shriveled, dried fruits. The cook yanks one off the branch, then peels off the ugly brown papery sack. Inside a white fruit glistens like a moist pearl.

"For you," he offers.

I sniff and take a bite. The fruit is sweet and juicy. An enormous seed hogs the center. Like a loquat, I think. Even though the large seed crowds the fleshy fruit, what fruit there is is wildly delicious and exotic.

Tashi, the Tibetan tonga driver, parks outside the hotel. Yesterday he waited all day for our business. Would he still wait if we weren't staying here? It's still early, before the heat of the day.

Beggars expect us. They squat by the side of the road, waiting for our tonga. They run after our horsedrawn cart. They're all kids younger than me.

The littlest have the most stamina, skinny as they are. They start out in a pack; slowly the weaker drop out.

"Mother, give them something." It's horrible to watch them.

"We must be firm," she says. "If we give in, they'll always pester us."

We ride on; voices whine behind. A girl of about seven with a baby tied to her back is the first to falter. A boy with smallpox facial scars pants "memsahib . . . meemsaaahib! Paisa. Paisa . . . memsahib!!"

"Mother! Do something!" She looks agitated but she sits

tight in the bouncy cart with a ridiculous parasol over us and Tashi at the reins. The whining is agony. I can't stand it. Nor can Mother.

"Tashi. Stop!" She gives in. Just a little. A few coins, some paisa. We wait for the girl with the baby to catch up, then I give her a few coins. Others get wind of the free-for-all. Paisa from the memsahibs. The word is out faster than a rooster's crow. Swarms of kids and adults head our way. "Tashi! Chello!" Mother shouts. She learned "chello" in Delhi. I think it means giddyup or just plain, Go!

Incredibly, they still follow. Like mother warned. We can't give enough. The same kids who received our paisa, tag along behind, whining again. The cycle starts all over as if we didn't give them anything.

Tashi turns around. "No give . . . memsahib. No give."

The Bodhi tree grows behind a temple with a large pointed spire. Mother carries her materials to a spot on the grass. I carry the lichee; Tashi carries the picnic tins. Does lichee grow in Tibet?

The grounds are large and parklike. Many sculptures of Buddhas are scattered about. The large temple is in the center of the park. A walkway surrounds both the park and the temple. Mother seats herself on some grass and begins to sketch in the outline of the temple in the background. I sit on the blanket a short distance away. Tashi sets the tins behind mother, then joins a group of Tibetans circling the temple. When he halts in front of an image of the Buddha, his hands automatically rise to meet in a fold below his chin.

An elderly Tibetan woman shuffles up to the tree in a thick, woolen dress. It's 85 degrees in the shade. Is she too poor to buy flimsy cottons? She tilts her candle wick to a flame, drips wax over a spot of stone under the tree and tries to stand the candle. It topples. There is a knack to planting a candle on stone. She drips a larger molten puddle then a forceful thrust lands the candle in the center of the puddle without extinguishing the flame. The air is scented with soot. Her candle doesn't want to stand up. Gravity, the height and heaviness of the candle, the temperature of the wax puddle are all factors to consider. She is not in a hurry, nor is she flustered. On her fourth try, she succeeds.

A commotion near the temple gate. A busload of Japanese tourists file out of a noisy bus. Each tourist wears a camera on a strap and a straw sun hat. When I glance back at mother, I see a tattered figure in flight. A scruffy boy carrying picnic tins. Our picnic!

"Mother! Look out!"

Mother looks up. The thief is running.

"Stacy. Get it!"

Even before her command I set off, running wildly.

The beggar scampers up the embankment and out of the temple compound. I follow, feet and arms pumping. My mind is racing faster than my feet. Behind a house, down an alley. Dogs bark. Kids jump up and down with glee. The alley suddenly deadends where three water buffalos are tethered, munching on tree leaves. The thief tosses the tins under the buffalos as if to hide his theft. The buffalos look up slowly when the metal clunks on the dirt.

"Eerooo . . ." a buffalo complains as if to ask, "What is the commotion?"

The bowls separate. Peanuts, lumpy potato curry and chapatis hit the dry, powdery India dirt. A man grabs the thief. Women appear from darkened mud houses, pulling up their saris to cover their faces. Quickly a crowd surrounds us. A gaggle of Hindi. My panting is heavy.

A boy crawls under the buffalo and retrieves the tins. A man, his father maybe, shouts. The boy hands the bowls back to me. The thief is younger than I am—maybe ten. His eyes dart from face to face seeking a way out. A small girl tugs at my pants. When I look down at the girl, she gives me a wide-eyed astonished look. What are you looking at? I glower to myself. She touches me, pinches me hard, then scampers to join her friends picking out the shelled peanuts from the dirt. She brings back a handful to give me, but I shake my head. A woman brushes off a chapati and tucks it into a corner of her sari. I turn to leave and my feet start to run. I'm running away, back down the alley, with the soiled and empty picnic tins. When I glance back, I see the man slap the thief, scolding him gruffly.

When I saw the potato curry lying in the dirt, I knew our picnic was spoiled. I didn't think of punishment or justice, I just thought, "the food is dirty and wasted." But I was wrong. In India dogs and chickens fight over spilled food. If I knew that a hungry boy would steal to eat, I would have given up my share. It's hard to know how to give. When the beggar kids held out their palms, asking for paisa, at least Mother and I had a clear choice: to give or ignore them. And we knew what to give.

I knew then that I would have a harder time ignoring the beggars. If I'm asked for money, there is a clear opportunity to give something that is needed. I'd try to give something however small the amount. Back home there are homeless men and women who camp in the creek near the El Camino. Some ask for money on the street. I wondered what I could give to help them sleep and eat.

I slow to a walk and glance behind me. No one follows.

Mother is disappointed the picnic is spoiled but she congratulates me for getting the picnic tins back. I don't feel hungry.

We stay in Patna for a week. Mother takes Tashi's tonga into Bodh Gaya three more times. I come with her once more and walk around by myself as she sketches. I bring a book but it's hard to read, hard to force my eyes down on the page when there is so much to see. People mostly. Some dogs, cows, and loose chickens. The steady flow of visitors to the temple.

I walk around the outskirts of the temple grounds, in front of a row of bungalows on the dirt road. A thin man in the soft cotton cloth that men drape around their waists watches me approach and as soon as I get in front of his house he waves. I nod back. Then he motions for me to come over and sit with him. I nod in the way that acknowledges someone in a general, absent-minded way but I am careful not to lead him on or worse, agree to what he is suggesting. Then he gets up and comes over to me.

"Namaste," he says.

"Namaste," I return bringing my hands together. He takes that as a signal to lead me to the shade of an enormous mango tree next to his bungalow.

"Sit down," he seems to suggest. He points to a lone stool. His wife pokes her head out of the dark kitchen and smiles before pulling her sari up over her eyes in that mysterious way.

The old man mumbles to himself and to me. He praises his tethered cow, a large off-white creature with a huge camel-like hump between her shoulders. He sits down and begins to milk her, lovingly, in a boastful, caressing way. I am glad for a place to sit out of the sun. He holds the milk pail up for me to admire. When he calls out his wife brings a clay cup. He fills the cup with bubbling milk and hands it to me.

"No," I say.

He urges me to take the milk.

"No, I can't. Thanks." He's got to be kidding, I think. There's no way I'm going to drink that.

He is disappointed. Then he puts the cup in my hands and raises the cup to my lips.

"Go on," he urges and points again to his cow as if she, too, wants me to drink. The wife comes out again and she urges me to take the drink, to be refreshed.

The consequences of what happen next fill my head as Mother and I ride back in the tonga. I've been warned a thousand times not to drink unboiled water. I know about amoebas and parasites that lurk in water, lemonade and probably milk. Any liquid that isn't boiled is unsafe. How could I drink unpasteurized milk from an Indian cow?

"You're awfully quiet," Mother says. "Did you have a nice walk?"

"I met a man milking his cow."

"Did he speak English?"

I shake my head. "He wanted me to drink the milk."

"You know better than that," she smiles with confidence.

I know better. The milk was straight from the cow, water-born amoebas wouldn't be present in the cow's udder. Still there could be germs. Didn't I read tuberculosis is present in unpasteurized milk? The worse part was I didn't enjoy the taste of the milk. It was warm, straight from the cow's belly, an uncomfortable, intimate temperature. The only other warm milk I drank was disguised with heaps of powdered cocoa and sugar. Except for hot chocolate I always drank refrigerated milk which had little taste.

Knowing what to give is not easy, as I discovered with the beggars. Refusing a gift is not easy. In this country where I was the one expected to give I accepted a gift from a stranger. This is what I'll remember. A poor villager's gift of milk from his cow's frugal yield, an Indian cow fed on mango leaves and twigs. I may get sick. I've heard stories of travelers breaking out with unrecognizable tropical diseases months after a trip. Maybe the milkman was a modern day Sujata, the milkmaid who fed the Buddha in his time of need. Maybe the milk was blessed. No sense worrying about something I can't change. I feel fine now.

LAZAR MALKIN ENTERS HEAVEN

Steve Stern

MY FATHER-IN-LAW, Lazar Malkin, may he rest in peace, refused to die. This was in keeping with his lifelong stubbornness. Of course there were those who said that he'd passed away already and come back again, as if death were another of his so-called peddling trips, from which he always returned with a sackful of crazy gifts.

There were those in our neighborhood who joked that he'd been dead for years before his end. And there was more than a little truth in this. Hadn't he been declared clinically kaput not once but twice on the operating table? Over the years they'd extracted more of his internal organs than it seemed possible to do without. And what with his wooden leg, his empty left eye socket concealed by a gabardine patch, his missing teeth and sparse white hair, there was hardly enough of old Lazar left in this world to constitute a human being.

"Papa," my wife, Sophie, once asked him, just after the first of his miraculous recoveries, "what was it like to be dead?" She was sometimes untactful, my Sophie, and in this she took after her father—whose child she was by one of his unholy alliances. (Typically obstinate, he had always refused to marry.)

Lazar had looked at her with his good eye, which, despite being set in a face like last week's roast, was usually wet and amused.

"Why ask me?" he wondered, refusing to take the question seriously. "Ask Alabaster the cobbler, who ain't left his shop in fifty years. He makes shoes, you'd think he's build-

215

ing coffins. Ask Petrofsky whose lunch counter serves nobody but ghosts. Ask Gruber the shammes or Milstein the tinsmith. Ask your husband, who is as good as wearing his sewing machine around his neck . . ."

I protested that he was being unfair, though we both knew that he wasn't. The neighborhood, which was called the Pinch, had been dead since the War. Life and business had moved east, leaving us with our shops falling down around our ears. Myself and the others, we kidded ourselves that North Main Street would come back. Our children would come back again. The ready-made industry, we kept insisting, was just a passing fancy; people would return to quality. So who needed luftmenschen like Lazar to remind us that we were deceived?

"The Pinch ain't the world," he would inform us, before setting off on one of his mysterious peddling expeditions. He would haul himself into the cab of his corroded relic of a truck piled with shmattes and tools got on credit from a local wholesale outfit. Then he would sputter off in some random direction for points unknown.

Weeks later he would return, his pockets as empty as the bed of his truck. But he always brought back souvenirs in his burlap sack, which he prized like the kid in the story who swapped a cow for a handful of beans.

"I want you to have this," he would say to Mr. Alabaster or Gruber or Schloss or myself. Then he would give us a harp made out of a crocodile's tail; he would give us a Negro's toe, a root that looked like a little man, a contraption called a go-devil, a singletree, the uses of which he had no idea. "This will make you wise," he told us. "This will make you amorous. This came from Itta Bena and this from Nankipoo"—as if they were places as far away as China, which for all we knew they were.

"Don't thank me," he would say, like he thought we might be speechless with gratitude. Then he would borrow a few bucks and limp away to whatever hole in the wall he was staying in.

Most of my neighbors got rid of Lazar's fetishes and

elixirs, complaining that it made them nervous to have them around. I was likewise inclined, but in deference to my wife I kept them. Rather than leave them lying around the apartment, however, I tossed them into the storage shed behind my shop.

No one knew how old Lazar really was, though it was generally agreed that he was far past the age when it was still dignified to be alive. None of us, after all, was a spring chicken anymore. We were worn out from the years of trying to supplement our pensions with the occasional alteration or the sale of a pair of shoelaces. If our time should be near, nobody was complaining. Funerals were anyhow the most festive occasions we had in the Pinch. We would make a day of it, traveling in a long entourage out to the cemetery, then back to North Main for a feast at the home of the bereaved. You might say that death was very popular in our neighborhood. So it aggravated us that Lazar, who preceded us by a whole generation, should persist in hanging around.

He made certain that most of what we knew about him was hearsay. It was his nature to be mysterious. Even Sophie, his daughter by one of his several scandals, knew only the rumors. As to the many versions of his past, she would tell me to take my pick. "I would rather not, if you don't mind," I said. The idea of Lazar Malkin as a figure of romance was a little more than I could handle. But that never stopped Sophie from regaling me by telling stories of her father the way another woman might sing to herself.

He lost his eye as a young man, when he refused to get out of the way of a rampaging Cossack in his village of Podolsk. Walking away from Kamchatka, where he'd been sent for refusing to be drafted into the army of the Czar, the frostbite turned to gangrene and he lost his leg. Or was it the other way around? He was dismembered by a Cossack, snowblinded in one eye for good? . . . What did it matter? The only moral I got out of the tales of Lazar's mishegoss was that every time he refused to do what was sensible, there was a little less of him left to refuse with.

It puzzled me that Sophie could continue to have such affection for the old kocker. Hadn't he ruined her mother, among others, at a time when women did not go so willingly to their ruin? Of course, the living proofs of his wickedness were gone now. His old mistresses had long since passed on, and it was assumed there were no offspring other than Sophie. Though sometimes I was haunted by the thought of the surrounding countryside populated by the children of Lazar Malkin.

So what was the attraction? Did the ladies think he was some pirate with his eye patch and clunking artificial leg? That one I still find hard to swallow. Or maybe they thought that with him it didn't count. Because he refused to settle down to any particular life, it was as if he had no legitimate life at all. None worth considering in any case. And I cursed myself for the time I took to think about him, an old fool responsible for making my wife a bastard—though who could think of Sophie in such a light?

●　　●　　●

"You're a sick man, Lazar," I told him, meaning in more ways than one. "See a doctor."

"I never felt better, I'll dance on your grave," he insisted, asking me incidentally did I have a little change to spare.

I admit that this did not sit well with me, the idea of his hobbling a jig on my headstone. Lie down already and die, I thought, God forgive me. But from the way he'd been lingering in the neighborhood lately, postponing his journeys, it was apparent to whoever noticed that something was wrong. His unshaven face was the gray of dirty sheets, and his wizened stick of a frame was shrinking visibly. His odor, no longer merely the ripe stench of the unwashed, had about it a musty smell of decay. Despite my imploring, he refused to see a physician, though it wasn't like he hadn't been in the hospital before. (Didn't I have a bundle of his unpaid bills to prove it?) So maybe this time he knew that for what he had there wasn't a cure.

When I didn't see him for a while, I supposed that,

regardless of the pain he was in, he had gone off on another of his peddling trips.

"Your father needs a doctor," I informed Sophie over dinner one night.

"He won't go," she said, wagging her chins like what can you do with such a man. "So I invited him to come stay with us."

She offered me more kreplach, as if my wide-open mouth meant that I must still be hungry. I was thinking of the times he'd sat at our table in the vile, moth-eaten overcoat he wore in all seasons. I was thinking of the dubious mementos he left us with.

"Don't worry," said my good wife, "he won't stay in the apartment . . ."

"Thank God."

". . . But he asked if he could have the shed out back."

"I won't have it!" I shouted, putting my foot down. "I won't have him making a flophouse out of my storehouse."

"Julius," said Sophie in her watch-your-blood-pressure tone of voice, "he's been out there a week already."

I went down to the little brick shed behind the shop. The truth was that I seldom used it—only to dump the odd bolt of material and the broken sewing machines that I was too attached to to throw away. And Lazar's gifts. Though I could see through the window that an oil lamp was burning beneath a halo of mosquitoes, there was no answer to my knock. Entering anyway, I saw cobwebs, mouse droppings, the usual junk—but no Lazar.

Then I was aware of him propped in a chair in a corner, his burlap sack and a few greasy dishes at his feet. It took me so long to notice because I was not used to seeing him sit still. Always he was hopping from his real leg to his phony, being a nuisance, telling us we ought to get out and see more of the world. Now with his leg unhitched and lying across some skeins of mildewed cloth, I could have mistaken him for one of my discarded manikins.

"Lazar," I said, "in hospitals they at least have beds."

"Who sleeps?" he wanted to know, his voice straining up

from his hollow chest. This was as much as admitting his frailty. Shocked out of my aggravation, I proceeded to worry.

"You can't live in here," I told him, thinking that no one would confuse this with living. "Pardon my saying so, but it stinks like Gehinom." I had observed the coffee tin he was using for a slop jar.

"A couple of days," he managed in a pathetic attempt to recover his native chutzpah, "and I'll be back on my feet again. I'll hit the road." When he coughed, there was dust, like when you beat a rug.

I looked over at one of the feet that he hoped to be back on and groaned. It might have been another of his curiosities, taking its place alongside of the boar's tusk and the cypress knee.

"Lazar," I implored, astonished at my presumption, "go to heaven already. Your organs and limbs are waiting there for a happy reunion. What do you want to hang around this miserable place anyway?" I made a gesture intended to take in more than the shed, which included the whole of the dilapidated Pinch with its empty shops and abandoned synagogue. Then I understood that for Lazar my gesture had included even more. It took in the high roads to Iuka and Yazoo City, where the shwartzers swapped him moonshine for a yard of calico.

"Heaven," he said in a whisper that was half a shout, turning his head to spit on the floor. "Heaven is wasted on the dead. Anyway, I like it here."

Feeling that my aggravation had returned, I started to leave.

"Julius," he called to me, reaching into the sack at his feet, extracting with his withered fingers I don't know what— some disgusting composition of feathers and bones and hair. "Julius," he wheezed in all sincerity, "I have something for you."

What can you do with such a man?

I went back the following afternoon with Dr. Seligman. Lazar told the doctor don't touch him, and the doctor shrugged like he didn't need to dirty his hands.

"Malkin," he said, "this isn't becoming. You can't borrow time the way you borrow gelt."

Seligman was something of a neighborhood philosopher. Outside the shed he assured me that the old man was past worrying about. "If he thinks he can play hide-and-go-seek with death, then let him. It doesn't hurt anybody but himself." He had such a way of putting things, Seligman.

"But Doc," I said, still not comforted, "it ain't in *your* backyard that he's playing his farkokte game."

It didn't help, now that the word was out, that my so-called friends and neighbors treated me like I was confining old Lazar against his will. For years they'd wished him out of their hair, and now they behaved as if they actually missed him. Nothing was the same since he failed to turn up at odd hours in their shops, leaving them with some ugly doll made from corn husks or a rabbit's foot.

"You think I like it," I asked them, "that the old fortz won't get it over with?" Then they looked at me like it wasn't nice to take his name in vain.

Meanwhile Sophie continued to carry her noodle puddings and bowls of chicken broth out to the shed. She was furtive in this activity, as if she was harboring an outlaw, and sometimes I thought she enjoyed the intrigue. More often than not, however, she brought back her plates with the food untouched.

I still looked in on him every couple of days, though it made me nauseous. It spoiled my constitution, the sight of him practically decomposing.

"You're sitting shivah for yourself, that's what," I accused him, holding my nose. When he bothered to communicate, it was only in grunts.

I complained to Sophie: "I was worried a flophouse, but charnel house is more like it."

"Shah!" she said, like it mattered whether the old so-and-so could hear us. "Soon he'll be himself again."

I couldn't believe my ears.

"Petrofsky," I confided at his lunch counter the next day, "my wife's as crazy as Lazar. She thinks he's going to get well."

"So why you got to bury him before his time?"

Petrofsky wasn't the only one to express this sentiment. It was contagious. Alabaster, Ridblatt, Schloss, they were all in the act, all of them suddenly defenders of my undying father-in-law. If I so much as opened my mouth to kvetch about the old man, they told me hush up, they spat against the evil eye. "But only yesterday you said it's unnatural he should live so long," I protested.

"Doc," I told Seligman in the office where he sat in front of a standing skeleton, "the whole street's gone crazy. They think that maybe a one-legged corpse can dance again."

The doctor looked a little nervous himself, like somebody might be listening. He took off his nickel-rimmed spectacles to speak.

"Maybe they think that if the angel of death can pass over Lazar, he can pass over the whole neighborhood."

"Forgive me, Doctor, but you're crazy too. Since when is everyone so excited to preserve our picturesque community? And anyway, wouldn't your angel look first in an open grave, which after all is what the Pinch has become." Then I was angry with myself for having stooped to speaking in riddles too.

But in the end I began to succumb to the general contagion. I was afraid for Lazar, I told myself, though—who was I kidding?—like the rest, I was afraid for myself.

"Sophie," I confessed to my wife, who had been treating me like a stranger lately, "I wish that old Lazar was out peddling again." Without him out wandering in the boondocks beyond our neighborhood, returning with his cockamamie gifts, it was like there wasn't a "beyond" anymore. The Pinch, for better or worse, was all there was. This I tried to explain to my Sophie, who squeezed my hand like I was her Julius again.

•   •   •

Each time I looked in on him, it was harder to distinguish the immobile Lazar from the rest of the dust and drek. I described this to Seligman, expecting medical opinion, and got only that it put him in mind of the story of the golem—dormant and moldering in a synagogue attic these six hundred years.

Then there was a new development. There were bits of cloth sticking out of the old man's nostrils and ears, and he refused to open his mouth at all.

"It's to keep his soul from escaping," Sophie told me, mussing my hair as if any ninny could see that. I groaned and rested my head in my hands, trying not to imagine what other orifices he might have plugged up.

After that I didn't visit him anymore. I learned to ignore Sophie, with her kerchief over her face against the smell, going to and fro with the food he refused to eat. I was satisfied it was impossible that he should still be alive, which fact made it easier to forget about him for periods of time.

This was also the tack that my friends and neighbors seemed to be taking. On the subject of Lazar Malkin we had all become deaf and dumb. It was like he was a secret we shared, holding our breaths lest someone should find us out.

Meanwhile on North Main Street it was business (or lack of same) as usual.

Of course I wasn't sleeping so well. In the middle of the night I remembered that, among the items and artifacts stored away in my shed, there was my still breathing father-in-law. This always gave an unpleasant jolt to my system. Then I would get out of bed and make what I called my cocktail—some antacid and a shpritz of soda water. It was summer and the rooms above the shop were an oven, so I would go out to the open back porch for air. I would sip my medicine, looking down at the yard and the shed—where Lazar's lamp had not been kindled for a while.

On one such night, however, I observed that the lamp was burning again. What's more, I detected movement through the little window. Who knew but some miracle had taken place and Lazar was up again? Shivering despite the heat, I grabbed my bathrobe and went down to investigate.

I tiptoed out to the shed, pressed my nose against the filthy windowpane, and told myself that I didn't see what I saw. But while I bit the heel of my hand to keep from crying out loud, he wouldn't go away—the stoop-shouldered man in his middle years, his face sad and creased like the seat of someone's baggy pants. He was wearing a rumpled blue serge suit, its coat a few sizes large to accommodate the hump on his back. Because it fidgeted and twitched, I thought at first that the hump must be alive; then I understood that it was a hidden pair of wings.

So this was he, Malach ha-Mavet, the Angel of Death. I admit to being somewhat disappointed. Such a sight should have been forbidden me, it should have struck me blind and left me gibbering in awe. But all I could feel for the angel's presence was my profoundest sympathy. The poor shnook, he obviously had his work cut out for him. From the way he massaged his temples with the tips of his fingers, his complexion a little bilious (from the smell?), I guessed that he'd been at it for a while. He looked like he'd come a long way expecting more cooperation than this.

"For the last time, Malkin," I could hear him saying, his tone quite similar in its aggravation to the one I'd used with Lazar myself, "are you or aren't you going to give up the ghost?"

In his corner old Lazar was nothing, a heap of dust, his moldy overcoat and eye patch the only indications that he was supposed to resemble a man.

"What are you playing, you ain't at home?" the angel went on. "You're at home. So who do you think you're fooling?"

But no matter how much the angel sighed like he didn't have all night, like the jig was already up, Lazar Malkin kept mum. For this I gave thanks and wondered how, in my moment of weakness, I had been on the side of the angel.

"Awright, awright," the angel was saying, bending his head to squeeze the bridge of his nose. The flame of the lamp leaped with every tired syllable he uttered. "So it ain't vested in me, the authority to take from you what you won't give. So what. I got my orders to bring you back. And if you don't come dead, I take you alive."

There was a stirring in Lazar's corner. Keep still, you fool, I wanted to say. But bony fingers had already emerged from his coatsleeves; they were snatching the plugs of cloth from his ears. The angel leaned forward as if Lazar had spoken, but I could hear nothing—oh, maybe a squeak like a rusty hinge. Then I heard it again.

"Nu?" was what Lazar had said.

The angel began to repeat the part about taking him back, but before he could finish, Lazar interrupted.

"Take me where?"

"Where else?" said the angel. "To paradise, of course."

There was a tremor in the corner which produced a commotion of moths.

"Don't make me laugh," the old man replied, actually coughing the distant relation of a chortle. "There ain't no such place."

The angel: "I beg your pardon?"

"You heard me," said Lazar, his voice became amazingly clear.

"Okay," said the angel, trying hard not to seem offended. "We're even. In paradise they'll never believe you're for real."

Where he got the strength then I don't know—unless it was born from the pain that he'd kept to himself all those weeks—but Lazar began to get up. Spider webs came apart and bugs abandoned him like he was sprouting out of the ground. Risen to his foot, he cried out,

"There ain't no world but this!"

The flame leaped, the windowpane rattled.

This was apparently the final straw. The angel shook his melancholy head, mourning the loss of his patience. He removed his coat, revealing a sweat-stained shirt and a pitiful pair of wings no larger than a chicken's.

"Understand, this is not my style," he protested, folding his coat, approaching what was left of my father-in-law.

Lazar dropped back into the chair, which collapsed beneath him. When the angel attempted to pull him erect, he struggled. I worried a moment that the old man might crumble to pieces in the angel's embrace. But he was substantial enough to shriek bloody murder, and not too proud to offer bribes: "I got for you a nice feather headdress . . ."

He flopped about and kicked as the angel stuffed him head first into his own empty burlap peddler's sack.

Then the world-weary angel manhandled Lazar—whose muffled voice was still trying to bargain from inside his sack—across the cluttered shed. And hefting his armload, the angel of death battered open the back door, then carried his burden, still kicking, over the threshold.

I threw up the window sash and opened my mouth to shout. But I never found my tongue. Because that was when, before the door slammed behind them, I got a glimpse of kingdom come.

It looked exactly like the yard in the back of the shop, only—how should I explain it?—sensitive. It was the same brick wall with glass embedded on top, the same ashes and rusty tin cans, but they were tender and ticklish to look at. Intimate like (excuse me) flesh beneath underwear. For the split second that the door stayed open, I felt that I was turned inside-out, and what I saw was glowing under my skin in place of my kishkes and heart.

Wiping my eyes, I hurried into the shed and opened the back door. What met me was a wall, some ashes and cans, some unruly weeds and vines, the rear of the derelict coffee factory, the rotten wooden porches of the tenements of our dreary neighborhood. Then I remembered—slapping my forehead, stepping gingerly into the yard—that the shed had never had a back door.

Climbing the stairs to our apartment, I had to laugh out loud.

"Sophie!" I shouted to my wife—who, without waking, told me where to find the bicarbonate of soda. "Sophie," I cried, "set a place at the table for your father. He'll be coming back with God only knows what souvenirs."

GONE

Susan Thames

THIS MORNING, I walked into my father's room. It's been empty these three years, but just today I saw the floor and ceiling sagging, the walls bulging and the windows buckling with ghosts, the weight and volume of restless memory. It's Benny's going, it's my son's leaving that's made the rooms of this apartment suddenly crowded with phantoms, asleep for so long, awake now. Already I know what they are, how they play like gleeful children all day and fight over me like vampires at night.

This is the last night we will have together, Benny and me. In the morning, he is moving across town to live in a little room in the yard of the Watertown Brick Works. Night watchman; he saw the sign hanging from the iron fence. "When did you see it?" I asked him. We were closing up for the night. He was sweeping the floor of the smoke shop and newsstand, I was chewing a Mary Jane and counting the day's receipts. "You saw it today?"

"No, I saw it about a week ago," Benny answered. He swept in rhythmic pairs of strokes, long-short, long-short, long-short, the long strokes to push the pile of dust, gum wrappers and cigarette butts toward the front door, the short ones to empty the bristles of the broom. The kind of job they give to the retarded.

I pushed a handful of dull pennies into a red coin wrapper. "They probably got somebody already. You got to act fast if you see something like that." Benny drove the day's sweepings out onto the sidewalk with a firm shot of the broom, the muscles of his back and shoulders rippling like dancing water beneath his shirt. A boy of sixteen with no light behind his eyes, a Jewish bodybuilder with a neck like a gladiator and a thing for Nat "King" Cole. I called to him a little louder, "Anyway, how come you're in such a hurry to go live over there? How are you going to eat?"

Kicking at an imaginary nothing in the doorway, he answered me with his chin nearly touching his chest, "It's not that I'm in such a hurry. It was just an idea."

It wasn't just an idea. He hadn't been too late. "You want to come over and see the place?" he asked me, as I stood watching him fill paper bags with neatly paired socks and stacks of underwear.

I waited for a piece of strawberry taffy to grow soft in my mouth. "No," I said. "What do I have to see it for? You want to go, you go. What do they give you? You got a toilet? You got a sink? You got running water?"

"A bathroom, a kitchen sink, and a little hot plate. A desk with a chair. Plus the bed, and a corner for my weights. It's nice, Ma. You ought to come over and take a look." He folded a half dozen shirts from the closet and placed them in another bag.

"And you got to sit up all night watching the place?" I asked.

"No," Benny said, turning to me, "it's not like that. It's not a guard job. It's just to have somebody there. While I'm working I'm going to be sleeping. Not bad, huh?"

That was three days ago. Maybe it was four. I chew my lip to help my concentration. Four days ago was Sunday. I mark time by Sundays because it's the one day of the week I reserve papers for regular customers. It started out as a favor, my own idea, but it turned out to be popular. People like seeing their names printed neatly in the corner of the paper. Several people even said they'd never seen their names written in such a beautiful hand. One woman insisted over and over that I must have learned penmanship in a Catholic school. "I learned from my mother," I told her, but only the first couple of times, and then I let the woman enjoy herself with her Catholic fantasy of me, Sophie Topilsky, then Sophie Liffschutz, only daughter of Karen, who sculpted in stone and played a reckless piano; Karen, whose cough was a mocking laugh, whose laugh was a song; asthmatic Karen Liffschutz, and Malcolm, Malcolm D. Liffshutz, Malcolm the mystic, the mauler, the molester.

Three days it's been, with Benny doubling his curls and tripling his knee presses because, as he explained to me, sweating through another set of plunges, the shiny metal bar resting on his shoulders like a piece of the temple on Samson's back, he might have to miss a workout or two till he gets settled and he doesn't want to lose ground. He packs a little every night. I follow him from room to room. He takes only what is his, and still every room is empty with the echo of his going, and his going is already forgotten and remembered again, already a useless and terrible piece of the past that leaves room for little else.

"The sheet"—my mother's voice calling from the room above, what was it she had said? "Malcolm, please, bring me a sheet." She was asking for something to spill her cough into, the blood. Then the opening and closing of doors, the sound of my father's wedding ring scraping the railing as he groped for a hold in the dark stairway, the leaden tread of his descent. What about you, Sophie, waiting on the narrow cot, cold with sweat, damp with fear, a pulse like a hammer between your legs, pounding, demanding, hopeless? What about Sophie?

Sophie Topilsky—I call myself by my full name—Sophie Topilsky, don't *hoch* me. Is that the fat of your back pinched under the weight of your own too-big shoulders, pressed against these yellowing sheets? I can only answer yes. Yes, this is me, my chest and stomach buried under the open pages of the paper, my hands black with the ink of the news, the reports, the cartoons and UPI photos, the endless columns of classified ads, Help Wanted. I live among newspapers: by day I sell them, by night I read them. I am surrounded by current events. Still, I can make little sense of the world. I turn to candy. I love the crinkle of the cellophane wrappers, the names like old friends, Baby Ruth, Milky Way, Sugar Babies.

On the front page of the *Herald* is tonight's article about the space satellite. I read it all. Outside the window, the first star shines faintly, a speck of white gold in the blue sky of twilight. I remember the little girl named Sophie who lay in the grass so close to her father, waiting for such a sight. And how waiting had a smell, his smell, pungent, sharp, and sweet, a smell that made her nose run and her tongue grow thick in her mouth.

I turn my face from the window. On page three the advertisements for summer sales, swimsuits, halter tops, Bermuda shorts, patio furniture. Is $14.95 a good price for an aluminum table with an umbrella?

Enough. I throw the paper to the floor, where it takes its place at the top of what Benny calls my newspaper geology, layer after layer carpeting the room, a newsprint plain, and in some places tilting stacks like Monument Valley columns. Come, I coax myself as I heave my fifty-eight-year-old body onto its side. I am a tired slave of gravity, my heavy thighs and fleshy upper arms always seeking the nearest horizontal surface. The bold red and green plaid of my dress flashes in my eyes like blinking neon.

How he pulled me to him with the power, I was sure, of Almighty God, and moved me across the few inches that separated us like I was as weightless as an angel. In the distance between us young grass, the pebbles and clotted earth thrown from our newly planted garden, a fat-bottomed black ant trudging the same distance with a small bit of apple core, all that was left of my father's nightly ritual, the horn-handled paring knife, the clean handkerchief, coils of shiny red apple skin spiraling into his mouth, into mine, the fruit pungent, sharp, and sweet, the distance always too great, the distance always too small.

I part my lips and bat my tongue against the back of my candy-coated teeth, la-la-la, and up from the place behind my breastbone rumbles the sound of a song. Years ago there were words to the song, words formed through my father's smile, words that played on my upturned face, showered on me from his merciless golden eyes, *"Unter a klein beymele, Zitzen yinglich tzvey."* All the while he was tracing the curl and wave of my infant ear, patting the rim of the downy nameless shoot between my nose and my mouth, knuckling the hollow at the base of my throat. Sophie, star-gazer, what could you do?

From Benny's room comes the rattle of a window rising, the static of the radio, the pop of a bottle cap and the fizz of warm soda. Bottles of soda he drinks every day in the shadows in the back of the store: the caramel-colored froth he sucks from the round bottle top, the dance of his swelling Adam's apple in his strong neck, his massive adolescent hands, the thick fingers smearing the condensation along the curves of the bottle, the stripes of his short, damp hair stuck to his temples with dried work sweat, la-la-la. Now the groaning bed frame, his shoes tumbling to the floor, a talk-show radio voice, "Hello, you're on the air."

I strain to hear the caller, lifting my head from the bed, my whole upper body trembling with the effort. The words are muffled, something about an election, something about a candidate, a Jewish candidate, something about Jews. Benny turns the dial, static, and then that voice, "Mona Lisa, Mona Lisa, men have named you." He turns up the volume. I know what comes next: a long, vague swelling in his pants, the butterflies in his stomach, the swelling growing to a familiar shape—like my mother's hand guiding my pen, like my father's hand guiding my perfect, tapered fingers against the flimsy white cotton of his shorts, guiding my hips, now above him, now below—and Benny, drawing each breath from his intestines, gasping, "Mona Lisa."

I grip the top of the iron headboard, crushing the cool molded tubing into my palms until my skin burns and my fingers ache. Sobs like a churning sea roll inside me, choked back by the barbed edges in my fever-scarred throat and the memory of my mother's crying. "Go to her, Papa, please," I begged him. He had only pushed more forcefully against the red floor of the porch and sent us and the swinging love seat in a wider, higher arc, the rusty chain squeaking in my ear, the squeaking always a half note off from the pitch of my mother's shriek, the two sounds as difficult together as the music my father's friend Isaac Rubnitz played on the Victrola in the front of the house on Queen May Street.

"Stravinsky, Sophie," Mr. Rubnitz said, as he brushed the fine blond hair on my arm with the back of his hand, "a brilliant composer."

More static and then the crack of a baseball bat against the ball, "Looks like a single for Mantle. First hit in this game."

What, I got nothing better to do than lie here listening to a lousy ball game? When I got a cupboard full of Campbell's and an empty stomach? The hours and years on my feet in the shop speak back to me as I ease myself to the floor. I roll my gartered stockings down my calves and flex my short toes. They alone, among all the parts of my body and the features of my face, have hardly changed with age. They are still lined up perfectly, each one squared firmly against its neighbor like ten good soldiers, each nail like a tiny cap. This is the way my mother described them to me when she bathed me in the white tub in the kitchen in Brooklyn. Each toe had a name, but both of the little toes were called Napoleon. "Why," I once asked my mother, "why do they have only one name?"

"Because," my mother answered, "they are both so small they need only one name between them." She laughed, her head thrown back, her perfect, small white teeth gleaming, her face beyond my reach. Then she knelt and kissed each of the little Napoleons. But it ended in a bad coughing spell, and my father came in from the bedroom to send her to lie down. "I'll be all right, Malcolm," she wheezed.

"You should rest," he said. "I'll finish Sophie's bath. The doctor says you shouldn't be near her when you are having a seizure."

"It isn't a seizure," my mother insisted, "it's a . . ." But the horrible grinding in her chest rose again. I stared owl-eyed and stiff-necked at my father, his suspenders pressing against the bare skin of his chest, his immense hands swirling the soap into a lather which covered the long dark hairs on the back of his fingers.

On the shelf in the cabinet above the kitchen sink there are cans of tuna fish, sardines, corned-beef hash, cling peaches and a half dozen different kinds of Campbell's soup. Last night for dinner I mixed chicken rice with vegetable gumbo and Benny made a pot of macaroni and cheese from a box. Tonight I look at the labels of the cans until I come to my favorite, tomato. I stir a cup of milk into the red condensed soup in a pot. The two mix slowly as the temperature rises, the Campbell's red and the Brockton's homogenized white. Small and then larger coral-colored bubbles roll up from the bottom of the pot. The color is like salmon, fresh salmon, which I ate once in a fine restaurant with my father and his new wife, Natalie. Papa ordered fresh oysters and salmon for the three of us. I couldn't get one oyster down my throat, not even after Natalie covered it with horseradish and cocktail sauce, not even after Papa demonstrated with oyster after oyster, sliding each one from the shell into his mouth, sliding one from his mouth into Natalie's purple lipsticked mouth.

The stove top is dotted with cream of tomato. The soup is too hot to eat now. I turn off the gas burner and set the pot in the refrigerator to cool.

Benny calls from his room, "What's for supper?" He leans in the doorway, rubbing his eyes like a sleepy child. "I'm getting hungry."

"I didn't think you wanted anything. I made myself some soup." I open the refrigerator door and test the soup with the tip of my finger. It's just right now. I tuck Sunday's *Parade* supplement under my arm, let myself out the back door, and sit down on the third-floor landing. From the kitchen of a new family on the second floor comes the television broadcast of the baseball game. Someone has hit a home run and the announcer is shouting, "The season's first grand slam! Look at them go!" The voices of too many children, squealing with delight, hurrahing, whistling.

I round my lips and try to whistle. Once, and for a long time, me and my father and mother were famous for our trios, she with her hands dancing among the black and white keys, Papa and me breathing sound. We did Chopin nocturnes and études and passages from the *Scheherazade* Suite. Even after Mama died, me and Papa continued the tradition.

Then I was sick. My mother's cough tore at my throat and racked my chest. Natalie went to live in Hartford for the winter and Papa sat beside me, night after night, rubbing liniments and mentholated oils into my chest, sleeping only in the minutes between the eruptions, breathing for both of us when the bed shook with the violence of my coughing. When the illness was over, Natalie came back and Papa closed my bedroom door at night. But if, before morning, he thought he heard me cough, he stood outside my door and listened, and sometimes, even when there was silence, he let himself in. To lie down beside me, lie down behind me, circle my new hips with his strong legs, spread the lips of my sleeping sex with fingers made wet in my uncertain mouth, drive himself into my young darkness and whistle in my ear.

"I'm going to have some cereal, some oatmeal," Benny calls to me through the screen door. "You want some?"

"No," I answer, "it's too hot for oatmeal."

"You're eating hot soup," Benny says, standing with his nose and forehead pressed against the fine mesh, his body outlined in a blurred silhouette behind the screen. "I got some bananas," he adds.

"Okay, make me a little," I say. "You going to eat it in there?"

"Yes, I'm going to sit down here at the table, and sprinkle some sugar over it, and a big pat of butter . . ."

"We only got margarine."

"So a big pat of margarine, and then the sliced bananas and a little milk. I think I'll make some coffee too."

"I don't want coffee. Just a little cereal." I let myself into the house. Benny is standing at the stove stirring the oatmeal, wearing only a pair of khaki-colored pants, no shoes, no socks, no shirt, no undershirt. His belt buckle dangles from the loop of his pants. I set the empty soup pot in the sink and lean toward his back as I move to the table. I can feel the warmth of his young skin. His pants stay up without the belt; though he has his grandfather's narrow hips, he has the full, high fanny of Harry Topilsky. From a chair at the table I say to him, "You look like your father more and more."

"Not like the pictures I've seen of him," Benny answers.

"You can't see everything in the pictures." I go into the living room and return with a silver picture frame, which I set on the table.

"So why do you bring the picture in here," Benny asks, "if you can't see anything from it?"

"No reason, just because I never look at it."

"There's no reason to look at it," Benny says, "no reason even to have it." He sets a bowl of oatmeal on the table in front of me. "You want a little milk?"

"Yes, pour me a little milk. But listen," I say to him, "what is it you got against him?" I turn the photograph toward myself. "You didn't even know him. You never heard a bad word about him from me. How is it you have such a bad feeling about your father?"

Benny puts his supper on the table and stirs milk and sugar into his coffee. He takes a big spoonful of cereal with a slice of banana. He chews slowly. He's thinking. "Grandpa," he says.

"What do you mean, you mean Malcolm, you mean my father? What? Did he say something?"

Benny nods his head while he chews another mouthful. He swallows and then he trims the edge of his bowl with the spoon. "Yes. Grandpa Malcolm."

"So what did he say?"

"He said there was someone before my father, someone who really loved you, who would have taken good care of you, but you wouldn't have him." He takes another mouthful of cereal.

So unflinching in your evil, Papa, so reckless, with your Tchaikovsky burning out tubes in the radio and rattling the glass of every window in the house, your stomping, slippered feet kicking at chairs, at walls, at doors, while in my room, my husband, Harry, panted—I was someone's wife, Papa—and threw himself despairingly over my senseless body.

"Of course there were other men," I insist to Benny. "I was nearly forty when I married your father. I was thought to be, well, a very attractive woman. But Harry Topilsky was a gentleman. And he was kind."

I am making excuses for the dead. Kind tonight was dull, unthinking, unseeing so many years ago.

The man in the picture is wearing an Air Force uniform, with the cap set back on his head and his hand shielding a high-browed face from the sun. Even with no other soldier to measure him by, you can tell he was a big man, over six feet tall, barrel-chested, but with a hesitancy about him, in the set of his eyes, in the almost-smile. Some things don't show yet, the stoop of his shoulders. Maybe they weren't so rounded then, maybe it was only after the war, after a year or two working with Malcolm Liffshutz, that Harry Topilsky bent his back and shrunk his neck. But Papa must have known those shoulders could round, must have sensed that back could bend. He heard it in Harry's stutter, and saw it in his eyes so ready to tear, a man who could die that fast, choking on the bone of a boiled chicken.

Harry was the last of a dozen men—my father called them boys—soldiers, sailors, an officer or two, a mechanic who was one of two gentiles, the other was a doctor. Eleven young men, and there could have been dozens more, because, Papa said, I was a beautiful woman.

In the bedroom closet, in a box of photographs and newspaper clippings, there is a picture of me wearing a little black hat with a veil, a borrowed fox fur over my arm, and a corsage of roses pinned to the lapel of my suit jacket. Above the photograph, this title: THE BEST-DRESSED WOMAN ON THE BOARD-WALK. On that spring day, I walked into the finest tearoom in Atlantic City on the arm of Mr. Samuel Levitsky, a salesman with a good line of well-placed housewares—he sold only to department stores. He was the cousin of a Mrs. Levinson, a wealthy friend of Natalie's mother, one of a large party invited to spend the day taking in the sights and the salt air on the Jersey shore.

After Atlantic City, Mr. Levitsky used to come into the shop for cigars. He liked to stand and talk with Papa while he kept his eye on me. One day when Papa was out, Sam—he said I should call him Sam—he told me he had big dreams for me, because I was gorgeous—that was his word. He pressed himself against me in the back of the store. His breath was heavy with the sour smell of Havana tobacco. He kissed my neck roughly, he buried his face in my breasts, he drove his tongue into the pit of my arm. He told me he could get me into the pictures.

I was foolish. I told my father. "What does a goddamned salesman know about the pictures?" he shouted at me, and I never saw Sam again. Then there were years without a date. I worked, Natalie left, we moved to Connecticut. Then came the war, and the USO, the boys home on leave, and Harry.

"Your cereal's getting cold," Benny says.

"I lost my appetite." I take a toothpick from a little glass I keep on the table and pick at the last of this morning's rye toast, a caraway seed lodged between two of my back teeth. As it turned out, I had the kind of good looks that didn't last. Right after Benny was born my knees started to fall. And that was just the beginning. Not that it matters now. How beautiful do you have to be to sell newspapers and cigarettes? My customers aren't looking for anything but a clean front page. Like Mr. Creely, who shuffles down the stairs from his third-floor apartment above the store to buy the evening paper and torture me. "Is this the only paper left?" he asks every night, examining the print of the paper in his hand.

"No, old man, there's another dozen papers just like it," I tell him, making myself busy emptying cartons of cigarettes and chewing on an occasional stick of licorice. "I order an extra dozen, twelve more than I sell, just to make sure you have a good selection, so that when you go back to your cell and lock your door and pull down the shade you can be sure you have the right paper." What drives people to such loneliness and isolation?

"I guess it's getting late," Benny says, drinking the last of his coffee.

"It's not so late," I say. "You're so busy?"

He makes a stack of his dishes on the table. "I still got some packing to do," he says.

The clock above the stove says 8:45. It's about three quarters of an hour slow. The black round face with glowing green numbers and hands was a premium I bought from a magazine distributor who tried to sell me on a line of movie and love-story magazines. "This is a newsstand," I explained to him.

"These magazines *are* news, Mrs. Topilsky," he said. He was clear-eyed and clean-cut, the kind of young man who ought to have a regular job, an office, and a lunch hour.

"These magazines are heartache," I told him.

"But heartache is news, Mrs. Topilsky," he insisted.

"Only when you're young," I said. But I took the clock anyway, and the *TV Guide*, eighteen copies a month to start. For every ten copies I sold, I got a quarter back on the price I paid for the clock. I made a couple of bucks back before it started to slow down. I took it across the street to the jeweler to see if I could get it fixed. He said it wasn't worth the price of the repair to fix it. So I brought it home. I figure in about thirteen years, and for maybe a whole day, it will tell exactly the right time.

"You want to take the clock?" I ask Benny.

"It's broken," he says over the rim of his coffee cup. "Anyway, they got a clock there. A big one."

"How are you going to wake up in time to go to school?"

"The gatekeeper said he'd knock on my door," Benny answers.

He's a smart kid. He's got an answer for everything. But he's shy with strangers. It's just me who knows what a good kid he is. I reach across the table and tousle his hair. Young hair. He ducks his head down and lowers his eyes like a shy little girl. "You going to come home and see me once in a while?" I ask him.

"What do I got to come home and see you for?" he asks. "I'm going to see you every day in the store." He puts his dishes in the sink and runs the water. What do I care? He's no company to me. He wipes his face with his wet hand and ducks his head in uncertainty. "Sure, I'll come and see you. We'll fix this place up. Make it nice. I'll bring my friend over."

I reach for another toothpick and upset the glass. "What

friend?" I ask, as I pick up the toothpicks and put them back in the glass.

Benny turns the water on a little harder and puts some soap on the sponge. "Maria," he says.

I never saw him wash the dishes before. I know he does it once in a while, when the sink gets full. But I never actually saw it myself. I was always reading the paper. "What Maria?"

He washes each glass and dish with soap and makes a pile of sudsy things on the counter. "She's just somebody I know," he says.

Now I got a terrific appetite. "What kind of somebody? You got a girlfriend all of a sudden?" I ask as I feed myself a mouthful of cold, tasteless oatmeal.

He turns the hot water on harder to rinse the dishes. "No," he says, "she's just a friend. From school."

The cereal is like papier-mâché in my mouth. I can hardly get it down. "What is she," I ask Benny, "she's Italian? That's an Italian name?"

"I don't know what she is," he says, shaking the water from his hands. "She's Tony DiStassi's sister. Yes, I guess she's Italian."

"So," I say, pushing the empty bowl toward him, "you got a friend. That's very nice. You got a friend, you got a room, you got a clock. Sixteen years old. You're doing very nice for yourself, aren't you?"

"Mom," Benny says, like he's asking me for something, there's a question, an asking in his voice.

"What, Benny, what do you want?" I say to him.

He can't answer me. He puts my bowl in the sink and runs the water again. He braces himself against the counter, his shapely arms straight, the heels of his hands pushing against the trim, his fingers spread like claws. On either side of him are stacks of old newspapers discolored with time, stacks Benny sorts and tends carefully, useless stacks of newspapers he prefers to the random collections in the bathroom, in the hall, Benny's work, his futile pleasure, lifting weights, sweeping the floor, and making stacks.

If I could eat newspapers, I would have a feast, a hundred-thousand-course meal. As it is, I got a lump in my throat the size of a golf ball and a horrible cold sweat covering my body, a cold dying feeling all over me like a rubber sheet. Over my shoulder, behind my eyes, a black and endless hole, and at a distance I cannot measure, Papa grinning at me. Benny dries his hands on the sides of his pants and leaves the kitchen.

"I've been thinking," I say, following him to his room. He's stripping the sheets from his bed and folding them properly. The bed linen he treats like silk. That's how I should have treated him. Then he wouldn't be going away. "I've been thinking I might take in a boarder. An older person, maybe. I hate to see the room empty."

"Sure," Benny says. "Sounds like a great idea. Got anybody in mind?"

I sit myself down on a corner of the bare bed and run my hand over the striped mattress ticking and the buttons. "No, I didn't think that far ahead yet. I thought I'd wait a while. To make sure it's okay, to make sure everything works out for you over there."

He is making a pile by the door, great bars and disks of steel—the toys of a young Atlas—bags of clothes, boxes of papers, odds and ends. "I'm sure it's going to work out," he says. "I was by there today. They cleaned it up nice for me. I got a new lamp by the bed. And a radio."

"You don't need a radio, you got this radio. Here you got the AM and the FM, and with an antenna you could hear broadcasts from Europe, from South America." I unplug the radio and wind the cord.

"They got me a transistor, Ma. It's little. It doesn't take up a lot of room." He puts the old Admiral back on the bureau. "Maybe your boarder will use it."

"You got such a small room you have to worry about the size of a radio?" I unwind the cord and plug it back in. "Never mind, I'm going to do just like you say. I'm going to keep it for my boarder. I think I'll get a new TV set too, a color TV. I'm going to get an RCA Victor with a big screen."

"RCA," he says.

"That's what I said," I say. What's he going to sleep on tonight is the question in my mind.

"No, you said RCA Victor," Benny says. "They don't call it that anymore."

"How come you stripped the bed?" I ask him. "You going to sleep on the bed without any covers? No pillow?"

He checks the drawers of his bureau one more time. He's only moving across town but he's acting like he's going across the country. "No," he says, turning to me. He's still without a shirt. The muscles in his stomach are taut and his hands are tightly fisted at his sides. His father was never this handsome. He's got a waist like a girl, a wasp waist, and skin wrapped around his muscles and bones like a fine jersey, seamless, supple, beautiful like I've never seen before in a boy, a man, sixteen, a know-nothing kid, his nipples like crushed pomegranate seeds.

I stomp my foot on the floor. A welcome pain shoots up from my heel to my hip. "So where are you going to sleep?" I say.

"Over there," he answers.

"Over where?" I say. "What are you talking about?"

"Over at my room, at the brick works," he says.

"I thought you were going tomorrow. In the morning." My mouth is dry. I feel in the pocket of my dress for the Life-Savers. Butterscotch, they are stuck together. Three of them fit in my mouth with enough room for my tongue and my questions. "You're going tonight? How are you going tonight? I thought we'd have breakfast together in the morning. I was going to make biscuits. Remember my biscuits? I was going to make a baked apple."

Benny grabs an undershirt from the top of a bag. "Maria and Tony are coming over after they finish eating. Tony's got his father's car. They're going to help me. It works out better this way." He lifts his arms into the undershirt. For an instant his head disappears inside the white cotton and he stands like a faceless god. "They'll be here any minute," he says as his boy face emerges again.

Benny fills his arms with bulging brown-paper bags and

walks to the kitchen door. When he has brought everything from his room, I look at all there is of my son's life. It's very little, it's only enough to fill the backseat of a car. When my father and I moved to Connecticut, when we sold the house in Brooklyn and moved to this Catholic town, we had little more. "Leave it," Papa said, "leave everything. We'll start over." Natalie went back to her mother again—"You don't need a wife," she screamed at him, "you got Sophie"—and Papa and me lived in the little room behind the store, and then the little room above the store, Mr. Creely's room. Every time we moved, we left everything, and every time there was less to leave. But we weren't starting over. There were no new beginnings. There were just the endless piles of newspapers, and every cigarette in the entire universe passing over the counter. Like shadows, they hid the thing between us, because since I was grown, a woman, we didn't know how to be together. He couldn't bring himself to touch me, but I saw how his hand lingered where my body had been, his palm vibrating from the heat my buttocks left where I sat on the edge of a chair. I was nearly his height and he was alone, and there was no one to love me, no one to challenge him, I was there every day, beside him, behind him, in front of him with my dress riding up the backs of my legs as I bent to tie my shoe. He couldn't bring himself to touch me, and I ached for him, and dreaded the sound of his breathing so near, the beard of two or three days of hopelessness on his falling cheeks.

Every day I hung our coats in the closet and ate my meals with him, our muted eyes sunk in the pages of editorials, advertisements, obituaries. And every night, alone in my bed, I dreamed: I set fire to young children and burned the skin off their innocent faces, tore from them their eyelids, their lips, their ears, their genitals. In the morning at breakfast I stirred two spoonfuls of sugar into his tea and folded his napkin just so.

And he brought me candy. Whitman's Samplers, foil-covered hearts, long strings of red and black licorice, yellow-and-orange candy corn, truffles. Customers returning from Paris, from Vienna, brought him candy to give to me, sent him boxes of sugar-coated pears and chocolate-dipped plums from Berlin, from Rome. For me, and they smiled, and imagined that they petted me, purred over me, plotted the use of my used body, imagined the paths he had taken, sucked at my breasts with their eyes. When finally there was Harry, they laughed into their snot-filled handkerchiefs; when Benny was born they made signs of devils and of the cuckold at his *bris*, at his *bris*, do you hear me? Only when Harry died, only then did they hide their faces, a momentary lapse into shame, and call Benny a Topilsky, you could see he was a Topilsky, that was the manhood of a Topilsky, how they never let up. And when Malcolm died—I thought I would go with him, I thought we would go together—they went to their offices, they opened their shops and answered their phones, and not one of them followed me to the cemetery, none of them came to watch him lowered into the ground, no one cared, or needed the assurance that he was really gone, or the promise that even if he changed his mind he had a half ton of earth, of dirt—are you listening, Malcolm?—hundreds of pounds of rock and soil to weigh him down while he lay for eternity with the memory of my wretched delight as his only companion, leaving me with the boy, the bastard child of Harry and Sophie Topilsky, Harry married to a woman forbidden him, Sophie promised and possessed from birth, the boy, Benny, his father's son, his grandfather's curse.

The buzzer, the door, this Maria, and Tony. "Here, children, sit down, a cup of tea. We have tea, don't we, Benny? I'm sorry there are no cookies. DiStassi, what's your father's name? Maria, you sit here. Have a piece of candy. Benny, pass Maria the candy. You like caramels, Maria? In the cupboard I have caramels. Joseph Junior? No, I don't know his name." Oh, she pats his hand, her fingernails pink and white, perfect edges, tender cuticles.

"Well, we better get going," one of them says.

"Sure, sure, I got things to do too. I got to clean up."

"So, I guess I'll see you tomorrow afternoon, Ma," Benny says.

"That's right, tomorrow afternoon." From the landing, Benny turns to wave to me, his herculean arm, his dumb face reaching toward me, he is frightened. I fumble in the pocket of my dress. What became of the lemon drops? The other pocket is empty too. In the kitchen, I search the countertop, the drawers, the cupboards, I scan the floor. Miniature lemon candies, each one the size of a pea. They come from England in a round white tin, a fancy habit.

Sophie, Sophie, such determination. I march methodically from room to room, certain, confident. I will find them. I look: here, in the medicine cabinet; no, there, behind the pillows of the sofa; maybe under yesterday's paper. Finally, of course, where they have always been—we've known each other for decades—in my room, between the mattress and the box spring of my bed. The lemon drops exactly where Papa kept them, kept count of them. Every night he selected one single sun-yellow sweet, placed it delicately between my lips, waited for the citrus perfume to fill my mouth. *Benny.* Pressed my high school lips apart with his skilled fingers. *Is gone.* Laid his father lips against mine, sucked my heart up into my throat, swallowed my breath and my life with one kiss. *Never. A kiss. Not one. Benny is, praise God, and damn Him, gone.*

SUN-DIALING

Beth Weatherby

My brother called me from his wind-surfer just off the coast of Rhode Island. He has one of those tiny wrist-phones. He said, "I was sitting here, doing nothing, waiting to be rescued, and I thought I'd check in with you."

I am out in the garden when he calls. It's November, time to put the garden to bed now. My hands are numbing up. I'm about to go inside and stick them in a sink full of warm water when the phone rings. I crawl a few feet, around the exhausted zucchini plants, and stretch for the cordless phone, which is on the tree stump with the rusting sundial. I hold the phone with my neck, squeeze my hands between my thighs. They burn as if receiving a message.

"So how's everything?" my brother says. "I meant to call you last month, but you know how things go. You get busy."

"Did you say *rescued*?"

My brother is silent.

I'm not letting go of this. He can't just throw that word out there and not deal with it, just say *rescued*, like when you say *How are you?*—they say *Suicidal, how are you?*—you say *Fine*—and the Suicidal skirts off under a bush, hides in the twigs there, dissolves there like compost, and all is fine, you've decided ahead of time, so why even ask the question?

My brother is silent. I press my ear closer. I hear his breathing, not normal breathing. This is muscled breathing, trying to control things, choppy breathing, unfamiliar, unbrotherly. Then a long sigh. This is some sort of Morse Code with air. I say, "Gregg?" But it's drowned out by the fog horn.

A fog horn? Ship horn? Roaring falsetto swallowing my brother?

"You there?" I say. "Hey! What are you doing?"

A ship horn? A freighter? A surf-board. Six feet of fiber-glass. A rainbow-striped sail wrapping round him. The water sloshing. Which water? Where? I hear engines, the engines so close I hear them moaning, pushing, brainless.

I'm not breathing. The ground has melted. Someone has flipped up the edge of it, like flapping a sheet out, and I'm riding muddy lopsided dirt-waves, the vines are tangling, I'm clutching that phone now, I'm whispering—not shouting, I won't be able to hear if I shout—I'm whispering, *Gregg*, then listening. There's nothing but engine. I press the * button, the # button, but I can't clear the static.

My body is stiff as his board now, up and down the wave-slopes, little fingers snapping off when I try to bend them. My ankles are dangling dead fish-things. We are nowhere, connected by sound-cords. And now drifting.

It's cold here, cold there. In the water. It said "Rescued?" This slick white plastic? This is my brother? I scream his name out over my garden. I've got that phone down on the ground now, strangling its no-neck, kicking my toes into the rye-grass. Digging a hole. He could appear there.

But I've got him. It's okay, Gregg. I've got you by the wristphone. Can you hear me?

And then the noise dissolves. My breasts slowly loosen their grip there. This is the unraveling, the finding out what happened, the part you have to make yourself calm for. I roll over onto my back, chew the dirt that's fallen into my mouth and swallow it deeply. I let the grit wash over my eyes. I look into the sun.

I say it into his wristflesh, wherever that may be now, in the air or in the water, the wristmachine still buzzes, I say, "Gregg, if you can hear me, I want you to know that I'm looking directly into sun now even though I know that I'm not supposed to do that, I'm doing it anyway."

"Jesus," I hear. "Jesus, that was a close one."

The seas smooth. The winds calm. Our hearts slow. The air clears.

"Beth?"

I don't answer.

"Beth?"

I feel mean. I feel like punching. I'm making him wait now.

"Beth? Sorry about that."

He's melting me, but I can't quite open my mouth yet.

"A freighter went by. Close."

My silent treatment explodes right out of the water. "No shit, Gregg," is all I can say, though.

"Well, I wasn't expecting it," he says. "The fog—it crept up on me. Little cat feet."

"Gregg? I've been lying in the garden, near the cabbages, screaming."

"If I'd known," he says, "I'd have tried to call you at a better time."

Silence and silence. And then I say softly, "It's okay. These things happen."

Once when he arrived for a visit, he said, "I did a three-sixty, the weather. Rolled over twice, dodging a semi. Then the cap flew off a pickup, glanced off my right front fender, broke the headlight—"

I sat down. I said, "These things happen?"

Once he ran across an enormous red gym-mat, a field of blood-colored vinyl. He rocketed and flipped over our heads three times without landing, not only flipping, but twisting at the same time—he'd learned it from the Japanese—to get a perfect score, you're supposed to land on your neck without breaking it.

He broke his neck that way and another way and yet one more way—three times broke the thing that's meant to hold your head up. They say he is very lucky. This is something we all agree on.

Our mother called. "He breaks his shoulder boat-racing,"

she said, "so he goes bike-racing. He breaks his ankle bike-racing—he's making me nervous."

Once I dreamed he was green bloated faceup under the surface of some scummy Floridian swamp-water. But when I awoke I realized that he was only in a hospital with a no-name tropical disease that he says you can get diving. He dives, heals, dives, heals, again and again in his own sort of order. You spend a fortune on get well cards. You call and say, *How you doing?* He says, *Fine, fine. No problem.*

"These things happen," I said, but I was shook. My voice was deranging. "Call me back," I said abruptly. I pressed the button that ends the phone call.

Then I tried to unpress it. Undo! I yelled. He wasn't, after all, in his kitchen, in his fluffy bathrobe, in his slippers. I remembered: He's in the water. He might be wearing a wet-suit. But he did say, *Rescued.*

So I waited. I walked around the garden, waiting. I could not pull out the overgrown radishes, waiting. I could not rake up the dead things, thinking, *What if it's serious this time?* I circled along the weedy edges, chanting, "Come on, call." My day is ruined, I was thinking. I needed a sandwich, I was jittery. I needed a dark beer. I was light-headed. I needed the phone to ring.

Then the phone rang against my palm. My palm pressed it to my cold skin.

"Hello?" I said.

He said, "This is Beth Weatherby?"

"Yes?"

"Mrs. Weatherby, this is Northernmost Windows calling. How are you today?"

"Suicidal," I said, "how are you?"

"I'm fine," he said, "and I'm calling to let you know that we'll be in your neighborhood this week to help you with your heating problems."

"Hello?" I said. "Mr. Windows? I have to hang up now. This may be an emergency."

"There is no obligation," he said.

"Thank you," I said and pressed the button that ends the conversation.

I didn't have the number of his wristphone. I was afraid to call his home-phone. What if Jane doesn't know? I thought. Doesn't know what? I thought. I don't know either.

I take the phone inside. I make a sandwich: mustard, lettuce and some stale bread. I drink two strong dark beers quickly. I want a cigarette, but I don't smoke. I imagine smoking and smoking, a chain of sweet-dreams. I imagine that the phone in my hand is a conch shell. In Gregg's hand is its sister. I blow into mine and he understands me. I hear the innocent falsetto of a shell-soul. I wish that we were pink shells or their slimy little inhabitants.

My big slimy brain, though, interrupts me. It urges me, "You should be worrying. That's right: Worry. Worry."

I can't call there or drive there or fly there or run there. I'm stuck here. He's somewhere. I run outside, taking the phone with me—to the neighbors, I'll look ridiculous, obsessive, taking the phone running. I wonder, Did the neighbors hear me? Was I screaming? I jog around the block nonchalantly for a minute. Then I run. I sprint. I do the dash, chanting, "Come on, call. *Call.*"

He swallowed a dime once. Was bitten on the ear by a Saint Bernard he had ambushed. Walked into a wall and split his lip, pretending to be a blind boy. Pulled the garage door down on himself; I found him stuck there. Flew off a trampoline into the arms of a football player. He likes to be upside down and crooked and sideways; he knows exactly where he is when up is down or angling off sideways. He was invented, I think, before they discovered gravity. He was meant to loop and whirl outside the limits of such computations.

I skinned my knee once. I bumped my head. I bit my tongue. I struck my funnybone.

Then the phone rang again. I was nearly back up my own driveway.

"Hello?"

"Hi," he said. "Sorry about that. My hands were numb. The waves were ten-foot. I couldn't press the little buttons. It was the current. Swept me right out into the ocean. I lost the sail. Tied myself onto the board. Prayed to the dolphins. Dreamed I was a baby."

"You're okay?" I said. I thought I heard a sea-bird.

He said, "The Coast Guard found me. They put me in a space-suit—I had hypothermia or something."

"You still on the wristphone?"

"No. I'm on my way home, on the car-phone. I'm going to pick up a pizza, sit by the fireplace, look at the atlas. I'd like to try cliff-jumping."

I sat down on the cold cement of my steps. The darkness under the bushes smelled of pine, spoke of danger. I heard a watery air-voice, circling, whispering into my pinkness, *Call.*

"Promise me," I said to him, "you won't leave me here alone." The dirt was forming into weird clumps, heaving and exploding, clearing its throat disgustingly.

"You want to go hang-gliding?" my brother said. He was eating something. It sounded like pretzels. My stomach growled.

"Sure," I said, backing into the house to get my car-keys. Suddenly I saw myself ski-jumping, back-stroking, steeple-chasing, fire-walking, cloud-flying, mountain-riding, volcano-leaping—"Fine. Sure. Hang-gliding sounds great. Whatever. I'm on my way. Just wait there, okay?"

I made him promise to sit there until I got there. For four or five hours to eat pretzels, tie himself to the sofa, just to hold his blessed horses—horses, yes. They've thrown him.

THANKSGIVING STORY

Kate H. Winter

It was already snowing the first time Jill saw the woman. Jill stood squarely at the kitchen sink peeling potatoes for Thanksgiving dinner. Afterward she wouldn't be able to remember the noise from the family boisterously watching the Macy's parade in the next room, but she could recall the imagined sound of the huge snowflakes thudding on the window in front of her as she stood with her hands plunged into the cold water. It was the sense of wonder at how heavy snowflakes could be that made her lift her eyes from the tangle of peelings and look into the backyard.

That's when she saw her. Just there—beyond the edge of the lawn, into the woods where they'd been cutting down the dead birches—the woman sat perched on one stump and stared through the veil of snow at the lighted kitchen window where Jill stood staring back.

At first she didn't really believe that the woman was there. She looked away, back at her hands, and shook her head as if to clear her vision. She turned the potato over carefully in her left hand and made a smooth stroke downward with the peeler before she raised her eyes to look again. The woman was still there. Jill touched the switch to the right of the window to shut off the fluorescent light above the sink and leaned against the countertop to steady herself as she searched the view and studied the stranger's figure.

She had dark hair, darker maybe than Jill's own, and it hung now damply on her shoulders. Within minutes it had become white—she was quickly shrouded in snow as she sat on the dead tree stump staring straight ahead into—Jill supposed—the Neville's Kitchen.

"What time did the turkey go in?" her mother-in-law hustled into the kitchen and eased herself into a chair at the table.

"It will be ready by 3:00, Mother." That wasn't, of course, the issue. "It will be ready by the time they get here." And it would. Jill's efficiency was the family's pride and humiliation. She made her husband and his family look slovenly by comparison. Jill could do anything right and on time. Her house and her office were masterpieces of order and priority. It made her mother-in-law hate her, she knew.

Jill turned back to the peeling and looked again. The stranger was still there, her hair and coat—a thin one, not enough protection against this kind of late November weather in Vermont—were thoroughly white. She looked more than before like an apparition, and Jill mistrusted her sight. Her mother-in-law lurched out of the chair when one of the small cousins yelped—not even she could tell which one of the seven assembled children it was. As she passed by the sink, Jill thought she saw her mother-in-law glance out the window—she *had*—yes, she was sure, she had looked. But she hadn't seen. Yet the woman was still there.

On the wall behind Jill, stark white against the blue wallpaper, the telephone was silent. And it would be all day. These were the hard times, when they couldn't be together, couldn't even talk on the phone. He was with his wife and her family and she—well, she was in her own cheerful kitchen surrounded by the blur of Thanksgiving dinner. Suddenly her arms ached for him. Jill hadn't believed that the first time it happened, thought it was the stuff of romance novels, but it was true. Her arms ached to hold him. The memory of him made her weak, made her eyes swim. She struck downward hard with the peeler and caught her thumb with the sharp edge. It was a minute before the hurt registered and the blood seeped into the water. She put her thumb to her mouth and sucked hard at the cut, biting the flesh around it.

The phone rang. As always she was first to yell "I'll get it!" It might be him. Her Lover. She always thought of him in capital letters. Never "Nick" or "Anne's husband." Always, "My Lover." In those months he'd grown beyond the beautiful incubus of first passion. Now he was her muse, the place where her heart beat, the room she felt most herself in.

Jill loved the assortment of economy motels they met at for afternoons of love-making. They were clean, efficient, anonymous rooms. She could never remember any of the names of the places, just where they were, which exit off the highway she had to take. There was curious pleasure in checking in and making herself comfortable in each new room. The anonymity was liberating. She would strip off the scratchy bedspread and the blanket too unless it was soft and fresh. She sometimes rearranged the furniture while she was waiting for him to arrive, and often he brought surprises for them—croissants or scented candles or a clutch of flowers. But she never made it a home, never tried to, never thought of cleaning it or redecorating or leaving anything behind or taking anything away. They simply spent the hours wound around each other talking.

"I'll get it!" she gulped again on the third ring.

"Can you talk?"

"Yes—a little." She barely breathed. He whispered cautiously into the phone the way he spoke to her when he was leaning over her in bed, their bodies joined at that dark triangle, their breaths coming in the same rhythm. "How is it?"

"Dreadful. I mean—everything's perfect—the children aren't even fighting—but I cut my finger, thumb actually—and I miss you so."

"I know. I couldn't *not* call, but . . ."

"You don't have to say it."

"Yes, I do. I need you to hear it. I love you. I want to be with you—want you. What's this about? Why aren't we together?"

"Because we're good people. Families. Houses. You know all the reasons."

"Yes, but they don't make the ache go away."

Jill leaned into the wall to keep from slipping into her desire. She wanted him. Wanted the brave disorder of days with him.

"I have to go. I love you."

"Yes. Monday again, right?" Her voice sounded crisp against the air of the kitchen.

"See you." And he was gone. Jill wondered again at the frailty of the connection, the voice on the wire that kept her alive some days, made her hurt from wanting him, left her mad with the impulse to clean, clear, sweep, arrange this place.

"It's two thirty! Where *are* they? Your brother can't ever be on time. No sense of obligation, responsibility."

"They'll be here. It's probably taking them longer because of—you know—her being so big—and then there's the snow." For an instant Jill imagined her sister-in-law round-bellied and awkward with this baby and pressed the palms of her hands against her own flat hips. It still surprised her that her family was so prolific when she herself had remained childless. It wasn't anyone's fault. The family had finally stopped asking her about children when she adopted her quiet, unresisting stare in response. It was simply a condition of her life, like her husband's silences. "Let's just let it rest today, Mother, ok?"

No answer. She was already gone, hefting the last pile of china onto the table, distributing the dinner plates. Jill noted that the pattern was upside down at some places, the flowers growing downward toward the diner's belly instead of thrusting upward. She knew she'd have to go in and move the plates before they sat down, otherwise the setting would be ruined. But first she had to put the potatoes to boil. The heavy pot pulled at her aching thumb while she filled it with cold water, tossed the diced potatoes in and settled it on the front burner. Sluicing her hands down the fronts of her thighs to get the water off, she moved toward the china cabinet and began to take out the wine goblets. Eleven. She pushed the sherry glasses over to get at the twelfth but her hand trembled, and it fell in a slow arc to the floor. Its impact was like a distant bell or the rustle of leaves. It was no sound at all compared to the gathering snow. She grabbed the sherry glass instead and set it at her own place at the table, its odd shape marring the symmetry of her design. She swept the shattered glass carefully into the dustpan, making sure the glistening shards were gathered up, giving the floor a last wipe with a wet paper towel to insure that every bit was gone. It the kitchen, the water surged over the rim of the pot in a boil. She was already whisking the pot to the sink while she called "I'll get it!" She didn't want to, but she looked into the yard again.

The woman still sat there, but she had moved slightly and just as Jill leaned to look, the woman turned her head keenly as a bird does. The day had gone gray, the light watery, and the trees' shadows made bars across the snow, their shadows as bare as they were. Jill's eyes brimmed again. The woman turned to her, looking into her, into the dark-hearted kitchen.

"They're here!" Yes, they would be. Jill clicked into action, dashed her apron onto its hook beside the stove and went to work. The bustle in the house occupied her. She became the house again. She had found this house the first year they were married, and together they had rebuilt its interior, meticulously maintaining its original character. Thanksgiving was the beginning of the season when the house would be filled with children and food. Her husband joined her now in the doorway, holding himself slightly apart from her. They were careful with each other always. Her brother and his wife stood on the threshold stomping the snow off their boots in unison. With a flick of his gloved hand he tossed the snow off his own shoulders, then bent to do the same for his wife. The snow lay in clusters on the gray slate floor of the foyer, the edges melting quickly away.

"We're here!"

"I see! Come in—dinner's ready, so just sit down. You can find your own place. Nana's here already—help her to a place." Jill's grandmother clutched the doorframe for support, steadied herself in the doorway to the dining room and grinned at no one in particular. Jill suddenly remembered a day when she herself was six, riding in the country on an autumn Sunday, curled against the flowered dress and cream-colored cardigan that Nana wore. The miles ticked by, lazy, Jill listening to the gossip and the "good stuff"—the stories her mother and her mother's mother traded across the back seat of the old Ford, who had run off with whose wife and who had the baby that didn't have a father. Nana had pronounced sentence on the old farm houses as they passed. "Vacant," she'd say, and sigh. Jill had finally looked up into her face and asked her what "vacant" meant. Today Nana held the doorframe as if to keep herself attached, her eyes as empty as the windows of those houses too many years ago.

"It's all right, Nana, there's a place here for you."

"Happy—happy—happy—hap . . . hap—happy," she gurgled, looking distractedly from one to another of the family faces, not knowing any of them for certain. "Meg? Happy—happy." Jill knew finally that it wasn't really a question. Hearing her grandmother say her mother's name startled Jill, made her forget for a moment that her mother had been dead those five years. Nana hadn't understood her daughter's going, eaten away by cancer and loneliness. Your children weren't supposed to die before you.

She touched Nana's cold hand and whispered, "It's Jill, Nana, and we're all happy too—and Happy Thanksgiving." Everyone sat patiently in front of the place cards she had lettered the day before. The food steamed along the surface of the table. Only Jill's eyes caught the dissonance of the single sherry glass. She picked it up and put it quickly back into the cabinet.

"No—no wine for me," she told her husband as he poured. Yes, that was better. A little thing, not having the wine, and see how it made the difference? Now all the glasses matched. Her husband didn't ask her about it. She had known for years why she had married him. His reasonableness, his lack of passion, made a place for her to hide from the abusive chaos of her parents' marriage. She had needed his calmness. Lately she realized that it wasn't so much that he had control of his feelings as that the feelings weren't there. It was like living with someone who was absent most of the time. The rhythm of their jobs and the house moved them through time, but there was no heart to what they did. They never spoke of it. They were like a house with a fireplace where no one ever makes a fire.

She went to the kitchen for more gravy and paused to look out the window again. It was all right. The woman was gone. Jill searched in both directions for a sign of her, a footprint maybe, but there was nothing. She was just gone. Jill was struck by her own neglect. She hadn't even thought to invite her in. Jill sat at the table and bit unconsciously at the cut on her thumb until the blood oozed again and she tasted its redness on her tongue.

Nana sat quietly in the corner place at the table. Only Jill saw her hand moving, fingers picking at the cloth. She was trying to hold on, to recognize the faces and voices and find her way out of the speechless confusion she spent her days in. They asked for dessert, but Jill could barely hear them. Jill didn't know if she herself had eaten, simply that it was time to pile on the pies and cream and pour the coffee. The family lingered over the disarray of nearly-empty dishes. The candles were half-burned. Nuggets of white wax had dripped down their sides and merged into the puddles at the base. This time when the phone rang, she didn't jump.

"I've got it," and she slipped from the chair to the kitchen phone. "Hello?"

"Come with me."

Jill looked toward the window. The snow was still coming. Behind her, the family began to shuffle the mess of napkins and plates, but the clatter sounded far off and she missed entirely her husband's request for another cup of coffee.

"Yes." She eased the telephone onto its cradle and stepped through the hall to the foyer. Without looking back, she swept her coat off its peg and slid her arms into the sleeves. She hesitated, then tossed her purse over her shoulder. No one noticed when she opened the front door and stepped into the snow. Her footprints surprised her. The edges softened and behind her the marks of her passing nearly disappeared as the whiteness and the darkness covered her going. By the time she reached the first corner, she was covered in drifting white, her hair a veil. At the second corner, his car pulled alongside the curb, its engine muffled by the gathering snow. It glittered in the half-light when Nick opened the car door and she got in. Then she looked back at the street, but she couldn't quite remember which house had been hers. If it hadn't been for the faint trail of her footprints, she wouldn't have known which door she had come out of. From where she sat, all the houses had the same impassive fronts and darkened, empty windows. She turned to Nick. There was only the sound of snow and their breathing.

WASHINGTON SQUARE MOVES*

CHARACTERS

AL, 32
BOBBY, 41
SAMMY D., 23
RANDALL, 39
MARGIE, 32
HOMELESS WOMAN, played by the same actress as Cop
COP
JOHN, played by the same actor as Passerby
PASSERBY

TIME

November of this year

PLACE

Washington Square, New York City

WASHINGTON SQUARE MOVES*

Matthew Witten

Scene 1

TIME: an early November afternoon.

SETTING: the chessboards at Washington Square, New York City. Behind the chessboards is a sign: "no gambling allowed."

A bunch of used books and magazines are laid out on an upstage bench and on the ground in front of it.

AT RISE: Bobby and Al play chess. They're not what you'd call well-dressed. Al is 32, black. Bobby is 41, white.

AL   I think I can do this. Yeah. (*Makes a move, punches the chess clock*). I got it down, you are gone. (*Bobby moves, punches the clock.*). What kind of a move, man? Tha's a Washin'ton Square move.
BOBBY   Bullshit. That move is strictly uptown.
AL   Uptown, my ass.
BOBBY   What do you know about uptown?
AL   I know it when I see it, an' that move ain't it. (*Moves, punches the clock.*)
BOBBY   Maybe I'm just too deep for you, brother! (*Moves, punches the clock.*)
AL   Yeah, you so deep, you diggin a hole! (*Grunts.*) Hunh! (*Moves, punches the clock.*)
BOBBY   A hole in your wallet! (*Grunts.*) Hunh! (*Moves, punches the clock.*)

---

*Act One from *Washington Square Moves.*

AL   (*Grunts.*) Hunh! (*Moves, punches the clock.*)

BOBBY   (*Grunts louder.*) Hunh!! (*Moves, punches the clock.*)

AL   (*Grunts even louder.*) Hunh!!! (*Moves, punches the clock.*)

BOBBY   Are you losing what's left of your mind?

AL   Take my queen, man, she waitin for ya, take her.

BOBBY   (*His face falls.*) Shit.

AL   You be owin me another dollar.

BOBBY   Shut up and let a man think.

AL   Go ahead. Think. I gotchou in a tough position. Ain't no Vaseline for this position.

BOBBY   I thought I had you this time. (*Sammy D. enters, carrying a small brown bag and wearing the same kind of clothes as Bobby and Al. He's 23, Hispanic.*)

AL   Sammy D.!

SAMMY D.   Hey hey hey!

AL   My man!

SAMMY D.   Whatchou playin Bobby for? He can't play chess.

AL   I know. Tha's why I'm playin him for money.

SAMMY D.   Candy from a baby, man.

AL   Whatchou got for me?

SAMMY D.   (*Takes a small bottle out of the bag.*) Whatchou think I got? (*He flips the bottle to Al. Bobby moves and presses the clock. Al doesn't notice.*)

AL   Fuck is this? Ain't enough juice in here to make a roach drunk.

SAMMY D.   You'll get a nice buzz off o' that.

AL   I wanted a buzz, I'd be a bee. See me flappin around with them little wings? Think I got honey under my shirt?

SAMMY D.   You asked me to getchou a bottle. You didn' say what size.

AL   You know I didn' want no half-pint.

SAMMY D.   You know I ain't got no money.

AL   We done hustled twenty bucks this morning.

SAMMY D.   I spent my dime. I got me some lunch.

AL   Lunch! Whatchou need lunch for, man, you had breakfast! Tha's jus' throwin money away!

SAMMY D.   I was hungry!

AL   Damn, junior. You keep on eatin all these meals, you ain't never gon save up enough for a jacket an' tie. (*To Bobby.*) Come you ain't movin?

BOBBY   You are squashed like a bug.

AL   Then how come you ain't movin?

BOBBY   Wanna make it two dollars? (*Beat*)

AL   Sammy D. It look to you like the King o' Washin'ton Square gittin squashed?

SAMMY D.   Looks to me like Bobby's brain is gone on vacation.

AL   Okay, dude. Two bucks.

BOBBY   Okay, Al. You've been so busy talking, I made my move a long time ago and your clock ran down to zero. (*Laughs.*)

SAMMY D.   Oh shit. (*Laughs, slaps Bobby five.*)

AL   That ain't right.

BOBBY   Maybe not, but you owe me two dollars.

AL   Fuck you, motherfucker!

BOBBY   Hey, I'm just pullin a hustle, like you always—

AL   This ain't no hustle, this is fuckin chess!

BOBBY   Two dollars, Al!

AL   Kiss my ass! Ain't got no two dollars, an' if I did, you wouldn' git 'em!

BOBBY   Then gimme the bottle.

AL   (*To Sammy D.*) Sonufabitch tryin to hustle me! (*To Bobby.*) Shit, you couldn' hustle your own granma, man. It wasn't for your motherfuckin trust fund an' your rent-controlled apartment, you be lost in this world! You ain't nothin but a vegetable, man, a fried onion!

SAMMY D.   (*To Bobby.*) Don' even talk to him.

BOBBY   I beat you fair an' square, you fuckin bum. You owe me some money. (*He starts to go.*)

AL   (*As Bobby goes.*) Tha's comical, you callin somebody a bum! You act like you got a Ph.D. from Bum University!

BOBBY   Hey. I beat you, bro. (*He exits*)

AL   (*To Sammy D.*) Damn, that guy's a fuckin onion. Why's he come out here every day, anyway?

SAMMY D.   Why do you?

AL　I'm makin much money here. You wanna play?

SAMMY D.　Not when you're like this.

AL　Like what?

SAMMY D.　Callin people onions. Who needs it? (*Gets up.*)

AL　Where you goin?

SAMMY D.　Walk around.

AL　Where you gonna walk around to?

SAMMY D.　Promised my aunt I'd look for a job.

AL　Bullshit, you ain't lookin for no job. Sit your ass down.

SAMMY D.　Hey, I got a fast metabolism. I need breakfast, lunch, *an'* dinner.

AL　Ain't no dinnertime yet. Come on, we'll think up a good hustle.

SAMMY D.　Later, man.

AL　Sit down before I sit you down, motherfucker, come on. (*He grabs Sammy D.'s arm and tries to lead him to the chess table, but Sammy D. pulls away.*)

SAMMY D.　Shit, why you gotta always act like this?

AL　Like what?

SAMMY D.　I got along jus' fine without you, man.

AL　Yeah? Wasn' for me, you never woulda made it outa the joint alive!

SAMMY D.　Wasn' for you, I never woulda gone to the joint in the first place.

AL　Tha's besides the point. Look, Sammy D., don' be rollin no dope. Ain't got no luck at that shit, ya always git busted! I mean, you already goin up front o' the judge next week behind this shit, man!

SAMMY D.　(*Points to the U. books and magazines.*) I ain't sellin no more bullshit for you, man, three-year-old *U.S. News an' World Reports,* damn! (*Starts to go.*)

ALL　(*Sets up the chess pieces.*) Yo, bro! You come here, I school you to the hidden mysteries o' the King's Gambit Opening. I make you a master o' the infinite tactical possibilities.

SAMMY D.　Don't take chess so goddamn serious. (*Sammy D. exits.*)

AL　(*Calls off-stage L.*) Then wha' should I take serious? (*He finishes setting up his pieces and sets the clock. A Homeless Woman enters, carrying her bags and dressed in black from head to toe.*) Oh shit, woman, why you gots to follow me around? You gimme the spooks. (*She walks up to Al and stands mutely in front of him.*) Look, you smell funky. Git the fuck away from me. (*She stands and waits. Finally he gives in, hands her the bottle.*) Go ahead an' finish the fuckin thing. (*During the following, the Homeless Woman goes U., sits on a bench and drinks, then lies down. Al calls off-stage L.*) Who wants to play the King o' Washin'ton Square? On'y one dollah! Yo' money back if you win! (*Pause.*) Special deal! Today only! I give you two dollahs if you win! Two dollahs! On'y gimme one if you lose! (*Pause; calls off-stage R.*) Three dollahs! (*Randall enters L., unseen by Al. He'd 39, black, well-dressed. Al still calls off-stage R.*) Get three when you win, on'y give one if you lose! That ain't chess, it's stealin! Git away from them wussy backgammon sets! Come here an' make some money! (*Al turns L., sees Randall. He stands up, stunned.*) Is that you?

RANDALL   How's it hangin, homeboy?

AL   Damn.

RANDALL   Surprise, baby. (*They hug.*)

AL   What the hell you doin here? (*Admiring Randall's clothes.*) Lookit these rags, man.

RANDALL   I been lookin for you all over town.

AL   I thoughtchou was in for another couple o'years.

RANDALL   I been out five months. Nobody knew where you cut out to.

AL   You musta done escaped.

RANDALL   No, man, they gimme time off for good behavior.

AL   Whatchou do, go down on some guards?

RANDALL   You talkin like you ain't glad to see me.

AL   I jus' cain't believe my peepers. Man, you lookin bad.

RANDALL   Whatchou doin, man, hustlin chess? (*Picks up a chess piece.*)

AL   Jus' tryin to keep my ass-pockets full o' coins without goin the joint. Come you all fancied up? Gittin set to rob a hotel or somethin?

RANDALL   (*Sits down.*) Damn, feels good to hold a chess piece again. Ain't played since I got out.

AL   The fuck is this?

RANDALL   What?

AL   On your finger.

RANDALL   I be a family man now.

AL   You gots to be jivin me.

RANDALL   I always liked women the best.

AL   Bullshit, man

RANDALL   Ain't no women in prison, man. You gotta take the best out o' what life offers you.

AL   Shit.

RANDALL   You wasn' in there long as I was.

AL   Your own damn fault, man, only a fool hold up a Congressman!

RANDALL   I didn't know he was a Congressman. He wasn't wearin no nametags!

AL   Yeah, bad luck. So wha's her name?

RANDALL   Desirée. French. Means "The Desired One." Nice, hunh?

AL   My man Randall done got married to a French girl named Daisy Ray?!

RANDALL   Make a move, man, let's play some chess.

AL   Damn. (*Moves.*)

RANDALL   (*Points at Al's move.*) Pawn to king four. You ain't changed, Al. (*Moves.*)

AL   You done changed enough for both of us. (*Moves.*)

RANDALL   I is gonna whup your ass. (*Moves.*)

AL   You is gonna die. (*Moves.*)

RANDALL   You gonna wish you already dead. (*Moves.*)

AL   You gonna feel like a jellyfish gittin run over by a truck. (*Moves.*)

RANDALL   You be cryin fo' St. Peter take you away. (*Moves.*)

AL   You be cryin fo' yo' Mama. (*Moves.*)

RANDALL   Don'tchou be talkin 'bout my mama! Damn, this is some kind o' sweet feelin, ain't it? Lord, I hated them paper pieces.

AL   Shit yes, every time you sneezed, they be flyin all over the place.

RANDALL   Kiss my foot, man, I ain't sneeze. You sneezed.

AL   You had allergies!

RANDALL   Not when I played chess! Every time you was losin, you sneezed! Now don' be tellin me you ain't do it.

AL   Chess is war, man. All's fair in war. You know chess is a African game? (*Points to the U. books.*) Says in one o' them books the oldest chess pieces ever found are from Morocco.

RANDALL   No shit. Tha's all right.

AL   So what was the score, anyway?

RANDALL   Three hundred forty-two for you, one hundred forty-six for me.

AL   You remember that?

RANDALL   How can I forget it? I was the only cat in the whole damn joint come close to you. (*Moves.*)

AL   You ain't lyin 'bout that.

RANDALL   Our last hundred games, I was whuppin you two out o' five.

AL   You was gettin might uppity. (*Moves.*)

RANDALL   I never knew I was smart til I beat you at chess. An' sittin down with you, man, studyin them openin's for weeks til we got 'em figured out, tha's the first time I realized if I put my mind to somethin I could actually do it.

AL   So wha's your game, Randall?

RANDALL   It meant a lot to me. Specially when Margie Williams put us on the radio—"Jailbird Chess Experts."

AL   She was a quality thoroughbred, man, she wasn' nothin like what I remembered from junior high.

RANDALL   I run into her at a party last week.

AL   You an' her go the same parties?

RANDALL   She was askin aboutchou. Y'oughta check her out man. She done got divorced.

AL   Aw, man, she ain't for me. Come on, what is this tie bull-shit?

RANDALL   This is for my j.o.b.

AL   You ain't got no job. I bet you plannin some kind o' late-night second-story work.

RANDALL   Well now, that was my intention. Made it out o' the joint, spent all my cash, (*Moves.*) met this brother was workin as a bicycle messenger. In the daytime. In the nighttime he go back the places he checked out in the daytime, an' take off their computers. So I decided, hey, be a messenger.

AL   Tha's dangerous, man.

RANDALL   Ain't no way rob people 'thout it bein dangerous.

AL   I'm talkin 'bout ridin around on them bicycles. Man, I rather rob a hundred banks full o' security guards with Uzis than ride around the streets like them crazy-ass bicycle riders. (*Moves.*)

RANDALL   So one day I'm deliverin a package to A.J. Advertisin Agency. I walk in, an' these two white dudes is arguin about how to sell blue jeans to black people. They got posters on the wall, an' they raisin all kinds o' ruckus which one's better. Thing is, they're all shit! So I git pissed off, 'cause I be smarter 'n these jokers—could whup their butts at chess—but they got money an' I'm ridin the streets riskin my ass. So I says to 'em, "Fools, them posters is some kind o' lame. Ain't gon sell nothin to nobody with this weak-ass diddlysquat." So this white dude laughs like I sayin somethin funny, an' he says, "You got any ideas?" So hell, I say, "How about a advertisement linkin up yo' blue jeans with freedom. 'Cause tha's all the black man wants: freedom."

AL   No shit.

RANDALL   Yeah, but they don' know that. So I start vampin on some slogans. "The blue jeans that bring you freedom." Shit like that. An' that joker's face starts goin through some changes! He says, "Come here," takes me up to his office, shows me all kinds posters an' flyers an' videos directed toward the black urban consumer, an' he asks my opinion. (*Beat.*) Al, you are looking at a fuckin executive consultant.

AL   No. No.

RANDALL   Twenty-five grand a year.

AL   Bullshit, man.

RANDALL   An' it's all because o' you. Playin with them

paper pieces an' findin out I was smart enough make you sneeze. (*Moves.*)

AL   Damn, man. I don' know what to say. I should ask you for money, tha's what I should be sayin. Seriously, man, can you lend me a dime? I'm short today.

RANDALL   (*Gets out his wallet.*) I owe you a lot more 'n that, homes. (*Gives him a bill.*) Twenty-five grand is what I owe.

AL   (*Looks at the bill.*) I don' need twenty, man, I jus' asked for ten.

RANDALL   Keep it, homie. Doin anythin besides chess?

AL   Hey, it pays the rent. Specially considerin I ain't got no apartment so I ain't got no rent.

RANDALL   Where you stayin?

AL   Man, you know how it is. I'm stayin with my sister. For now.

RANDALL   How's Peggy doin anyway?

AL   Too many damn kids, man, I sleepin on the kitchen floor. Only peace o' mind I git is comin out here.

RANDALL   I don' wanna lose you again, Al. You the one guy I always figured we was on the same track.

AL   I been around, I jus' hangin in different circles now. Tryin to cut loose from the guys what we used to get into shit together, ya know?

RANDALL   I thought you was applyin for college, I mean shit, takin all them practice SAT's in the joint, whatchou git, 1100?

AL   Eleven fifty, man. Bovine is to Ox as Ursine is to A: Bear; B: Lion; C:—Man, they must lay awake nights thinkin up that shit. Yeah, I'm gon apply for college, an' not no funky-ass joint neither. I'm talkin Columbia University. I been checkin out their catalog in the library.

RANDALL   Tha' be dynamite, man. 'Course, you should apply for a couple other ones too.

AL   Fuck that, I'm goin straight to the top, where I belong. I gon learn *all* them ologies.

RANDALL   All them what?

AL   *Geology, zoology, ety*mology. . . . 'Sides, they got some fine young ladies there, bitches with all kinds o' money, an' I gon git me one.

RANDALL   Go for it, man. 'Course you ain't as good-lookin as me, but give it a shot.

AL   I hate cats like you. You the kind o' cat my sister says, "Why cain'tchou be like Randall?"

RANDALL   Hey, I'm lucky. I know it. Got twenty in yo' pocket says I know it. Shit, two o'clock, I gots to git back to my major gig. They's pissed at me for comin in late all the time.

AL   So what's it like down there, man?

RANDALL   Dog eag dog, man, worse than the joint. I be back here tomorrow, homie, I show you how the game is played.

AL   I don' care what kind executive you is, I still whup your ass.

RANDALL   We see about that! Later.

AL   Later, man (*Randall exits. Al watches him go, shakes his head in amazement. To himself.*) Goddamn! (*Lights fade.*)

CONTRIBUTORS

Jennifer Armstrong is an award-winning author of children's books. Her historical fiction for young adults includes *Steal Away* and the Wild Rose Inn series; her children's picture books include *Hugh Can Do, Chin Yu Min and the Ginger Cat*, and *That Terrible Baby*. She has also ghostwritten dozens of paperbacks for a popular young adult series. Ms. Armstrong grew up in South Salem, New York, and graduated from Smith College. She now lives in Saratoga Springs, New York.

Mae Guyer Banner, born in Detroit, the oldest of four children, first published work in her junior high newspaper. After a 20 year career as a teacher of sociology, Ms. Banner went back to writing and reporting, specializing in dance and theater. She now freelances for several area dailies and other periodicals.

Maria McBride Bucciferro was born in Troy, New York where she worked as a city hall reporter for the local newspaper after college. She is presently vice president of communications for Capital Risk Associates, Inc. Her abiding interest in her hometown, Saratoga Springs, New York, and its history, results in many freelance articles for area periodicals and newspapers.

Michael Burkard's books of poems include *My Secret Boat, Fictions From The Self, The Fires They Kept*, and *Ruby For Grief*. He received a Whiting Writer's Award in 1988 and twice has received grants from the National Endowment for the Arts. He has taught at many colleges and universities, and his poems have appeared in numerous journals and magazines. He currently works as an alcoholism counselor and teaches in some local art programs in central New York.

Albino Carrillo is a native New Mexican. He attended the University of New Mexico and Arizona State University. His poems have appeared in *the Antioch Review, the Midwest Quarterly, Caliban* and many others. Most recently Carrillo taught creative writing and modern American literature at Union College, Schenectady, New York.

Lâle Davidson characterizes her writing as visionary fiction for the most part about and for women. She is a professor of creative writing and composition at Adirondack Community College in Glens Falls, New York. She gives workshops and performances in storytelling as a founding member of the performance group, The Snickering Witches. Her work has been published in *The North American Review, Phoebe, Mildred,* and *The Little Magazine.*

Ken Denberg was born and raised in Columbia, South Carolina. He earned a master of fine arts degree in creative writing and a doctorate in poetics and rhetoric. He has worked as a waiter, landscape gardener, farm laborer, truck driver, executive director of an arts organization, and has owned a bookstore. Currently, he lives in rural upstate New York where he small-farms, teaches English at a local college, and edits *The Snail's Pace Review.* His new book is *Driving With One Light Out.*

Marianne Gilbert Finnegan has lived in Saratoga Springs, New York since 1979. She taught literature and creative writing at the University of Connecticut where she completed the Ph.D. in English and American literature. As associate to the president at Empire State College and senior research editor for the Chancellor of the State University of New York, she wrote articles and essays on academic and policy subjects. In 1988 Ms. Finnegan and her husband began a four year residency in Portugal where she owned an international bookshop and wrote of her experiences as an American woman living in a foreign country.

Douglas Glover lives in Wilton, New York with his wife, four children, three dogs, and a cat. His stories have appeared in *The Best American Short Stories* and *Best Canadian Stories.* He has taught, intermittently, at Skidmore College and as visiting writer-in-residence at the New York State Writers Institute at the State University of New York at Albany. His most recent book is a novel called *The Life and Times of Captain N. (Knopf, 1993)*.

Amy Godine is a journalist and fiction writer living in Saratoga Springs. Her novellas have appeared in *TriQuarterly* and *The Quarterly*. She writes frequently on ethnic and social history in the north country for *Adirondack Life*.

Barry Goldensohn is the author of the following books of poetry: *St. Venus Eve, Uncarving the Block, The Marrano*, and *Dance Music*. He has taught at Goddard, Hampshire, the Iowa Writer's Workshop, and for the past dozen years at Skidmore College. His wife, Lorrie, has also contributed to this anthology.

Lorrie Goldensohn is a poet and critic who has published two collections of poetry, *Dreamwork* and *The Tether*. Her critical study, *Elizabeth Bishop: The Biography of a Poetry*, appeared in 1992, and was nominated for a Pulitzer Prize. Her poems and articles have been published in a wide range of journals and anthologies. She teaches poetry, criticism, and women's studies at Vassar College.

Elaine Handley was born and raised in western New York. Currently she is the director of a writing program at Empire State College, part of New York's state university system. She lives in the woods just outside of Saratoga Springs, New York where she is working on a novel and more poems.

William Hathaway came of age in Ithaca, New York, where he has recently returned to live. In the intervening years he lived in Europe, Massachusetts, Montana, Iowa, and Louisiana. He supported himself as a teacher of writing and literature for 25 years. He has published six books of poetry; the latest is titled *Churlsgrace*.

Bruce Hiscock was born in California but grew up in Michigan. He studied chemistry at the University of Michigan and got his Ph.D. from Cornell University. After a series of scientific jobs, including college teaching and drug testing race horses, he began writing and illustrating children's books, something he had always wanted to do. Now with a dozen books to his credit, Mr. Hiscock has two grown children, two ex-wives, and lives in a little house he built himself in Porter Corners, New York.

Kay Hogan has been writing for ten years. Her genre is the short story, but she is working on several plays and hopes to complete a novel. She brings to her writing a strong Irish-Catholic background and this duality is reflected often in her work. Her works have been included in many small press magazines. Presently Ms. Hogan teaches creative writing, adult education and writing workshops at area libraries. She is the mother of five children and resides with her husband in Saratoga Springs, New York.

Dennis Loy Johnson's work has appeared in numerous literary reviews and been featured in several short story anthologies, such as *New Stories From The South* 1993 (Algonquin) and *The New Generation* (Doubleday). His writing has also been awarded a Pushcart Prize and a fellowship from the National Endowment for the Arts.

Naton Leslie was born and raised and educated in Ohio, earning degrees in English and creative writing. His poetry, fiction, and nonfiction has appeared in numbers of literary journals and magazines. He recently was awarded a grant for poetry from the National Endowment for the Arts and has been twice nominated for Pushcart Awards. Currently he is assistant professor of English at Siena College in Loudenville, New York, and involves himself with editing and publishing projects as he has for the past twelve years.

F. R. Lewis's fictions have won two PEN Syndicated Fiction Project Awards and been included in many anthologies. Almost two dozen stories have been published in national literary and commercial magazines. Her essay on the Saratoga Spring Public Library's reading group appeared in *The Book Group Book* by Ellen Slezak. She has been a fellow of the Millay and MacDowell Colonies for the Arts and is currently at work on a novel.

George Liaskos was born in Manhattan, raised on Long Island, and graduated from Syracuse University. He has written literature for the past twenty years, from journalism and theater, to poetry and prose. *The MacGuffin* of Livonia, Michigan and *The Saratogian* of Saratoga Springs, New York are publications in which his work has appeared.

Ron MacLean has published a poetry chapbook and numerous short stories. Before becoming an English instructor at the State University of New York at Albany, Mr. MacLean was a copywriter for an advertising firm, and earlier, managing editor of a weekly newspaper group. Now with his doctor of arts in English he hopes to spend lots of time writing.

Shirley Nelson is the author of two prize-winning books, a novel, *The Last Year of the War,* and a documented narrative, *Fair Clear and Terrible: The Story of Shiloh, Maine.* Her work appears regularly in a variety of publications.

Paul Pines spent the sixties in Vietnam, Europe, Mexico, Belize, and New York City's Lower East Side. During the seventies he ran the Tin Palace, a Bowery jazz club. His critically acclaimed novel *The Tin Angel* is based on that experience. He received a CAPS grant for poetry in 1976 and a fellowship from the New York State Foundation for the Arts in 1984 among other fellowships. His poems, essays, and translations have appeared in many literary journals and a book of poems, *Onion,* was published in 1971. Mr. Pines lives in Glens Falls, New York with his wife and daughter.

Jay Rogoff's poems have appeared in many magazines and journals. His book of baseball poems, *The Cutoff,* won the 1994 Washington Prize and appeared from Word Works in 1995. He has also published reviews, essays, and critical articles. Other awards include the Poetry Society of America's John Masefield Award and fellow in residence at both the MacDowell Colony and Yaddo. At the Saratoga Springs Public Library Mr. Rogoff has presented readings, led the reading group, lectured on poetry, and served as resident scholar for a poetry study series.

Holis Seamon teaches writing and literature at the College of Saint Rose in Albany. She has published stories in many journals, including *The American Voice, The Creative Woman, One Meadway, The Hudson Review,* and *McCall's.* Ms. Seamon also serves as a fiction editor for *13th Moon: A Feminist Literary Magazine.*

Nancy Seid is a columnist for *Parents* magazine and an assistant professor of English at Adirondack Community College in Glens Falls, New York. She lives in Saratoga Springs with her husband, Matthew Witten, also included in this anthology, and their two sons.

Joanne Seltzer has had more than 500 poems published in *The Minnesota Review, The Village Voice, Sing Heavenly Muse!* and other journals. Her work appears in many anthologies, including the award-winning *When I Am An Old Woman I Shall Wear Purple.* She is the author of three poetry chapbooks, most recently *Inside Invisible Walls.*

Jordan Smith is the author of three books of poetry: *An Apology for Loving the Old Hymns, Lucky Seven,* and *The Household of Continuance.* He has been a recipient of fellowships from the Guggenheim Foundation and the National Endowment for the Arts. Since 1981, he has taught at Union College.

Marilyn Stablein grew up in the San Francisco Bay area. At eighteen she left home and traveled abroad for seven years. Her first collection of stories, now in a third printing from Black Heron Press, is *The Census Taker: Tales of a Traveler in India and Nepal.* A collection of personal essays, *Climate of Extremes: Landscape and Imagination,* was recently published. She lives in the Hudson River Valley.

Steve Stern was born and grew up in Memphis, Tennessee. His first collection of stories, *Isaac and the Undertaker's Daughter,* received the Pushcart Writer's Choice Award, and the title story of that collection won an O. Henry Prize. His second short story collection, *Lazar Malkin Enters Heaven,* won the Edward Lewis Wallant Award. His most recent book is *A Plague of Dreamers*, a collection of three novellas. He now lives in Saratoga Springs, New York, where he is associate professor of English at Skidmore College.

Susan Thames is a member of the creative writing faculties at Sarah Lawrence College and Columbia University. She is co-editor of *The Breast: An Anthology* and is finishing a novel, *Make My Bed and Light the Light*, part of which was written at Yaddo. She lives in Brooklyn, New York.

Beth Weatherby directs the creative writing program at Southwest State University in Marshall, Minnesota. She spends her summers in Greenfield Center, New York. "Sun-Dialing" is part of a collection of short stories, *The Monitor of Accidents*. Her work has been published or is forthcoming in *The Little Magazine, Groundswell, Capital Region, Open Mic: The Albany Anthology, River Oak Review*, and *Eureka Literary Magazine*.

Kate H. Winter was born in Mannsville, New York. She began writing poetry early, but after college turned to nonfiction prose and short stories. She teaches writing and American literature at the State University of New York at Albany where she received her doctorate. Her special interests are women writers, the literature of New York State, American regionalism, and the impact of landscape on writers. Winter has recently completed a novel set in Hawaii.

Matthew Witten's produced plays include *The Deal, Washington Square Moves, Sacred Journey, The Ties That Bind, Alaska Fire, Hadleyburg, U.S.A.,* and *The Body Parts*. Matthew has also written for film and television. He lives in Saratoga Springs, New York with his wife, Nancy Seid, and their two sons.